Development Strategies and the Status of WOMEN

Development Strategies and the Status of WOMEN

A Comparative Study of the United States, Mexico, the Soviet Union, and Cuba

MARGARET E. LEAHY

Lynne Rienner Publishers, Inc • Boulder, Colorado

Published in the United States of America in 1986 by
Lynne Rienner Publishers, Inc.
948 North Street, Boulder, Colorado 80302

© 1986 by Lynne Rienner Publishers, Inc. All rights reserved

Library of Congress Cataloging-in-Publication Data

Leahy, Margaret E.
  Development strategies and the status of women.

  Bibliography: p.
  1. Women in development—Cross-cultural studies.
  2. Women—Economic conditions—Cross-cultural studies.
  3. Women—Social conditions—Cross-cultural studies.
  I. Title.
  HQ1240.L43   1986   305.4'2   85-28246
  ISBN 0-931477-64-6

Distributed outside of North and South America and Japan by
Frances Pinter (Publishers) Ltd, 25 Floral Street,
London WC2E 9DS England   UK ISBN 0-86187-655-5

Printed and bound in the United States of America

To Sean and Maura

Contents

- Illustrations ix
- Preface xi
1. Women and Development: The Issues Defined 1
2. The Limits of Suffrage: Women in the United States 14
3. The *Casa* Prevails: Women in Mexico 47
4. Equality Creates a Double Burden: Women in the Soviet Union 65
5. The Revolution in the Revolution: Women in Cuba 91
6. What Have We Learned and Where Do We Go? 117
- Notes 122
- Bibliography 148
- Index 163

Illustrations

Figure 1.1 • Indicators of Women's Equality   11

Table 2.1 • The Female Labor Force in the United States   22

Table 2.2 • U.S. Median Wage or Salary Income of year-round,
             Full-time Workers, by Race and Sex (1974)   26

Table 2.3 • Bachelor's Degrees Awarded in 1979-80 in the United
             States   33

Table 5.1 • Percentage of Women Elected to Positions of Political
             Authority in Cuba   99

Table 5.2 • Percentage of Female College Students Enrolled by
             Field of Study (1972) in Cuba   107

Preface

This book does not purport to reveal new information about the condition and status of women in the United States, Mexico, the Soviet Union, or Cuba. With only limited exceptions, the information presented here reflects the hard work of others. What this book does is systematically use this information to examine and compare the effects of liberal/capitalist and Marxist development strategies on women's political, economic, and social status; this study also identifies particular factors in development logic that tend to either inhibit or facilitate greater equality for women.

Throughout the book, the specific contributions of various authors are cited. Others have contributed to this work in ways that require a different form of acknowledgment. Whatever analytic skills I may have were honed by the training I received from faculty at San Francisco State University and the University of Southern California. Special thanks go to professors Richard Ashley, Willard Carpenter, W. Ladd Hollist, Ted Keller, Charles Powell, John Sloane, and Judith Steihm. Particular thanks are also due to John Gerassi, my teacher, colleague, and friend, whose caring advice has consistently helped me to grow personally and professionally.

Research for this book could not have been completed without the assistance of many people. I am particularly grateful to Sally Shelly, who helped open many doors within the United Nations system, Susana Duran and Gonzalo Bravo, who made research in Mexico much easier, and Alfredo Almeida, Graciella Tabio, Catherine Rivas, and Joaquin Baez Gutierrez, for their invaluable assistance with my research in Cuba. My editors, Dianne Ewing and Janice Murray, deserve plaudits for making this book a reality.

My greatest thanks go to my friend and husband, Kevin McDonough, for his patient personal support and constructive academic criticisms.

Although each of the individuals named deserves credit for assisting me in this work, none should be expected to agree with my interpretations or conclusions.

Development Strategies and the Status of WOMEN

• CHAPTER ONE •
Women and Development: The Issues Defined

Interest in the condition and status of women is fairly recent in the international community of scholars and practitioners whose focus is international development. Although international pronouncements and an emerging literature introduced the issue of women into various development forums by the early 1970s, in many ways, recognition of women as a significant element in development policy was an unintended outgrowth of two United Nations conferences—the UN Food Conference and the UN Population Conference.[1] Convened in 1974 to examine food and population policies in the Third World, the conferences made similar discoveries: Most everyone involved with development issues—researchers, politicians, and policymakers—had neglected an important factor in food production and population levels. No one had considered the social roles of women as variables in production or reproduction.

At the start of the conferences, women were almost invisible. The role of women was all but absent from the agendas. The organizers, planners, and participants were overwhelmingly male, and most were working in the traditional development paradigm of modernization, which neither in its theoretical constructs nor its practical applications had identified women as a separate category worthy of investigation.[2] However, it soon became clear in analyzing the information from these two conferences that women could not be ignored, nor could they be subsumed any longer in the traditional categories of international development analysis. Women, the conferees discovered, were a distinct category that had to be separately examined and then integrated into development policy.

Specifically, at the United Nations Food Conference, the extant development paradigm had produced a mind set that associated the public production of agricultural commodities with men and assigned women the more privatized tasks of familial nutrition and consumption.[3] Such assumptions came under challenge as research revealed that women were actively engaged in food production; studies found that, on average, women's contribution to the food supply globally was approximately 44 percent[4] and in some regions, such as Africa, as high as 70 percent.[5]

The Food Conference also revealed that what women produced, how they produced it, and for whom differed from the production patterns of men. Studies found that the penetration of mercantilism and colonialism had drawn men into the production of cash crops for export and thus into employment for wages, while women continued to produce crops destined for home consumption and to do so for the most part without remuneration. Because previous assumptions had designated men as the primary producers, information on improving crop yields was disseminated primarily to men. However, the export-oriented sector of agricultural production where men dominated, although increasingly efficient, did not yield greater agricultural surplus for home consumption. Meanwhile, women, because they were not recognized as agricultural producers, were given little if any assistance in increasing their production and, as a result, still tended to produce the major home consumption crops with traditional methods and on small family plots. Because past development theory was based on inaccurate assumptions—placing men in the public and women in the private sphere of social existence—past policies were ineffective in achieving their goals of increased food production and consumption in the Third World.

The discoveries of the Food Conference were soon augmented by other insights that emerged from the UN Population Conference. Here, conferees ascertained that women were rational decisionmakers when it came to determining family size; women's decisions were conditioned not only by the availability of contraceptive devices, but more importantly by specific economic and social factors.[6] Women tended to have children when children were perceived as contributing to the economic welfare of the family. Agricultural societies, for example, viewed children as additional laborers on lands in which mechanization was not applied. In urban areas, the children of the poor engaged in a variety of service activities that brought in additional family income. Societies without extensive welfare programs regarded children as the only source of support during illness or old age. To the extent that a society valued males more than females, both legally and extralegally, women would continue to produce large numbers of children in order to be assured that a sufficient number of male children would survive in the face of high infant mortality rates and thus would be available to provide the sustenance and support the family required. In addition, to the extent that the community bestowed social status on women solely in accordance with their roles as wife and mother, and to the extent that other avenues of social identity were closed, women continued to want children in order to fulfill the only role that provided them with a measure of social esteem.

As research presented at these conferences and in subsequent investigations exposed the systematic links between the position of women in society and development concerns, some researchers began to see that a new variable needed to be included in development research—the status of women. But what was women's status? Never before confronted with this question, the international community of scholars and practitioners had little information to offer. At this juncture, a new field of inquiry emerged concerned with women's roles as they related to development.

A major impetus in these new investigations was the proclamation by the United Nations of 1975 as International Women's Year and the subsequent International Women's Year Conference held in 1975 in Mexico City. Working from the premise that not only should women's equality be bolstered by development, but that movement toward women's equality with men should have a positive impact upon national development efforts, the conveners of the conference sought to comprehensively examine the condition and status of women around the world and investigate women's roles in development and the effects of development on women.

The conference was a learning experience for all involved. Participants discovered quite rapidly that, although most governments proclaimed support for women's equality and assured the conference of their own commitment to women, few had much information on the condition and status of women in their own nations. Many nations had never thought to collect information on women as a distinct category. Basing their investigations on the reigning development paradigm, which assumed that the economic, political, and social relations of any given society would affect women in the same manner as all other groups, and often perceiving a woman's status as derivative of her relationship with a male, researchers had made little effort during the years to ascertain the specific condition and status of women. Where sufficient information on women as a distinct category was to be found—generally in industrial, "developed" nations—there was little and limited evidence to suggest that government proclamations in support of women's equality had found appreciable expression in government practices or in significant progress toward women's equality.

Women's role in the development process and the effects of development on women remained unanswered at the end of the Mexico City conference. But these new concerns were now added to a growing inventory that disputed the adequacy of the dominant development paradigm, which defined development primarily in terms of economic growth, which saw it bolstered by the maturation of pluralistic political institutions, and which assumed that such political and economic processes would, over time, benefit all in the society.[7]

To answer the specific questions concerned with women and women's role in national development became the task of the UN Decade for Women. Between 1975 and 1985, national and international investigators would systematically ask questions about women's condition and status in societies. In the process of analyzing the generated data, they would begin to ascertain how women's equality is affected by national development policies and then go on to examine how overall national development efforts might be affected by women's equality.

What has been learned since 1975? With the increase in the collection of data on women, we are now in a better position to examine, compare, analyze, and evaluate women's condition internationally in a manner that goes beyond supposition and to examine such data in correspondence with government policies that have attempted to effect women's equality.[8] A review of government policies adopted since 1975 suggests that a "sensitizing" process has occurred wherein "the integration of women into development has been formally accepted by most Governments as a desirable planning objective."[9] By 1985, "ninety percent of all nations [had] official bodies dedicated to the advancement of women [with] half of them created since the beginning of the decade."[10]

However, evidence also indicates that in no nation do women presently have equality with men; in no nation is women's political power, economic position, or social status equal to that of men. Based on the data generated, we can also conclude that, although a movement toward greater equality for women has been evidenced in some nations, little progress can be seen in others.[11] As a result of comparison and interpretation of the data, we have begun to ascertain which policies and strategies tend to afford women greater equalities over time and which factors hinder such progress.

According to the 1980 *Report of the World Conference of the United Nations Decade for Women,* positive progress toward women's equality will not occur with the "mere provision of equal rights" for women. Rather, women's equal rights and women's ability to use these rights will be conditioned by (1) the general level of economic development obtained by a nation; (2) the "priority Governments accord to issues concerning women"; (3) the degree to which women's equality is integrated in the overall development strategy of the nation; and (4) the extent to which governments take "positive and concerted action to change attitudes and prejudices" concerning women's social role.[12]

This book, which examines and compares the effects of liberal/capitalist and Marxist development strategies on women's status in the United States, Mexico, the USSR, and Cuba, tends to augment and reinforce the conclusions of the UN *Report.* Like the UN *Report,* it suggests that the granting of equal political rights to women, although important, does not in itself generate significant movement toward greater equality for women. In each of the nations studied, women have been granted equal rights to vote and hold office, but in each, women's ability to effectively use these rights to generate policies promoting greater equality for women has been conditioned by distinct economic and social factors.

Like the UN *Report,* the book also concludes that a growing industrial base will have an impact on the possibilities for women's equality. However, although economic growth is necessary in order to generate conditions favorable for women's equality, such growth is, by itself, insufficient. Other intervening variables are necessary to ensure progress: first, the degree to which reproductive and auxiliary home responsibilities are lifted off the shoulders of women and second, the degree to which social roles for male and female are redefined to encompass public and private personas.

Further, the studies in this book indicate that the ability of each of these factors to positively affect women's equality will be conditioned by the degree to which the government and the institutions of any society equate women's equality with overall national development strategy and offer leadership in promoting such conjuncture. Additionally, the emergence of a separate, nationwide women's organization that is recognized as a legitimate political force with institutionalized access to policymaking is important in conditioning both the manner in which women are affected by industrialization and the propensity of the state to adopt policies that facilitate women's entrance into the public realm and promote a redefinition of male/female social roles. A comparison of women's equality across the nations examined also suggests that the particular development strategy chosen by a nation will condition the inclination of that society to facilitate greater equality for women.

In order to familiarize the reader with the methodology employed in this study, the remainder of this chapter offers an overview of the liberal/capitalist and Marxist theories of development and the strategies of each for engendering women's equality in the process of development. I also explain the rationale employed in choosing the nations included here and set forth the criteria used to assess women's equality.

• AN OVERVIEW OF THE COMPETING THEORIES •

In the framework put forth by liberal/capitalist theories, a developed society should exhibit particular sets of social relations and institutions.[13] Economically, the society should be based on private ownership of the means of production and private or market mechanisms for the reallocation of monies back into the economy. Further, it should have a solid and growing industrial base. Politically, the society should manifest equal political rights for all citizens. Socially, it should be organized such that all individuals and groups have equal rights that allow access to and participation in the society's institutions. In these socially, economically and politically "fair" ground rules, society encourages competition between individuals and between groups to enhance overall development.

The development strategies that flow from this perspective focus on the diffusion to less-developed societies of the more modern forms of economic, political, and social relations and institutions associated with the capitalist democracies of Western Europe and the United States. In particular, with regard to the economic sector, such strategies stress policies and institutions supportive of private property and capital accumulation in order to mobilize the society for industrialization and economic growth. The concept of democratic pluralism is the cornerstone of strategies for a political system characterized by equal rights. Such strategies stress democratic elections, universal suffrage, and equal rights to run for office. Greater economic growth and democratic pluralism are additionally bolstered by developments in social organizations—greater role differentiation and specialization that lead to increased social mobility.

In this tradition, capitalist industrialization and political pluralism are the necessary components for a strategy of development that, in turn, would give rise to women's equality. Not only is capitalist industrialization the most efficient means for generating economic growth, it is also the mechanism necessary to lessen the physical requirements of labor that, according to this logic, have historically acted to limit women's role in employment and adversely conditioned women's overall social mobility and equality. Equal political rights for women are an additional prerequisite for women's equality because such rights will, when granted in conjunction with opportunities for greater social mobility, afford women equal opportunities to influence policies that affect their lives.[14]

A Marxist logic sees a developed society and the strategies necessary to get there quite differently.[15] In the Marxist context, a developed, industrialized society should exhibit communist social and institutional relations. With regard to political relations, although there is no state per se, all persons should possess what amount to equal political rights.

The development strategy offered by the Marxist approach is that of proletarian revolution and socialism: a transformation of the entire social formation in its various production, political, and sociocultural relations such that, over time, class antagonisms in all their forms will be eliminated. The initial transition from capitalist to socialist relations will produce state ownership of the means of production as well as state control over accumulation and reallocation. The socialist state will represent and serve the needs and interests of the proletariat in these matters. In addition, institutional arrangements will be organized and social norms altered to favor this class. According to Marxist analysis, it is only as these new sets of social arrangements begin to dominate the material and intellectual life of the society that the vestiges of socially antagonistic class relations will disappear. Only when the state is no longer needed to support the interests of one class over another will the society be transformed from a socialist to a communist one.

In this development strategy, women's equality is a function of changes in women's relations to two material concerns—production and reproduction.[16] In order for women to participate equally in social production and to gain equitable benefit with men from such endeavors, a resocialization of the society and its institutions must occur such that women's public as well as private roles are recognized. Additionally, the society must accept responsibility for the burdens of reproduction and its traditional auxiliary functions that have acted in the past to preclude women's equal participation in and benefit from the general social order. Under socialism this resocialization of attitudes and responsibilities should lead to greater equality for women as publicly sponsored child-care facilities are instituted, rights to paid maternity leave are legislated, and housekeeping is transformed first from a woman's private responsibility to an equal family responsibility and later into a public function. Such arrangements will assure that the development of equal rights for women in the public sphere do not place an unequal and double burden on women because of their reproductive capabilities and traditional private responsibilities.

At present, no society fits into a purely liberal/capitalist or purely communist model. Although some nations claim to have had a proletarian revolution, no nation that claims to be pursuing a Marxist strategy fully exhibits communist social relations, if for no other reason than they all continue to be statist. Similarly, no industrially developed nation that professes capitalism does more than approximate capitalist production relations. For the purposes of this study, however, it is possible to differentiate between nations according to the dominant character of their overall social organization and the dominant thrust of their development strategy and examine women's equality as it proceeds from different strategies for national development.

• THE CHOICE OF RELEVANT CASES •

In the general category of liberal/capitalist societies and at a level of high industrialization, the United States in an obvious choice as a relevant case for examination. Not only has the United States put itself forth as a model of this form of development, but it fits quite well in the liberal/capitalist logic. All citizens are assumed to have equal political rights and the potential to affect government decisions in matters that concern their needs and interests. Although there is state intervention into the economy, the government acts either to provide collective goods that otherwise could not be produced profitably or to provide the preconditions or stimulus for profitable private investment through fiscal or monetary policies.

The strategy promoted in the United States to generate greater equality for women also fits well in the liberal/capitalist framework. The conditions of industrialization and economic growth should afford women greater opportunities for employment and social mobility. Because women have been granted equal political rights and are assumed to have the potential to influence policy equal to that of all other groups, the general thrust of government policy concerning women's equality is to intervene only when women's equal civil rights are not recognized.

In the category of highly industrialized and socialist countries, the Union of Soviet Socialist Republics immediately stands out as an obvious choice. Not only has the Soviet Union put itself forth as a model of socialist development, but it fits fairly well in the Marxist logic. It has had a proletarian revolution, and the state presently owns and operates the means of production, controls accumulation from production, and reallocates these monies as well as the products of production in the name of the proletariat.[17]

With regard to a development strategy for women's equality, the USSR also fits fairly well in the Marxist logic. In the Soviet Union, women have been granted equal political, economic, and social rights and responsibilities. Further, legislation has been effected and institutional arrangements organized that recognize women's dual social roles in production and reproduction. Attempts have also been made to change attitudes toward women's social role.

However, the Soviet strategy for development has differed from traditional Marxist theory in one substantial way. At the time of the Russian Revolution, what were traditionally viewed as the "material and human preconditions for socialism—a technology of abundance and an educated, urban working class capable of mastering it"—were not present.[18] Although Russia had a growing industrial base and was participating in a capitalist world economy by 1917, its pervasive economic character was far from industrial, and it was still unable to provide abundantly for the Russian society, even if production had been organized differently and its products distributed more equitably. Additionally, there was no organized tradition of political participation among the class that under a socialist system would direct the production and distribution of economic surplus and social benefit—the proletariat. Nor was the population "educated" in the ways necessary to run or reorder the society.

Because of this difference in its emergence, the Soviet state has not followed the traditional Marxist schema for socialist development. With regard to production relations, the Soviet state not only had to function as owner and operator of the means of production and act as the mechanism for the reallocation of surplus and benefits, but it also had to mobilize and allocate resources for industrialization and the production of abundance. Similarly, Soviet political relations differed from those envisioned by traditional Marxist theory. Political power was not transferred immediately to an organized and politically educated proletariat; rather, power to determine social direction fell into the hands of individuals who claimed to represent the needs of the developing proletariat.

These factors may well have an effect on the relevance of the Soviet case, but all other nations in the general category of industrially developed and socialist have similar and often more profound drawbacks.[19] In addition, some modern theoreticians writing in the Marxist tradition have modified Marx's classic theory concerning the need for industrial abundance prior to the establishment of a socialist state. Contending that in the twentieth century, nations cannot hope to industrialize sufficiently (because of the international system of capitalist relations), some Marxist theorists have called for a new type of socialist revolution brought about through a coalition of proletariat and peasantry. Socialism, in this new interpretation, is not the result of class struggles, in a condition of surplus, initiated to redesign society, but rather an alternative strategy to develop such surplus without prior capitalist inequalities.[20] Although not all these writers would look to the Soviet Union as a model of this new strategy for socialist development, Soviet society does fit within the boundaries of this new interpretation.

In the category of less-developed countries, methodological integrity demands that the choice of representative nations take cultural attributes into account—history or religion, for example—in order to avoid the effects extreme variations in these areas might have in more traditional societies. This book examines representative nations from the Latin American region because the author has greater knowledge of the nations of Latin America than of the nations in Africa or Asia and is thus better able to assess the effect of cultural attributes on these societies.

Cuba is the only Latin American society that espouses a development logic derived from Marxist theory.[21] A proletarian-peasant revolution attained power in 1959. Since the early 1960s, Cuban development efforts have stressed the achievement of greater equality and greater industrial growth in the context of a socialist political economy. The Cuban state presently controls the means of production and the accumulation of surplus as well as its reallocation. Although political power is not directly in the hands of the proletariat, the revolution attempted early on to mobilize the population in political activities, and recently it has moved toward a decentralization of political power and elections.

The Cuban strategy for women's equality also fits well in a Marxist logic. Women in Cuba have gained equal political, economic, and social rights, and in order for women to actualize these rights, Cuban society has developed institutions to socialize the burdens of reproduction and home responsibilities. The state has also attempted to change attitudes toward male and female social roles through its control of the media and educational institutions.

Two Latin American nations were initially identified as possible representatives of the less-developed, liberal/capitalist type—Mexico and Brazil. Each is industrializing but has yet to reach the category of industrially developed. In both nations, the strategy for economic growth and industrialization fits well in one form of capitalist economic relations, that of state capitalism. In other words, although each has instituted industrial development policies that rely on a large measure of government intervention in the free market, each has done so within the parameters of modern capitalist development principles. However, Mexico exhibits a modicum of democratic pluralism and verbally supports its intervention in the economy with proclamations that such intervention is needed to benefit all of the people through more channeled economic growth. Brazil, on the other hand, achieved its economic growth during the 1960s and 1970s despite (or maybe because of) its lack of democratic institutions. Because of this factor, Brazil does not reflect the democratic and pluralistic component of the liberal/capitalist logic and was rejected for this study.

In Mexico, the development strategy put forth for women's equality is similar to that of the United States. Although neither nation granted women equal political rights for a considerable time after independence, women in Mexico now enjoy equal political rights with men. Because women have these rights, it is assumed that women can be elected to office themselves and/or can elect persons who will represent their interests. Neither political power nor social mobility have diffused successfully throughout the society, but within the realm of civil rights, Mexican law does not discriminate against women simply because they are women. As industrialization increases, it is believed that women will be drawn into the public realm of paid employment and, like all other groups, increasingly gain the social mobility necessary to achieve social equality.

Each of the four nations selected, although a representative case of different development logics, has important differences in social organization and level of development that make any comparable assessment of women's equality challenging. The following section explains the framework used for examination and comparison in the case studies that follow.

• INDICATORS OF WOMEN'S STATUS AND EQUALITY •

The liberal/capitalist and Marxist perspectives differ as to the key variables conditioning women's equality and status, but each defines women's equality as equal access to, participation in, and benefit from the political, social, and economic arrangements of society. Each perspective, although to a different degree, is also concerned with women's equality in the public sphere and in the domain of the family—i.e., with women's rights and accepted role in family structure and with the effects women's familial role has on their ability to participate equally in the public sphere. However, although each logic offers strategies to positively affect women's equality and status in society, neither offers guidance for developing specific indicators by which to assess women's equality. Interestingly, national reports on women's equality and women's status from the four nations do use similar indicators.[22] The same indicators also are present in international reports on women that have been compiled from a much larger sample of nations.[23] An extensive review of these sources as well as the social science literature concerned with definitions of female status and indicators of women's equality allows for some general conclusions.

There tends to be general agreement that in any social system and at any level of development, female status can be defined in both public and private spheres with reference to (1) women's power and authority and (2) society's perception of women's acceptable roles. Women's equality relative to that of men's, in this regard, is generally measured by (1) women's abilities to acquire and exercise influence, power, and authority as compared with men's abilities; and (2) the parameters of acceptable social activity and social roles allowed to each sex. Additionally, although reports may focus on only one aspect of women's social relations, there is general agreement that in any society "the position of women represents a coherent structure in which all the elements [of social relations] are integrated: ideology, the role of the family, role in society, economic role, sphere of activity and sphere of forbidden activity, etc."[24]

As such, any comparative study of women must be cautious and take as many relations into consideration as possible. Indicators of women's status and measures of women's equality must be defined to include the totality of social relations—economic, political, and social. Additionally, the indicators must be flexible enough to probe the issue of women's equality in various and differing contexts. (See Figure 1.1 for a more comprehensive and specific breakdown of the indicators used throughout this study.)

The question of where to chronologically begin such comparative studies is crucial if any attempt to evaluate the effectiveness of different development strategies on women's equality is to be made. Fortunately, the logic of each theory is quite specific with regard to what might constitute the starting point. In the liberal/capitalist logic, the strategy for women's equality necessitates two conditions: (1) that a society be industrializing and (2) that women exercise equal political rights. From the time that these two conditions are met, positive changes in women's social equality should be evidenced. Therefore, in the United States and Mexico, the period for examination should extend forward from that time when the process of industrialization was joined with women's suffrage—1920 for the United States and 1954 for Mexico. To assess changes wrought by such a strategy, however, an assessment of women's social equality during the period immediately proceeding such a conjoining is also important.

In the Marxist logic, a similar break point is available. Before positive changes in women's equality will be evidenced, a socialist revolution, equal political rights for women, the social recognition of women's dual role in society, and the development of institutional and ideological supports to lessen the

FIGURE 1.1 Indicators of Women's Equality

Women's Political Power

A. Legal Entitlement
   1. rights to equal protection under the law
   2. rights to suffrage
   3. rights to hold political office
   4. rights to serve on policymaking bodies

B. Political Influence
   1. the existence of women's political organizations
   2. the percentage of women who participate in women's political organizations
   3. the percentage of women in politically influential organizations
   4. women's effect on legislation

C. Political Authority
   1. the percentage of women elected to office at various levels of government
   2. the percentage of women appointed to office at various levels of government
   3. the percentage of women participating in preparatory paths to positions of political authority

Women's Economic Position

A. Economic Rights
   1. employment rights
   2. wage rights
   3. job security rights
   4. trade union rights
   5. maternity rights

B. Economic Participation
   1. the percentage of women in the labor force
   2. the percentage of the labor force, both full time and part time, that is female
   3. the composition of the female labor force by age, marital status, and age and number of children

C. Occupational Distribution
   1. the percentage of each economic sector that is female
   2. the percentage of various occupational groups that is female
   3. the percentage of managerial positions, overall and within various occupational groups, that is female
   4. the percentage of women occupying high- and low-status occupations

D. Remuneration
   1. women's average wage as compared with men's
   2. average female/male wage rates in particular occupational categories
   3. a comparison of female/male nonsalary benefits

E. Education and Training
   1. the percentage of women completing various levels of education
   2. areas of educational specialization for males and females

Women's Social Status

A. Social Rights
   1. rights and duties in marriage
   2. rights regarding divorce
   3. rights regarding child custody
   4. responsibilities regarding child support
   5. rights to control over maternity

B. Recognition of Women's Dual Role
   1. availability and quality of child-care
   2. costs of child care
   3. availability of surrogate household services

C. Social Identity
   1. portrayal of male and female social roles in media and government institutions
   2. percentage and type of male participation in household maintenance

private burdens of this social role must have taken place. Therefore, in the Soviet Union and Cuba, the period for examination should extend from just prior to the development of such conditions—1921 for the USSR and 1959 for Cuba.

In this book I use historical narrative to describe and illustrate changes in women's political power, economic position, and social status in the four nations being examined. Following the country studies, an assessment of the effects of the different strategies on women's equality allows some conclusions to be drawn about the relationships between development strategy and women's political, economic, and social status.

• CHAPTER TWO •
The Limits of Suffrage: Women in the United States

In examining the effects of the liberal/capitalist strategy on women's equality in the United States, the year 1920 emerges as a watershed. Prior to this time, women were without uniform rights or legal status, although a few states had granted women limited political rights. It was only with the ratification of the Nineteenth Amendment to the Constitution in August 1920 that women finally emerged as citizens with voting and certain other political rights equal to those of men. By this time, the United States also had emerged as a modern industrial economy. Between 1870 and 1920, the United States experienced a period of rapid economic growth and industrialization. Factories multiplied and agriculture became increasingly mechanized. By 1920, the economy was transformed into an industrial one, and with it evolved a more mobile and urban society. The joining of industrialization with the political rights granted under the Nineteenth Amendment appears to satisfy the preconditions for the unfolding of the liberal/capitalist strategy for women's equality.

This chapter examines the following question: has the granting of equal political rights to women in the United States allowed them to benefit equally with men from the industrial development and economic growth of the nation? Or, more specifically, to what extent has the combined advantage of political rights and industrial expansion allowed women in the United States to attain greater equality relative to men in the marketplace, in political arenas, and in general social hierarchies? The following sections attempt to shed some light on these questions, first by offering a general description of women's condition prior to suffrage, and then by tracing changes in women's economic, political, and social equality from 1920 through the mid-1980s.

• THE ROAD TO SUFFRAGE •

Women's Economic Position

Impoverished women have traditionally been employed outside their homes. Although primarily employed as domestic servants, poor women also worked as teachers, especially at the elementary level.[1] However, this pattern of female employment altered after the Civil War as the quickening pace of industrialization and mechanization created a larger market for unskilled workers, and the adoption of publicly funded education, combined with the development of compulsory schooling, allowed greater numbers of women to gain an education.[2]

Between 1870 and 1920, two major changes in women's economic position occurred. First, women became a greater proportion of the labor force. Second, for the first time, educated women from the middle class began entering the work force in large numbers. Although poor and immigrant women flocked to the factories, the newly developed typing machine opened up the realm of office work to women with an education. Between 1890 and 1900, more than 1 million women joined the labor force. By 1920, 20 percent of the total labor force was female.[3]

The occupational composition of employed women also changed. Whereas in 1900, women's employment was limited to a few areas—domestics, farm laborers, unskilled factory operatives, and teachers—by 1910 women had begun a steady climb into the ranks of white-collar occupations.[4] During the decade 1910-1920, more than 1 million women joined the pool of clerical workers, bringing the percentage of clerical workers who were women up to 21 percent. By 1920, women were 30 percent of all clerical workers, and women also represented 85 percent of all teachers.[5]

Federal government recognition of the tremendous influx of women into the work force came in 1918 with the creation of a special Women's Bureau in the Department of Labor. The bureau observed that although women were being educated in greater numbers and were steadily entering the work force in both manual and white-collar occupations, their employment still tended to bring them less remuneration than that received by men. Although women attempted to organize themselves to collectively bargain for better wages and working conditions, their attempts were rarely successful. In the ranks of organized labor, recruitment efforts were concentrated primarily on skilled, blue-collar workers, whereas women predominated precisely in the unskilled areas of blue-collar employment. In 1910, the percentage of women wage-earners who had succeeded in becoming unionized was only 1.5 percent.[6]

Women's Social Status

The prevailing attitude toward women's role in society was a key determinant of women's political and economic position. In general, society viewed women as fulfilling a different role than men. Conventional wisdom held that women were created to fulfill a "higher and holier" purpose.[7] A woman's accepted social function was to ensure the moral character of the society through her influence in her immediate family, and, thus, her social role was depicted almost exclusively in the context of her private roles as wife and mother. Men, on the other hand, were expected to participate in the public realm of economic and political activity and in doing so fulfill their domestic role as provider and protector.

Women's Political Power

Until 1920, this social perception defined and circumscribed women's political role as an adjunct to men. During the struggle for the abolition of slavery and later, during debates on the Fourteenth and Fifteenth Amendments to the Constitution, which were designed to enfranchise the former slaves, the issue of women's political rights emerged quite forcefully. Speaking before his fellows during debate on the Fourteenth Amendment, Senator Williams of Oregon summed up the prevailing social attitude when he observed that equal political rights for women would be the downfall of the family and the ruin of U.S. society, which he asserted was built on the concept of the patriarchal (i.e., male-dominated) family:

> When God married our first parents in the garden according to that ordinance they were made 'bone of one bone and flesh of one flesh'; and the whole theory of government and society proceeds upon the assumption that their interests are one. . . . The woman who undertakes to put her sex in an adversary position to man, who undertakes by the use of some independent political power to contend and fight against man, displays a spirit which would, if able, convert all the now harmonious elements of society into a state of war, and make every home a hell on earth.[8]

According to the legal scholarship of this time, a woman's legal person was suspended upon marriage. The husband and wife were viewed as one entity, with all legal standing being "encorporated and consolidated" into the person of the husband.[9] In the various states, different legal traditions gave women differing rights, but none afforded women total legal equality. For instance, women's rights to property often altered with marriage, and in most instances the rights of wives were subservient to the rights of husbands. Because women could not legally sign contracts in many states, they were legally denied even the few benefits men might acquire through collective bargaining. Because women could not exercise the franchise, elected officials placed laws for improving women's wages and working conditions low on, if not off of, their policy agendas.

Until 1920, women were without any direct political power. Although their influence had grown in some states, in general, women's legal rights were not recognized as equal to those of men. In some respects, however, women's economic position was beginning to change. Not only was the female labor force growing, but women were beginning to occupy white-collar as well as unskilled, blue-collar positions. However, the jobs for which women were hired still tended to be concentrated in quite limited and narrow bounds and offer salaries lower than those offered to men. Because much of the occupational and remunerative discrimination against women was believed by those supporting suffrage to emanate from the circumscribed social and political roles attributed to women, hopes were high that the granting of suffrage would remove the barriers to women's economic and social equality.

• **WOMEN'S POLITICAL POWER:
SUFFRAGE AND BEYOND** •

Women's Legal Rights

Women in the United States have made some dramatic strides since 1920. Once the necessary two-thirds of the states ratified the Nineteenth Amendment, women attained equal political rights—equal rights to vote and hold office in all states and at all levels of public office. By the 1970s, women comprised more than one-half the electorate and had been elected or appointed to a variety of local, state, and national offices. However, to fully appreciate women's legal position in the U.S. political system, an examination of state as well as national law is important because, according to the Constitution, all powers not vested in the federal government fall to the individual states. Although a constitutional amendment assuring that "equality of rights under the law shall not be denied or abridged by the United States or any state on the account of sex" was first proposed in 1923 and passed Congress in 1973, it was defeated in June 1982 when less than the two-thirds majority necessary for ratification voted in favor of the amendment's passage. As a result, although federal law presently gives women in all states specific rights, women's legal rights in many areas of important jurisdictional matters differ between states.[10]

Women's Political Influence

Women's influence on public policy diminished in the years immediately following suffrage and only recently has reemerged as a factor in policy formation. With passage of the Nineteenth Amendment, both Democratic and Republican parties "appointed women as equal members [although not in equal numbers] to their respective national committees, and each named female aspirants to governmental positions."[11] Lobbyists from women's organizations flooded congressional offices in an attempt to get a variety of bills passed onto the floor. From all reports, between 1921 and 1924 women's organizations seemed very effective in getting legislation passed. However, the positive response by legislators seems to have been prompted not by sympathy or agreement, but by the fear that male politicians had regarding the strength of the new female vote.

The battle for women's suffrage was "waged on the premise that females had a special set of interests which distinguished them from men and made it necessary for them to have a separate voice" in political decisions.[12] By 1924, when it was fairly obvious that women neither exercised the franchise in large numbers nor constituted an automatic voting bloc, women's organized political influence began to decrease. Additionally, whereas the struggle for suffrage had united women on a common issue, once suffrage was granted, no such unifying factor remained, and women's organizations lost a large portion of their constituency. Although in the decade of the 1890s there were 800 active women's groups and in 1920 the major women's suffrage organization, the National American Women's Suffrage Association, "boasted a membership of 2 million women," by 1925, the women's movement comprised but a "small cadre of activists."[13] This further eroded women's political influence.

Women's political influence remained low throughout the rest of the decade. Beginning in 1932, however, women again gained a modicum of influence in political circles. This increase in women's influence is not generally attributed to women's organizations, however, but to the roles played by two particular women—Mary Dewson and Eleanor Roosevelt. In 1932, Dewson revitalized the nearly moribund Women's Bureau of the Democratic party and utilized the platform of the proposed New Deal to mobilize women in support of the Democratic candidate for president, Franklin Roosevelt. Her efforts were extremely effective. Recognizing that women could mobilize support for the administration's programs, Roosevelt appointed Dewson and a number of other women to positions in the many social service agencies that developed during the 1930s.

Eleanor Roosevelt's contribution to women's increased political influence during the Roosevelt administration was considerable. Not only was she the wife of the chief executive, and therefore in a unique position to influence him on a variety of matters, she was also an articulate spokesperson for many issues of concern to women. Her presence at the White House, in combination with the other women appointed to various New Deal agencies, assured that issues of concern to women would at least get a hearing. According to William Chafe, when women in the New Deal programs asked other agencies of the government for assistance with regard to women's issues, they often sent a duplicate copy of such requests to the White House. Perhaps more importantly, it was common for the White House, in turn, to forward a copy of the request to the appropriate agency along with "a personal note of endorsement from the president or his wife."[14]

Overall, however, women's political influence remained sporadic and individual, at best. Although women worked in greater numbers in both parties, they did not work on women's issues per se. Rather, throughout the Depression and World War II, women who were active in party politics focused their attention on more general national issues, for example, the social and economic policies of the New Deal or winning the war. This is not to suggest that women were without their own organizational affiliations. Women continued to join a variety of organizations throughout this period—for example, the American Association of University Women, the National Federation of Business and Professional Women, and various organizations affiliated with the General Federation of Women's Clubs.[15] However, most were without a direct political thrust, and there was no common political goal that connected these organizations. As a result, there was no national cohesion among women's groups. It was not until the late 1960s and early 1970s that women once again organized on behalf of political issues of specific concern to women. In the interim, women's groups that were concerned with politics, such as the League of Women Voters, tended to address issues of "good government" rather than issues specific to women or their concerns.

In the mainstream of party politics, women have organized caucuses in all the major parties, and they have been appointed to many party positions. However, they have not generally been able to positively influence their parties on issues of specific concern to women, and at times they have become frustrated. For example, when Jill Ruckelhouse—a woman who has been appointed to many federal boards and commissions concerned with women's issues—spoke in 1978 of her role as a feminist in the Republican party, she compared it to her first lesson in ballroom dancing: "In my first class, I put my hand on my partner's shoulder and realized I was going to spend the rest of my life dancing backwards. Now I realize that this was perfect training for becoming a Republican feminist."[16]

The Republican party is not alone. From the mid-to-late-1970s, during the administration of a Democratic president and with a Democratic Congress, women's issues did not fare well either. One year after a National Women's Conference was sponsored by the federal government with a mandate to examine women's role in the United States and to recommend specific legislative changes, a review of the legislative record of the Congress indicates that there was minimal action taken. Few of the recommendations had been debated, and the provisions of those that became law were of a much more limited nature than was originally proposed.[17]

On the whole, women have not been influential in getting male politicians and political parties to reorder their priorities, and as a result women's issues have remained low on the executive and legislative agendas well into the 1980s. Speaking to this point, Eleanor Smeal, president of the National Organization for Women, commented that "for too many years candidates have pledged support for women's rights, but action after elections has been sadly lacking."[18] Women have also had limited success in becoming part of the political power structure that determines such priorities.

Women's Political Authority

In the fifty-odd years since suffrage, the percentage of politically authoritative positions held by women has not changed as dramatically as was expected by the supporters of suffrage. Whereas in 1920, only one woman was a member of the

House of Representatives, by 1984 women had increased their ranks to only 5 percent: 22 out of a total of 435 representatives were female.[19] Although the number of women in the Senate has varied, there have never been more than two women senators at any one time. Until the late 1960s and early 1970s, Emma Bugbee's 1930 remark that women in elective office played a "widow's game" rang true. The overwhelming majority of women elected to Congress "succeeded their dead husbands, most for only a single term."[20] At the state level the pattern was similar.[21] Not until 1974 was a woman elected governor in her own right—Ella T. Grasso of Connecticut.

Although conventional wisdom holds that women concentrate their political activities on the local as opposed to national level, a combined picture of women's political authority at all levels of elective office is not encouraging. In the mid-1970s, women held only "5 percent of all local, state and federal elective positions."[22] In the state legislatures, women held only 13 percent of the elected positions in the early 1980s.[23] At the local level, female elected officials were still rare.

Women in appointive positions fare a bit better. Women began to appear in positions of national authority during the administration of Franklin Roosevelt when, for the first time, a woman was appointed to a cabinet position—Frances Perkins was given the position of Secretary of Labor in 1932. However, fifty-odd years later, women in cabinet positions are still rare. From 1932 through 1976, only three women served in cabinet positions. During the Carter administration, three more women were variously appointed.[24] During the Reagan administrations, up to 15 percent of the cabinet has been female at any one time.[25]

Florence Allen, also appointed by FDR, was the first female federal judge. She sat on the U.S. Circuit Court of Appeals. However, until the end of the 1970s, the number of women appointed to the federal bench increased very little. Out of 675 federal judges sitting in 1974, for example, only 8 were women, and at that time, only 10 women had ever received appointments to the federal bench.[26] During the Carter administration, some 152 federal judgeships were created, and 40 women were given appointments, raising the percentage of women in the federal judiciary to an all-time high of 5 percent.[27] Until Sandra Day O'Connor and the Reagan administration, no women had ever been appointed to the Supreme Court, and it was not until the latter part of the 1970s that a woman served as judge at the level of a state supreme court, Justice Rose Bird of California.

When state and local levels are combined, the percentage of women in appointive positions is somewhat higher but still far from impressive.[28] In 1975, thirty-nine states responded to a questionnaire on women's participation on appointive state boards and commissions. The percentage of women varied from state to state, ranging from a high of 23 percent (in Arizona, Hawaii, Iowa, and Washington) to a low of 11 percent, (in Arkansas, Indiana, Louisiana, New York, Ohio, and Texas) with the percentage of women appointed averaging only

15 percent of all appointments. On more than 53 percent of the boards and commissions studied, there were no female members.[29]

Although women are not excluded by law from participating in positions of political authority, traditionally women have not participated in those activities and occupations that society views as routes to elected or appointed office, nor is society at large socialized to view women as political actors. Commenting on this social perception of women's public role in her book *In The Running: The New Woman Candidate,* Ruth Mandel concludes:

> Centuries of history and custom have taught that women belong in the private sphere. Rather than seeking elective office, a single woman is still thought to be better off seeking a good husband; instead of serving in office, a married woman is expected to be serving her husband's and children's needs first.[30]

At the national and state levels and in most local elections, individuals running for political office need to get the endorsement of one of the major political parties. In these parties, nominations for office usually go to individuals who have proven themselves at other levels of elective or appointive office. Or, if an individual has not previously held office, she or he is usually expected to have demonstrated leadership qualities through previous business, professional, or party work. Because there are few women in positions of political authority and women in general have not risen to the levels of administrative responsibility that would afford them the background skills considered important for elected officials, few women receive party backing either financially or organizationally.[31] Further, women do not constitute a significant percentage of the one occupation whose practitioners seem to dominate the political arena in the United States—the legal profession.

• WOMEN'S ECONOMIC POSITION: SUFFRAGE AND BEYOND •

Women's Economic Participation

In many ways, women's position in the U.S. economy has changed dramatically since 1920. As can be seen in Table 2.1, between 1920 and 1980 the proportion of females entering the labor force continued the steady climb begun during the first waves of industrialization. A closer examination also shows that the most dramatic shifts in women's overall economic participation came after 1940. Each decade between 1940 and 1970 saw the number of women workers as a percentage of the total labor force grow by 4 percent. However, 1980 figures suggest that this trend may be moderating. Figures on married women who are employed also show their most dramatic rise in the postwar period. Between 1940 and 1980, the proportion of married women who were working grew from 17 to 56 percent.

TABLE 2.1

The Female Labor Force in the United States

Year	Female Labor Force as Percentage of Total Labor Force	Female Labor Force as Percentage of Female Population	
		Total	Married
1920	20	23	9
1930	22	24	12
1940	25	27	17
1950	29	31	25
1960	33	35	32
1970	38	43	41
1980	39	51	56

Source: U.S. Department of Labor, Women's Bureau, 1975 Handbook of Women Workers (Washington, D.C.: Government Printing Office, 1975), pp. 9, 11, 17; Rosalyn Baxnell, Linda George, and Susan Reverby, eds., America's Working Women (New York: Random House, 1976) p. 405; Ruth Leger Sivard, Women...a world survey (Washington, D.C.: World Priorities 1985), pp. 14, 20.

Although insufficient data exist to explain what may be a leveling off of women's labor force participation in 1980, the increase in the number of women workers that began in the 1940s is generally attributed to the economic and social changes wrought by World War II. The war wrenched the U.S. economy out of the Depression, creating large numbers of jobs in traditional occupational fields as well as in the new wartime industries. Because a large proportion of the male labor force was under arms, women workers were called upon to fill the nation's employment needs. Between 1940 and 1945, the size of the female labor force increased by 50 percent as 6 million women joined the ranks of the employed for the first time.[32]

Immediately after the war, however, women's participation in the labor force diminished. U.S. Department of Labor statistics show that in April 1945 women were 36.1 percent of all workers, but by April 1947 only 29.1 percent of the labor force was female.[33] There is a simple explanation for much of this drop: Men who had previously been removed from the labor force during the war were reentering the job market, and, thus, the overall number of male workers increased dramatically. At the end of the war, women did not leave the work force in the numbers some commentators anticipated, nor to the degree that tradition has led many to believe. Although females comprised 60 percent of all workers released from employment in the early months after the war, and women were laid off at a rate of 75 percent higher than men, an increasing number of women continued to seek employment. Although 3.25 million women left their wartime employment between September 1945 and November 1946, nearly 2.75 million were hired at new jobs. As Chafe suggests, women "did not disappear from the labor market," but they did lose "some of their better-paid war positions."[34]

The demands of World War II also brought an increasing percentage of women with children into the work force. Estimates suggest that one-quarter of the women who entered employment during the war had children under eighteen years of age.[35] Women with children also remained in the labor force after the war. By 1974, the proportion of employed women with children under eighteen represented 38 percent of all women workers. By March 1980, the figure had increased to 56 percent.[36]

Apart from the experience of the war, the increased degree of labor force participation by women since 1920 has been attributed to the combined effects of two trends: (1) the growth of the service sector in the United States and (2) women's rising educational level. These changes have not, however, dramatically altered either the working conditions women have encountered, women's occupational choices, or the parity of women's wages as compared to men's.

Women's Occupational Distribution

Any description of women's occupational composition during the two decades between 1920 and 1940 paints a rather bleak picture. When women's economic participation is broken down according to occupational category, and employment categories are placed in rank order according to the number of women employed in each, the types of jobs that form the top ten occupations for women do not change dramatically.[37] Although shifts in occupation rankings do occur, until World War II women were employed primarily as unskilled workers or as clerical help. Although women increased their participation in factory work, and this occupational category entered the top ten female occupations by 1940, one area of industrial employment—the garment industry—accounted for more than 40 percent of all women working in industry. Although the percentage of female professionals (most of whom were nurses or teachers) grew to 14.2 percent by 1930—mainly due to the influx of nurses following World War I—the percentage of women professionals actually dropped during the decade of the Great Depression, falling to 12.3 percent by 1940. This decrease was due in large measure to the drop in the percentage of women employed as teachers. In the field of teaching, however, women had made some tremendous gains since 1920.

Although women educators remained clustered at the elementary level, the proportion of women college teachers had risen to 35.2 percent by 1930. This figure is somewhat offset, however, by the fact that within these ranks, women constituted only 4 percent of the full professors. In all occupations, in fact, few women were employed in higher ranks or in supervisory and administrative positions.[38]

Female occupational mobility did begin to shift as the U.S. economy geared up for World War II. The percentage of women in overall manufacturing occupations shot up 110 percent between 1941 and 1945, and women's participation in such war-related occupations as welding, shipbuilding, and other highly skilled crafts rose by 460 percent. Additionally, in industry and government, women flocked to provide the clerical support services necessary to run the war.[39]

Changes in women's employment opportunities were especially advantageous for black women. Whereas prior to 1941 black women were twice as likely to work as white women, they were disproportionately concentrated in two occupations: 70 percent of all working black women were domestics, and another 20 percent were employed in agriculture. By 1945, the percentage of black women working as domestics had dropped to 48 percent, and only 7 percent were still employed in agricultural labor. In this same period, the percentage of black females employed in industry more than doubled, rising from 7.3 percent in 1941 to 18.6 percent in 1945.[40] Although by 1947 nonwhite women were still more apt than white women to work outside the home, the gap between nonwhite and white women who sought employment had narrowed to 14 percent (down from 50 percent in 1940).[41]

The trend of women joining the ranks of skilled workers did not continue after the war, however. Many of the war industries changed to other types of production, and women workers were dismissed during the interim conversion periods in greater numbers than men.[42] Many women had been placed on seniority lists separate from men, and male lists were used fully before women were retained. Further, when it came to new hirings, returned veterans were given preference over female war workers. By the mid-1970s the percentage of females employed in skilled jobs remained almost negligible, and the percentage of women in all blue-collar occupations, skilled and unskilled, remained low.[43]

Today, women are still more likely than men to be concentrated in a few occupations and in lower paying positions. In 1973, according to the U.S. Department of Labor, more than 40 percent of all employed women worked in just ten occupations: secretary, retail trade salesworker, bookkeeper, private household worker, elementary school teacher, waitress, typist, cashier, sewers and stitchers, and registered nurse. One-third of all working women were employed in clerical work. Male employment statistics do not show the same pattern of concentration. In the same study, the Department of Labor found that only 20 percent of all male workers were employed in the ten most common male occupational categories.[44] In 1980, Ellen Goodman reported that "80 percent of the women in this country work in the 20 job categories that are overwhelmingly female."[45]

In the general category of professional work, women constituted only 14.5 percent of all professionals in the mid-1970s and were represented in appreciable numbers in only two professions—nursing and teaching. These are the same professions in which women dominated at the turn of the century. Almost 98 percent of all nurses were female in the mid-1970s, and nursing accounted for approximately 17 percent of all professional employment for women. Elementary and secondary teachers represented an additional 43 percent of women's professional employment.[46]

Until 1980, the number of women employed in higher education had dropped continuously since the early 1930s when women accounted for approximately 35 percent of all college teachers. By 1973, only 27 percent of college faculties were female, and in the universities, women clustered at the lowest ranks—45 percent of instructors, 15.2 percent of associate professors, and 9 percent of full professors. In total, college teaching employed only .4 percent of all women professionals. By the academic year 1983-84, women in higher education had yet to regain their 1930s status, averaging only 27 percent of all instructional personnel. The pattern of female employment in higher education has not altered much, either; women remain concentrated in the nontenured ranks.[47]

In other professional endeavors, women's proportion of employment is still exceedingly low. By 1980, for example, women made up only 14 percent of all those employed in the legal profession[48], and although the percentage of women medical doctors had more than doubled since 1920, women were but 9 percent of all physicians and surgeons in 1973[49] and only 13 percent by 1980.[50]

Although the percentage of women in the labor force has grown in the years since suffrage, women have continued to be employed in fewer occupations than men, and perhaps more importantly with regard to social mobility, women have increasingly been concentrated in occupations that have low social status and offer low wages.

Women's Remuneration

Working with U.S. Department of Labor statistics from 1910-1960, Dale L. Hiestand developed an Index of the Status of Occupations, using occupational wage rates as a main measure. A summary of his findings was reported by Abbott L. Ferris as follows:

> His results show an improvement in the relative occupational position of Negro females relative to white females, an improvement slightly greater than that of Negro males relative to white males, 1910-1960. The position of females relative to males, by color, improved from 1910 to 1940 but since 1940,

both have deteriorated, owing primarily to the entrance of women after 1940 into lower paying positions.[51]

In 1974, according to U.S. Department of Commerce information, the wage distribution pattern was similar, with white males making greater salaries, on average, than nonwhite males and women's salaries trailing behind men's (see Table 2.2).

Interestingly enough, the earnings gap between females and males has actually risen over time. Whereas women, on average, earned approximately sixty-five cents for every dollar a man earned in the 1930s and 1940s, by 1974 women only earned fifty-seven cents,[52] and according to data compiled by the U.S. Census Bureau, this was part of a pattern during the two decades from 1960 to 1980 wherein women's wages as compared with men's continually fluctuated between 57 and 60 percent.[53] In the 1980s, a woman's color as well as her sex continued to condition her paycheck. On average, white women earned fifty-nine cents for each dollar of male earnings, but black women earned only fifty-four cents and Hispanic women just forty-nine cents.[54]

Level of education does not account for such disparities. In 1968, a man with less than eight years of schooling, on average, would make more than a woman with one to three years of college, and a man with only a grammar school education would earn about the same as a woman with a college degree—$5,096 for the man, $5,305 for the woman. A man with a university degree, on the other hand, would earn an average of $11,257.[55] In 1973, the median income

TABLE 2.2

U.S. Median Wage or Salary Income of Year-round,
Full-time Workers, by Race and Sex (1974)
(persons 14 years of age and over)

Race	Women	Men	Dollar Gap	Women's Earnings as a Percentage of Men's
Minority	$6,611	$9,082	$2,471	72.8
White	7,025	12,343	5,318	56.9
Total	$6,967	$12,072	$5,105	57.9

Source: United States Department of Labor, The Earnings Gap Between Men and Women (Washington, D.C.: Government Printing Office, 1976), p.12.

for women remained far below that for men at all educational levels. U.S. government reports of the 1980 census concluded that in the same occupations and with the same level of education, men and women were still paid at different rates with permanent, full-time women workers averaging $11,200 and their male counterparts receiving $18,006.[56]

Women's Economic Rights

The fact that women in the United States have traditionally made lower salaries than men is not surprising when women's economic rights are examined. Until very recently, legislation affecting wages and working conditions has been of limited value to women and has often explicitly discriminated against them. Further, whereas males oftentimes secured better wages and working conditions through unions, women's role in organized labor has been limited, at best.

New Deal legislation brought greater government intervention in the economy, but government action in the areas of wages and working conditions had little impact on women workers. Although the National Recovery Act (NRA) of 1933 gave workers the rights to organize collectively and to bargain for higher wages and better working conditions, and further allowed the federal government to establish minimum wage rates in various industries, "one out of every four industry codes permitted women to receive a lower minimum wage than men, and the businesses affected were precisely those which employed the largest percentage of women."[57] Even when the provisions of the NRA were found to be unconstitutional, and the Fair Labor Standards Act replaced the NRA in 1938, the minimum wage provisions of the act applied only to industries engaged in interstate commerce. At that time, women were without rights to a minimum wage in twenty-one out of the forty-eight states.[58]

Government policy during World War II did not greatly alter women's chances for more equal remuneration either. Although in 1942 the National War Labor Board (NWLB) attempted to enact guidelines for equal pay in war-related occupations, the guidelines the board developed were so riddled with loopholes that it was quite easy for industries to engage in discriminatory wage practices. One of the most important loopholes declared that "the equal pay doctrine did not apply to jobs which were 'historically' women's nor to inequalities which existed between two plants, owned by the same company." Even in industries that had a history of wage discrimination, the NWLB could not force the issue of equal pay because a presidential order, which focused on the inflationary effects of higher wage rates, empowered the NWLB to grant wage increases only to correct "substandard conditions."[59]

Union policies also affected women's wages. When the war effort necessitated that women work alongside men at the same jobs, the unions that had jurisdiction over those jobs sometimes fought to have women receive wages equal to their male counterparts'. However, unions frequently insisted that women be placed in different job categories than men, and in these categories, women received a lower wage. More often than not unions also sought to have women war workers placed on separate seniority lists.[60] Because of such practices, even though women had a greater proportion of skilled jobs during the war, by 1945 the wage differential between male and female that existed prior to the war had not changed. On average, for every dollar a man earned, a woman earned sixty-five cents.[61]

Although legislation enacted during World War II did not substantially affect the differential between male and female wage rates, legislation did have an effect on women's working conditions. During the 1920s and 1930s, innumerable state regulations limited the occupations open to women by regulating the number of hours or shifts a woman could work and the weight a woman could lift. Some states legislated certain occupations as fit for men only.[62] However, with the growing need for labor generated by the war, women workers were in greater demand, and two types of changes occurred with regard to women's working conditions. In some states, protective laws were formally or informally held in abeyance for the duration of the war effort. Here, the particular conditions under which some women worked deteriorated. Individual companies in other states complied with the regulations by redesigning their operations so that women might be legally employed. Here, women gained both in occupational mobility and improved working conditions.[63]

The first federal legislation that really attempted to limit sexual discrimination with regard to wages was the Equal Pay Act of 1963. However, the provisions of this statute only applied to persons already covered by the minimum wage provisions of the Fair Labor Standard Act and allowed "differences based on a seniority system, a system measuring earnings of quantity or quality of production or any other factor other than sex."[64] The provisions of the law only covered nonprofessional employees and, even within this category, exempted many fields of employment dominated by women.[65] Although in 1972 executive, professional, and administrative personnel were included under the provisions of this law, important features of the legislation were retained that continued to allow discrimination in the important area of benefits, such as pensions, where "employers are permitted to maintain fringe benefit policies which have a differential effect on persons because of their sex, if equal contributions are made for both groups."[66]

In 1972, the Civil Rights Act of 1964 was amended, and Title VII of the act now "prohibits employers, labor organizations and employment agencies from discriminating on the basis of race, color, religion, and national origin, as well as sex."[67] Although all employers are not required by law to abide by the statute—for example, neither the federal government nor the District of Columbia is included under the act—greater numbers of workers are now protected against discriminatory practices. Also in the 1970s, Executive Order 11246, as amended by Executive Order 11375, extended the coverage against discrimination outlined in the Civil Rights Act to include any company or institution contracting with the federal government. Further, these orders attempted to ameliorate patterns of past discrimination through a variety of affirmative action programs. However, interpretation and enforcement of these orders have varied.[68]

Federal nondiscrimination policies do not affect all aspects of women's employment in every state. Where women rely on state laws, they do not always have equal protection under the law. Although Michigan and Montana enacted equal pay laws in 1919, as late as 1975 only thirty-seven of the fifty states had laws "specifically prohibiting pay differentials between the sexes for substantially equal work in private employment."[69]

Provisions with regard to pensions, health plans, leaves, and unemployment rights have altered in recent years, but women's economic rights remain unequal in some areas. Where equality has been legislated, the social position of women and women's traditional role in the family structure often act to limit the provisions of the law such that equality under the law affects women in an unequal and adverse manner. In the area of unemployment compensation, for example, women and men have equal rights to benefits based on their previous salaries and length of employment. However, benefits cannot be claimed if an employee quits his or her job to join a spouse whose job has been relocated. Neither can benefits be claimed if an individual has to take a temporary leave of absence to care for an ill family member. Because women are "more likely than men to follow spouses to a new job location or to leave work temporarily to care for an ill family member," the provisions of the law, although equal, act in a manner that in fact, discriminates against women.[70]

Progress has been made with regard to retirement benefits, but here again, regulations still do not effectively cover all employed women. For example, although the Employee Retirement Income Security Act of 1974 allowed for greater pension benefits for full-time workers with short work records and made provisions for those with interrupted work records, thus being of particular benefit to women who, because of family responsibilities, often interrupt their careers, the act did not extend protection to the great number of women who work part-time or only part of the year.[71] This category of female employment has been growing. Whereas in 1973, 68.4 percent of the part-time labor force was female, by 1981 women's share of part-time employment had risen to 70.3 percent.[72]

Women's capacity for maternity has also led to problems in the area of economic rights. A 1974 government survey of legal precedent concluded that "although the issue of pregnant women *staying on the job* seems to be fairly well settled, the issue of *benefits* is another matter."[73] In the same year, a survey of employer practices regarding maternity leaves found that only 58 percent of the employers surveyed granted paid maternity leave, and the duration and payment given differed between employers.[74] Although the 1978 Pregnancy Discrimination Act mandates that pregnancy be treated like any other disability, the law "does not require employers to provide benefits for illness or pregnancy."

Within the fifty states, only five allow state disability payments for maternity, and these are usually granted only when involuntary complications arise. Recent studies indicate that "60 percent of the working women in the United States are not protected by disability insurance during pregnancy." Although most employers offer women some form of maternity leave, "at least one-third of the women in [the U.S.] are still not guaranteed the same or a comparable job when they return to work."[75]

That women's economic rights were recognized so late, and even in the 1980s recognized so little, can be explained, in part, by the fact that women have very little influence in the labor organizations that have developed to promote worker interests. Women were not actively recruited by the major unions until World War II, and, as late as 1972, male employees were two and one-half times more likely than women to be members of a union. Although male union membership hovered at 30 percent between 1972 and 1984, the percentage of working women who are union members has varied little and remained low—only 12.5 percent in 1972 and 13.8 percent in 1984.[76]

The fact that women are not employed in occupations that tend to be organized can explain some of the variance between female and male union activities, but it begs the question of *why* women do not go into these fields. A partial answer can be found through an examination of the occupational training and education women receive.

Women's Education and Training

For the most part, women in the vanguard of the suffrage movement were drawn from among the ranks of highly educated women. Maybe for this reason, feminists and women's rights leaders of the 1920s viewed education as a key element in women's struggle for equality.[77] Indeed, women's educational experience has changed since the 1920s. Today, greater numbers of women are partaking in higher education. However, the fields in which women concentrate their study remain primarily those that train women either for the home or for those jobs that are lower-status, lower-paying occupations.

Until World War II, vocational training for women was not a major concern of either government or industry. Although women received a basic education comparable to that of men, and on average completed high school in greater numbers than men, for the vast majority of women who did not go to college after completing high school, there were few programs that trained women in anything other than domestic and secretarial skills, or as telephone operators. In 1941, for example, women were less than 1 percent of those receiving government-sponsored vocational training. But within four months of the bombing of Pearl Harbor, the proportion of female vocational trainees rose to 13 percent, and although women continued to enroll predominantly in more traditional "female" courses—sewing, homemaking, and secretarial classes—they also began to train in a variety of other skills that were necessary to the war effort.[78]

During World War II, the federal government joined with private industry to train women for war-related occupations. Commenting on this fact for a 1945 *National Geographic* article on women's wartime employment, La Verne Bradley wrote:

> In less than four years the Government alone has trained more than 2,000,000 women for war jobs. Working with industry, schools, and on farms, it has taught them to build, design, analyze and plow. At the 200 colleges operating under the War Training program, 235,000 women have been trained for technical and professional jobs in war industries.[79]

Although women continued to enroll in vocational schools in greater numbers once the war was over, women's vocational training resumed its predominantly segregated character. In the early 1970s, although women made up 55 percent of the enrollment in publicly sponsored vocational training courses, close to three-quarters of the women were receiving training in just two areas— 45 percent were enrolled in consumer and homemaking courses, and an additional 28 percent were learning secretarial skills.[80]

In the more formal sphere of education, the pattern is similar: Women have increased their numbers at all levels of education but have not generally studied for entrance into high-paying, high-status occupations. In 1980, women received 49 percent of all bachelor's degrees, 19.7 percent of the doctorates, and 23.6 percent of first professional degrees (i.e., in law, medicine, dentistry, and so on). In graduate school, however, women continue to concentrate their efforts in only a few fields of study. In 1980, more than 50 percent of all the master's degrees granted to women were in one field—education. Women also accounted for 81 percent of the M.A. degrees in library science and 70 percent of those in foreign language, but less than 22 percent of those studying business and management.[81]

The picture of women's participation in professional schools is not very heartening either. It was not until the 1980 census that the number of female medical students rose dramatically. Whereas in the academic year 1902-03 women medical school graduates numbered 1,280, in 1974 they numbered but 1,262, or 9 percent of the total.[82] In 1980, 3,486 women graduated from U.S. medical schools, increasing their percentage of medical graduates that year to 23.4 percent.[83] This is a dramatic increase in just a few years, but it is not a major improvement when viewed in the context of half a century.

When women first began studying at colleges and universities, their curriculum was not different from that of male students. It was not until after suffrage that what women studied began to differ from what men studied. In the 1920s, a movement away from the traditional academic programs and toward more "womanly" fields of study began—a movement whose purpose was, in the words of a major financial contributor to Vassar, "to raise motherhood to a profession worthy of the finest talents and greatest intellectual skills."[84]

Throughout the nation, programs began to proliferate in home economics and domestic science.

Although women received college credit during the war years for such nontraditional activities as auto repair, map reading, airplane spotting, and the work experience they gained while employed in war industries, after 1945 women's educational endeavors soon reflected the prewar pattern.[85] The fields of undergraduate study for women have remained steady throughout the postwar period. Most women have gotten their degrees in education, the humanities, and the social sciences. A review of the female/male ratio of bachelor's degrees awarded in 1979-80 attests to the fact that male and female students still tend to follow different academic patterns (see Table 2.3).

According to a 1977 University of California, Berkeley study, the "subject sexism" evident in Table 2.3 has roots that run deep and develop prior to a woman's entrance into the university. These roots spring from the "deeply entrenched sexual biases concerning subject matter" that prevail in elementary and secondary schools and are reinforced by society at large.[86] Particular social roles are attributed to men and others to women. Females are expected to excel in the more creative spheres, males in the more analytic. This sexual stereotyping is reflected most specifically in math and science training.

Women have developed what is termed "math anxiety." Females are not expected to excel in math; therefore in the early grades they are not pressured to hone their mathematical skills to the same degree as males, and by high school most female students believe they are incapable of learning advanced mathematics and do not enroll in these courses. Women's lack of mathematical training has major consequences for future educational choices. Of the freshmen who entered UC Berkeley in 1973, 57 percent of the male students but only 8 percent of the females had completed four years of high school mathematics.[87] According to the Berkeley study, when it came time to major in the variety of academic fields the university offers, this lack of mathematics training went far in explaining why women chose to concentrate their studies in only a few disciplines.

> All but five of 20 major areas of subject concentration required some kind of college level calculus and statistics background for which the majority of women did not qualify. This left only five areas of concentration for 92 percent of the women—humanities, music, social work, elementary education, and guidance and counseling.[88]

According to the National Center for Educational Statistics, the pattern was similar in 1980. Of all the high school seniors surveyed that year, approximately 40 percent of the males but only 28 percent of the females took three or more years of mathematics, and approximately 27 percent of the males but only 19 percent of the females completed two years of science.[89]

The social perception of women has a great effect on women's training and, as a result, on women's position in economic production. The next section examines the social perception of women in the United States since 1920 in

TABLE 2.3

Bachelor's Degree Awarded in 1979-80 in the United States

Discipline, Division, or Specialty	Females	Males
Education	87,206	30,896
Letters	24,108	16,525
Sociology	12,611	6,270
Health Professions	52,529	11,391
Fine and Applied Arts	25,827	15,065
Foreign Languages	8,402	2,731
Home Economics	17,550	861
Business and Management	62,719	123,964
Physical Science	5,546	17,864
Anthropology	2,255	1,337
Foreign Area Studies	1,506	983
Secretarial Studies	1,556	64
Library Science	378	20
Agricultual and Natural Resources	6,757	16,054
Engineering	6,405	62,488
Computer and Information Sciences	3,372	7,782
Law	311	372
Genetics	38	35
Nutrition, Scientific	85	31
Military Sciences	10	241

Source: United States Department of Education, Digest of Educational Statistics, 1982 (Washington, D.C.: Government Printing Office 1982), pp. 117-121.

order to ascertain whether or not positive changes have occurred in this realm of women's experience.

• WOMEN'S SOCIAL STATUS: SUFFRAGE AND BEYOND •

Women's Social Identity

At any given time, the social status of women in the United States is conditioned by two factors. First, the dominant *Weltanschauung* defines women's role in society as a function of the private sphere of the family; men's roles are defined primarily in the public spheres of economic and political activity. However, a second factor acts to modify women's accepted roles at any given time: National economic needs condition the degree to which women are socially rewarded for or are actively discouraged from undertaking more publicly oriented roles. When the nation requires a larger work force, or when inflation necessitates that family incomes be augmented, women are socialized and trained to perform a greater proportion of public economic roles. However, even at these junctures, women's public roles continue to be conditioned by the overriding social value placed on women's domestic roles.

In general, traditional female occupations are those that women can enter into prior to marriage and motherhood and to which they can return if family economic problems arise. Employment is seen as a transitory phase in a woman's life. Not viewed as careers, but seen only as temporary endeavors that a woman engages in to fill time before marriage or to which she returns in order to supplement family income, traditional "women's jobs" are characterized by low pay and low status.

Although the decade of the 1920s saw expanded educational opportunities for women and more women sought employment outside the home, the social perception of women's role remained tied to the dominant *Weltanschauung*. The vast majority of women who sought advanced education and a career did not consider themselves able to combine domestic and public roles. Neither did society at large. Magazines of the day portrayed a career for women as threatening to family stability and women's happiness. The most common plot in novels and magazine articles during the 1920s was that of a woman finding a man to support her and happily leaving her job to enter a life of "marital bliss."[90]

Women could work prior to marriage, but once married, a woman's career was to be bounded by the walls of her home. Speaking to this attitude at the time, Margaret Mead commented: "A female has two choices. . . . Either she proclaims herself a woman and therefore less an achieving individual, or an achieving individual and therefore less a woman." Women, in other words, had to make a choice. A woman could be a wife and mother or she could be a career woman. But she could not be both. Given these attitudes, it is not surprising to find that only about 12 percent of the women engaged in professional activities during the 1920s were married. Men, on the other hand, were presumed to play the roles of breadwinner and husband—indeed, much of the definition of the latter found substance in the role of the former.[91]

Although women continued to increase their participation in the ranks of the employed during the 1930s, the unemployed dominated national attention, and women's predominant role, that of wife and mother, colored the national perception of women's place. During the Depression, the government, the media, and society's institutions joined together to urge women not to seek employment. Males were viewed as heads of households, and to the degree that employment was scarce, the society believed that men rather than women should be given the opportunity to receive wages. A Gallup poll conducted in 1936 showed that 82 percent of the respondents were opposed to married women working. Gallup again polled the population in 1939 and found that 85 percent of the men and 79 percent of the women who responded continued to feel that married women should not be employed.[92]

In general, society still saw women's social role defined primarily within the context of the family. Although single women were afforded an opportunity to participate in the public sphere, once a woman married, her social identity and her social role were defined through the private domain of the family. This point was highlighted during the height of the Depression when Secretary of Labor Frances Perkins asserted that any woman who could support herself without employment should do so. A woman, she claimed, should "devote herself to motherhood and the home" and leave the role of provider to the man of the house.[93] This statement from the first female cabinet officer, combined with the Gallup polls, suggests how pervasive this restricted view of women's role was in society.

The accepted *Weltanschauung* was partially eclipsed during World War II, as the national emergency necessitated greater female participation in the labor force. In order to encourage women to enter the work force, the government and the media made a concerted effort to portray the woman war worker as an essential part of the national effort to win the war. Rosie the Riveter became a national heroine. A perusal of the national magazines of the time reveals that women were prominently portrayed in numerous occupations and women's contributions to the war effort lauded.[94] No longer were women exhorted to stay at home and develop themselves within the context of the family. Now they were called upon to win the war on the home front. In one especially hard-sell effort, then Secretary of State Henry Stimson sent out a pamphlet entitled, "You Are Going to Hire Women." Although not exactly an order, all who received the pamphlet must have known that the government was behind the effort to get more women into the work force.

All of this had a great effect on the social perception of women's roles. Whereas the Gallup polls of the mid- and late-1930s had found the majority of Americans opposed to the idea of married women working, by 1942 only 13 percent of the population objected to a married woman seeking employment.[95] According to a study conducted at the same time by the War Manpower Commission, 71 percent of the respondents felt that more married women should take jobs outside the home.[96]

As soon as the war was over, however, women were expected to return to the domestic scene. The war had lifted the specter of massive unemployment from the land, but the end of the war, and the return of thousands and thousands of male war veterans, threatened to revive the high unemployment rolls of the 1930s. Women were the expendable labor reserve, and the government, the media, and educational institutions quickly banded together to redirect the energies of women. Women did continue to work, but the support networks and social approval that made work easier for them during the war were removed. When women worked outside the home after the war, they did so in spite of what seemed to be a conscious attempt to dissuade them.

In contrast with magazine articles of the war period, articles written after the war "revived shibboleths about women's inferiority and questioned the ability of females to compete with men."[97] Although a survey taken by the Women's Bureau of the Department of Labor in 1945 showed that three-quarters of the women who had taken jobs during the war wanted to continue working, opposition to married women working was the dominant theme in surveys published in 1946 by both *Fortune* magazine and the American Institute of Public Opinion. In general, public opinion surveys conducted in the late 1940s reported that the majority of respondents approved of women working (1) to the extent that jobs were not scarce; (2) to the degree that female employment did not adversely impact on the ability of males to find work; and (3) as long as wives who worked did not have children under sixteen years of age.[98] Women could work, but the level of social approval given to women's employment was directly linked with the degree to which women's work did not impinge upon male employment possibilities, did not inhibit men's traditional role as family provider, and did not detract from a woman's domestic role as mother.

After the war, inflation was a major factor in women's decisions to remain in or to enter the work force. Between 1945 and 1947, the price of meat alone rose 122 percent.[99] In order for families to maintain or to achieve middle-class status, it was often necessary for both husband and wife to work. However, a woman's employment was not viewed as career-oriented. Rather, such work was viewed as a temporary activity engaged in to make life better for the family as a whole.

During the late 1940s, the majority of magazines, newspapers, and social opinion polls described women's attitude as one of frustration. Women were no longer the traditional homebodies, but neither were they accepted into the work force on an equal basis with men. Women's proper social role became the topic of the day. How could a woman be both a good wife and mother and a good employee? Could she be both? If a woman had to work, could she seek personal fulfillment from a career rather than simply putting time into a job? Although no answers were provided to these questions, the prevalence of the questions themselves suggested that women could not successfully fulfill public and domestic roles at the same time. No such questioning of the male roles occurred.

In the early 1950s, the idea of the professional homemaker reemerged. Such diverse magazines as *McCalls, Ladies Home Journal, Atlantic,* and *Saturday Review* all began to run features that elevated the tasks of mother and homemaker. The professional homemaker was not just a housewife; now she was a gourmet cook, a household accountant, and a nurse.[100]

In educational institutions women's expertise was again judged to be in areas different from men's, and once again the training women received began to reflect distinct sexual stereotyping. Women, many educators contended, should not be taught to compete with men in the sciences, in mathematics, or in "areas of learning which placed a premium on the ability to think abstractly"; rather, women should learn "the tasks of creating a good home and raising good children." One college president even went so far as to suggest that learning the "theory and preparation of a Basque paella" was more appropriate for women than learning theories of philosophy.[101]

Debate about women's social identity continued throughout the 1960s and 1970s. Although the number of women in the work force increased, and married women and women with children became an increasingly important segment of the work force, there was still social ambivalence as to women's acceptable social roles. By the 1970s, it was socially acceptable for women to have careers outside the home. It was also socially acceptable for women to remain in the home and concentrate their attention on their families. However, the conjoining of these public and domestic roles was not generally accepted or supported, and discussion advocating a greater domestic role for men remained infrequent.

Television monitoring studies undertaken during this period indicate that presentations of women were not only a misstatement of social reality, but acted to reinforce stereotypes about women. Not only were women underrepresented as a group in television programming, but even when women were present, it was rare to find a woman who was gainfully employed outside the home in a "legitimate" profession or who had a mind that was as well developed as her body.[102] Analyzing various media monitoring studies for her article "Media Maketh (Wo)man!" Kathleen Newland concluded:

> Most tv women are economically and psychologically dependent, deceitful, incompetent, indecisive, foolish and cruel or competitive towards other women. Women rarely occupy positions of authority and are often portrayed unsympathetically when they do. They are much more likely to have their problems solved for them by a man than to solve their own or someone else's.[103]

Although media portrayals of women have changed since the 1950s and 1960s when most women were portrayed as either sensual or motherly, few positive images of women have emerged. Indeed, in the 1970s, something of a backlash appeared. The increased public activity of women—women's increase in productive labor and women's collective attempts to exert political influence through pressure groups—became an item for ridicule. The "liberated" woman was increasingly portrayed as either a woman of easy virtue, hopping into bed with each and every man she encountered, or a woman who had to be shown her place in life through accepting emotional or physical dependence on a man.

Media portrayals of women were somewhat altered by the early 1980s, but they still offered a distorted picture when viewed against the realities of women's lives. Occasional films highlighted the exceptional woman. Some women's magazines focused on the Superwoman who, because of a supportive husband or uncommonly high income, successfully combined public and domestic roles. But these depictions of women, although more positive, presented a stark contrast to the lives of the majority of women.

Media portrayals of men have also changed. In earlier decades men were often portrayed in family situations—Ozzie Nelson in "The Adventures of Ozzie and Harriett," for example. By the 1970s and early 1980s, however, the image of the family man had all but disappeared from television. Male characters might well be married, but the television viewer watched them in their public, work role, not in their private, family role. Women were rarely seen as capable of controlling their own lives, but men could often solve their problems easily by use of their minds or muscles.

The portrayal of men and women in the media affects the society in which they live. To the extent that young children do not see positive images of men and women attempting to combine public and domestic functions, they are without role models. To the degree that people look at what is depicted in the media as reflecting social realities and accepted relations, they pattern their roles and relations accordingly. Because the media and institutions of society still portray women and men within the traditional *Weltanschauung,* traditional social roles for males and females are reinforced, and neither social institutions nor familial relations alter in ways that would relieve women of the double burden they must assume if they undertake to perform dual roles.

Recognition of Women's Dual Social Roles

The first official recognition of women's dual responsibilities for production and reproduction came during World War II when employers found female job turnover and absenteeism to be both disproportionately high when compared to their male counterparts and detrimental to the war effort. In 1943, a survey was conducted among workers at major war plants to determine why women had such poor work records. The results of the survey showed that "40 percent of all females who left work cited marital, household and allied difficulties as the reason, while only 9 percent spoke of poor wages or working conditions." Additional surveys concluded that (1) approximately one-quarter of the newly recruited female labor force had at least one child that needed supervision during the mother's work shift; (2) "approximately 20 percent of all female absenteeism was due to the need to supervise infant and school-age children"; and (3) nearly 2 million children needed supervision.[104] The war effort required women to work, but their home responsibilities adversely affected their efforts in this regard. Winning the war necessitated that something be done.

What emerged during World War II was a limited attempt by government and industry to provide those services that women needed in order to perform their wartime duties. Because the child care and other auxiliary services that emerged were viewed as emergency devices developed to meet a temporary wartime need, they were of a transitory and limited character. In 1943, federal assistance was made available to the various states in order to create day-care facilities for women war workers whose individual employers did not provide such services. Some companies, particularly those whose major production efforts were geared directly to the war effort, instituted twenty-four-hour child care in order to attract female employees. Some industries also began to provide household services, such as mail-order shopping, shoe repair and precooked meals, at their facilities.[105] However, the prevalent ideology, which viewed women's role as primarily that of wife and mother, maintained a definite hold on the workplace and was reflected in serious opposition to the development of surrogate domestic institutions.

The fact that women's domestic role even took precedence over women's role in the war effort was most directly stated during the height of the war when Paul McNutt, head of the War Manpower Commission, said: "The first responsibility of women with young children, in war as in peace, is to give suitable care in their own home to their own children." Given this sentiment, it is not surprising to find that federal as well as private expenditures for such services as child care were limited and the number of centers available less than needed. Although the number of children cared for by federally assisted programs varied continually during the war, at the peak of the program of federal assistance to the states, in July of 1944, only 129,357 children, out of an estimated 2 million who needed care and supervision, were enrolled in day-care centers.[106]

Once the war ended, even the limited assistance that the war effort necessitated was discontinued. In 1946, all federal assistance for child care was ended except for workers who were receiving unemployment.[107] For the most part, all state assistance ended by 1948. In New York State, for example, although surveys indicated that "7 out of 8 families using centers could not earn a living wage unless the mother worked. . . . The state Youth Commissioner suggested that working mothers might better go on relief so that they could care for their children in their own homes."[109]

To a large degree this sentiment continues to prevail in government, even though studies have concluded that "freedom of choice for married women to enter or not to enter the labor market is conditioned by the community devices available to them" for child care.[109] The federal government, for one, has not demonstrated a great commitment in this regard. When, in 1971, Congress passed a comprehensive day-care program that was "designed to make childcare facilities available to every working mother in the country," the bill was vetoed by President Nixon. In explaining his reason for the veto, Nixon declared that he could not commit "the vast moral authority of the National Government to the side of communal approaches to childcare," because such actions would undermine the family, which he viewed as "the keystone of our civilization."[110] Congress did not attempt to override his veto. Throughout the 1970s, no progress was made to reenact such comprehensive legislation, although by 1980 reports estimated that more than 50 percent of the women who had children under six years of age worked outside the home, nearly two-thirds of those with children over six were employed, and 9.4 million families were headed by women.[111]

Federal assistance to parents needing help with child care has come primarily through income tax credits. When these deductions were first granted in 1972, a working parent or a family in which both husband and wife were working full time could "deduct up to $200 a month for one child under 15 years of age, $300 for two children and $400 for three or more children." At the same time, however, "if the adjusted gross income of the couple or individual exceed[ed] $18,000 the deduction [was] reduced by one-half of the amount over $18,000."[112] Although such provisions did give a degree of recognition to the cost burden of child care, they gave little benefit to women who were employed in high salaried occupations—limited in number as they were—or to women whose husbands made a high salary. Women who made up the bulk of the employed female labor force did not receive substantial benefit either. In 1972, the median yearly income of women with full-time jobs outside the home was $5,903.[113] Although eligible to deduct child-care expenses from their taxable income up to the specified limit, thus paying less in taxes, if these women paid $200 a month for child care, such an expense would account for more than 40 percent of their salary. For those women who were at the lowest end of the wage scale, the percentage would be even higher.

During the 1980s, as women's participation in the labor force increased, the private sector once again began to link child-care responsibilities with business productivity. Citing the need to combat increased female absenteeism and resignations due to family responsibilities, a limited number of employers—primarily major corporations—addressed the issue of child care. Some offer a referral service to increase employee awareness of child-care options. Others make use of a 1981 federal law that allows child care, like health insurance, to be included in the category of nontaxable benefits employers may offer. A smaller number have even begun to subsidize a portion of child-care expenses either directly, through the operation of company facilities, or through voucher systems, where payment goes directly to private providers. The impact of such programs is limited, however: only 2,000 out of an estimated 6 million employers are involved in any manner with employee child care. Most still perceive child care as a personal problem that should be solved on the individual level, not something that should be of concern to business.[114]

The services that sprang up during World War II to assist women in fulfilling their domestic tasks disappeared even more quickly than did child-care supports. No longer needing to attract women into the labor force, nor wishing to have women compete with men for jobs, industries that provided precooked meals, shopping services, and the like quickly eliminated them. Today, unless an employed woman has the financial resources to hire someone (usually another woman) to function in the capacity of housekeeper and cook, the day-to-day chores of running a home fall solely on her shoulders during her "second shift." In the late 1970s, a study prepared by the Harvard-based Project on Human Sexual Development found almost no change in male/female domestic roles: 90 percent of the wives and 85 percent of the husbands surveyed said that the wife, whether or not she was employed outside the home, did "all or most of the household chores."[115]

Although women continue to enter the public domain of economic production in greater numbers, they do so not because the society accepts and supports a dual role for women, but almost in spite of the social pressures. The comment Margaret Mead made in the early part of this century still rings true: Women must choose between a public and a family life. Because a man's domestic role assumes a public career, such a choice on his part need not be made.

Women's Social Rights

The social perception of women affects women's legal rights in a variety of ways. Since 1920, however, most inequalities have been tied to women's marital status. Although single women have generally developed a more equitable legal standing with men during the years, married women's rights have often been defined differently and inequitably. As late as 1940, "eleven states provided that a wife could not get hold of her own earnings without her husband's consent," and "sixteen states denied a married woman the right to make contracts."[116] Although all fifty states removed such discriminatory laws by 1975, the rights of a married woman often remain secondary to those of her husband. This form of discrimination is particularly important in the area of property rights.

In the United States, systems of property law are not homogenous. Those states whose systems have legal roots in French, Spanish, or Mexican law operate on the basis of community property in marriage. States that developed legal systems based on the British tradition follow precepts of common law. Not only do women's rights to property in marriage differ between states with different legal traditions, they also differ between states with similar legal histories. For example, although eight states—Arizona, California, Idaho, Louisiana, Nevada, New Mexico, Texas, and Washington—as well as Puerto Rico, acceed to the notion that property in marriage is held in common by both parties, a 1975 review of state statutes concludes that the right to control common property differs between wife and husband:

> The husband has control of community property in Louisiana and Puerto Rico. Either spouse may control community property in Arizona, California, Nevada and Washington. In New Mexico, the spouses share control, but the husband has preference in managing business property. In Texas, each spouse has control of that property which he or she would have owned if both spouses were single.[117]

Forty-two states and the District of Columbia are under common law jurisdiction, wherein "all property is owned separately or jointly in accordance with the name or names on the title document." As of 1975, statutes in four of these states—Rhode Island, Tennessee, South Carolina, and Alabama—limit a wife's rights to "$1/3$ of the real property owned by a husband at any time during the marriage." However, in two of these states, Rhode Island and Tennessee, a husband's rights were not equally circumscribed. On the birth of an heir, a husband automatically acquired a lifelong interest in "all real property owned by his wife during marriage.[118] Since 1975, state equal rights amendments and other legislative endeavors have changed some, though not all, of these legal inequalities.

Even when women have equal rights to property under state law, a wife's rights are often subrogated to the husband. Such is the case with homestead laws, which prohibit foreclosure on homes for payment of creditors or taxes. Although such laws were designed to protect the entire family, the person having legal right over the disposal of family property, the person designated "head of household" is often limited by statute to the husband, thus giving him the sole right to control the property and its disposition.[119]

As with property rights, no consistent national law exists with regard to marriage, divorce, child custody, or other family laws. Some general conclusions can be drawn, however. In states that do not have an Equal Rights Amendment, state regulations can differentiate between male and female simply on the grounds of sex. For instance, women are often allowed to marry at a younger age than men, and the grounds necessary to file for divorce can differ for men and women.

The prevailing ideology concerning male and female social roles comes into play most predominantly in the areas of child custody and child support. Even though both parents are usually presumed to have equal legal obligations for the well-being of their children, in the majority of divorce cases, custody of children, especially young children, is granted to the mother. Women are expected to dedicate themselves to motherhood and the family, whereas fathers are presumed to have careers that preclude full-time parenting.

Although legal sentiment assumes that a woman is the more fit parent, legal precedent does not grant women either the legal recourse or the services necessary to ensure the financial stability necessary for full-time parenting. Studies indicate that after divorce men's income increases by 42 percent, whereas women's income decreases by 73 percent.[120] Although the courts usually assess a certain amount of child support to be paid by the parent who is without custody, if the amount goes unpaid, legal recourse is limited. Therefore, unless a woman has the opportunity to provide for herself and her family independent of court-imposed child support, her ability to generate a supportive home environment will be diminished.

Women's rights to control their own maternity also vary between states. Although contraceptive devices have been available since the 1920s, a 1975 congressional committee report concluded that "nearly 40 percent of low and moderate income women, some 3.5 million across the country, [were] still without access to any kind of family planning services." Various states have also erected legal barriers that limit the dissemination of family planning information and services. Although the same report estimates that 30 percent of the females between the ages of fifteen and nineteen are sexually active, many state and local ordinances prohibit the teaching of sex education in the schools.[121]

The United States Supreme Court granted women the legal right to medically safe abortions in 1973. Before then, only seventeen states allowed abortion for a variety of medical reasons.[122] Women's rights to determine their own maternity are not secure, however. Attempts to restrict or eliminate women's control over maternity through state initiatives and constitutional amendment persist. Legally, women's roles as wife and mother continue to color women's rights as individuals.

• SUMMARY •

The liberal/capitalist strategy for women's equality asserts that when capitalist industrialization and modern sociopolitical forms combine, women will begin to participate equally in and benefit from society. An expanded and representative political system that guarantees women equal political rights will allow women to promote their economic and social concerns through electoral procedures and legislative initiatives. When augmented by the greater employment opportunities generated by a growing industrial base, such rights will lead to greater overall social mobility for women. Through these processes, women will gain equality with men.

Although women in the United States have made some impressive gains since these processes have conjoined, their status is far from equal to that of men. Contrary to what this theory portends, equal political rights have not allowed women, as a group, to make major strides toward equal political power, economic position, or social status. Women have not gained a significant number of politically authoritative positions, nor have they acquired sufficient influence, either independently or in traditional lobbying groups, to significantly impact public policy decisions that concern women's equal economic and social rights.

Women's lack of political power is directly related to their limited social mobility. Neither equal political rights nor industrialization has affected women's ability to transcend traditional employment stereotyping. Although greater numbers of women have secured employment, women do not tend to participate in those sectors of public life that act as recruitment arenas for public office. Neither do women participate equally in organizations, such as labor unions or corporate groups, that have established varying degrees of political influence. Women tend to remain concentrated in low-paying, low-status occupations, with little economic power or political clout.

Industrialization and equal political rights have not challenged the traditional social perception of separate social roles for men and women, either. Despite the fact that women have gained the legal right to political participation and employment, their public activities are still viewed as necessarily, and almost naturally, constrained by their private lives if they choose to marry or become mothers. Unlike men, women are socialized to choose between a family and a career. Such socialization is reinforced in the employment arena, where limited support is given to the development of surrogate domestic services. When women attempt to have both a family and a career, they consequently assume a double and unequal burden that hampers their ability to compete on an equal level with men. As a result, the vast majority of employed women cannot pursue a career that will afford them greater social mobility; rather, they tend to work in positions that generate limited chances for social mobility but do not preclude or compete with parenting and homemaking responsibilities.

Equal political rights and a growing industrial economy certainly do benefit women by offering them greater opportunities to participate politically and economically in the society. However, in the United States such factors are insufficient to engender the social mobility necessary to allow women equal political, economic, or social status with men. A variety of explanations have been put forth to explain this failure, and in the liberal tradition, additional strategies for future success have been proposed. Some liberal critics assert that national legislation mandating equal rights for women would be sufficient to promote women's equality, as such laws would prohibit those discriminatory practices in employment, for example, that act to limit women's social mobility.

Although the proposed Equal Rights Amendment would standardize antidiscrimination legislation throughout the United States, it would not necessarily alter two of the major determinants of women's social mobility. Neither the dominant perception of women's social role as wife and mother nor the availability of surrogate domestic institutions and support structure would be affected. Indeed, depending on judicial interpretation, provision for equal rights might actually preclude the development of unequal services and benefits for women, such as paid maternity leaves. Even if the provisions for nondiscrimination enunciated in the Equal Rights Amendment were not interpreted to preclude the development of such services and benefits, the prevailing ideology in the United States may further constrain their development.

Competitive capitalism defines the economic system of the United States. In such a system, certain guiding principles relevant to women's equality obtain. Although greater equality between men and women may be a desired social end, the promotion of such equality is not seen as the primary function of business. Firms are in business to make profit. That is not to say that business activities within a capitalist structure cannot have a positive social impact, but a firm cannot promote social goals at the expense of profit. Take the issue of child care, for example. In order for a firm to institute free or subsidized child-care services, it would have to justify such decisions by demonstrating that they were necessary to increase production or profits. To the extent that additional female labor is required, or the costs to business limited, such decisions may well be made, as we have seen. Such actions are not, however, the general rule.

In capitalist economies, however, governments increasingly intervene in the economy to provide necessary social services that are too costly for the business community to assume. Governments may intervene in another manner, as well, by legislating that all firms and institutions provide such services. Many European countries, for example, require uniform paid maternity leaves and have developed national standards for child care and its expenses.

Proponents of women's equality who follow a liberal/capitalist logic might well see such government actions as possible in the United States. However, the dominant political ideology in the United States imbues government with a more circumscribed role, and other segments of the society might logically argue against such government intervention, citing the unequal treatment and benefit of such policies as unconstitutional on the one hand, and the increased costs and inefficiencies of such programs as bad economics, on the other.

It is impossible to predict which interpretation of the liberal/capitalist logic might prevail in the United States. One conclusion can be drawn, however: The degree of government intervention necessary to make such services and benefits available to all women would necessitate a major shift both in the social perception of women's role and in the nation's dominant ideology.

Although many proponents of the liberal/capitalist logic assert that a change in the social perception of women's role can occur within the existing framework of U.S. social relations, and that the political economy of the United States has modified in the past to accommodate increasing social demands and can do so again, a Marxist analysis would assert that progress toward women's equality with men would necessitate changes so basic they would significantly alter the liberal, capitalist character of the nation. In this analytic framework, neither the recognition of reproduction as a social need nor the socialization of the burdens of reproduction can occur in a political economy where efficiency and private profit take precedence over equality and social need. Prior to any governmental action taken to secure services and benefits for women, such a recognition would have to be forthcoming, either from the general electorate, or from those who are in politically authoritative and influential positions. However, present social institutions act to reinforce the existing perception of women and promote the virtues of competitive capitalism—efficiency and private profit. As such, neither the necessary recognition of women's needs nor the institutional and social policies allowing women equal opportunity will come about until the system of capitalism is overthrown.

Women in the United States have not achieved economic, political, or social equality with men. Future progress toward these ends can be disputed; the following examination of the condition and status of women in Mexico sheds further light on the viability of the liberal/capitalist strategy.

• CHAPTER THREE •
The *Casa* Prevails: Women in Mexico

The status of women in Mexico must be analyzed in light of those aspects of Mexican development that have combined to characterize the social, economic, and political life of the nation. The present social structure of Mexico, and women's role in it, cannot be appreciated without some understanding of the influence of Spanish conquest; neither can current political relations and ideologies be fully grasped outside the context of the Revolution of 1910. Therefore, a summary of important political, economic, and social forces that have historically conditioned the status of Mexican women precedes an examination of the effects of the liberal/capitalist strategy on women in Mexico.

• THE ROLE OF WOMEN BEFORE SUFFRAGE •

Women's Political Power

Although Mexico gained its independence from Spain in the early part of the nineteenth century, the country did not achieve full sovereignty until the 1860s. Up to this time the political rights of all Mexicans were limited, and the legal rights of women further circumscribed by Spanish law and, for a short time, the Napoleonic codes of French jurisprudence.[1] Under the 1857 constitution, which defined the rights and duties of citizens in the new Mexican Republic, women were not "explicitly excluded . . . from voting or holding office, but the election laws restricted the suffrage to males."[2] The Revolution of 1910 did bring changes in women's legal position, but women's political rights remained unclear and unequal to those of men.

The goals of the 1910 revolution—economic justice and political democracy—found form in the slogan "land and liberty." However, both the slogan and the goals it signified were variously interpreted. While Mexican peasants fought for a return of their traditional land rights, the urban middle and upper classes fought to overthrow the dictatorship of Diaz and institute free elections with effective suffrage. Workers fought to gain political recognition and economic rights. During the revolution, women participated in a variety of ways. Some took part in the actual fighting, and a limited number even rose to leadership positions.[3] Others gained a degree of political influence through their role as private secretaries to important male leaders.[4] At the close of the revolution, however, women's role in the revolution and the struggle for women's suffrage were overshadowed by the new government's fear of the Catholic church.

Although women's organizations developed with the express purpose of ensuring women's rights within the new governing structures, they could not dispel government fears that women's suffrage would hinder the revolution through church control of the female vote.[5] Such fears sprang from the historical role played by the church in Mexico, and from the traditional allegiance women had to the church. The institutional church continuously supported colonial rule during the struggles for independence in the nineteenth century, and a strong anticlerical feeling emerged that was reinforced when the church actively opposed the revolution. On assuming power, the new government sought to restrict the secular power of the church. For example, in order to limit the economic power of the church, the new government wanted to confiscate church lands. To erode church influence on the young, the government wanted to ban parochial education. Because women were perceived to be more religious than men, and thus more susceptible to church manipulations, the leaders of the revolution feared that a female electorate would become the voice of the church and would act to impede the goals of the government.[6] As a result, the constitution of 1917 left women's political rights unclear. Although it "did not specifically deny women the vote," the constitution was interpreted in such a way as to grant suffrage solely to males.[7]

Women's rights to national suffrage were not clarified for many years, although in 1922 the state of Yucatán allowed women to vote in local elections, and in 1925 Chiapas followed suit.[8] Commentators on these events make it clear, however, that the granting of limited suffrage was not a response to organized attempts on the part of women's groups but was due in large measure to the actions of progressive governors, and one or two women who had influence with those governors.[9] Limited suffrage did have an important demonstration effect, however; it gave women's groups and progressive forces the evidence they needed to counter the belief that women would vote with the church and against the government. As a result, by 1946 women were granted suffrage in all municipal elections.[10] In 1947, the first woman was appointed to a major judicial position: judge of the Superior Court of Mexico City and the Federal Districts.[11]

Effective national suffrage came about in 1953.[12] In 1955, women voted in national elections for the first time, and a limited number of women ran as candidates for national office.[13] The effects of suffrage on women's status can only be evaluated, however, against the backdrop of women's economic position and social status prior to suffrage.

Women's Economic Position

Although the constitution of 1917 had little effect on women's political rights, it did afford women greater economic rights. The constitution granted women equal rights to make contracts, sue and be sued, and to hold property.[14] The labor provisions of the document "also entitled working women to childbirth benefits, to protection against night work and against certain types of heavy and dangerous work."[15] However, only a minority of women were covered by these provisions—women who were educated, employed in large-scale industries, or in the socioeconomic position to personally acquire property. For the vast majority, these laws had little effect. One provision of the constitution did adversely affect many women, specifically rural women. According to Article 27, which concerned land reform, married women were specifically excluded from rights to *ejido,* or communal village lands.[16] Upon marriage, rights to the major determinant in agricultural production—land—became the sole prerogative of men. This provision reflected the separate social role assigned to men and women at the time: Men were viewed as economic providers; women were considered to be without an economic role. As a result, once a woman married, the society assumed that she would be provided for by her husband, and she had no independent claim to economic personage in the village.

Until the later part of the 1940s, the overwhelming majority of the population lived in the countryside and engaged in agricultural labor. Here, the majority of women continued to combine domestic chores, such as gathering firewood and water, cleaning, and cooking, with agricultural labor. However, their role in agricultural production was not given public recognition.[17] This lack of recognition may be due to the fact that women's labor was outside the public economic sphere. Unlike men, who tended to produce crops for the market and who received wages, women geared their labor almost exclusively to the nonremunerated production of food for home consumption.

In the cities, women's economic activities were conditioned by their economic status and education.[18] Poor and uneducated women, especially those who had recently migrated to the cities, found their economic prospects limited primarily to domestic service and street peddling. Beginning in the late 1800s, women of higher socioeconomic status gained limited admission to some forms of higher education, and by 1900 "a small number of outstanding women participated in the professions of law, medicine, and pharmacy, and a larger number in the teaching profession."[19] However, most women were not employed outside the home; they confined their activities to the domestic sphere.[20]

Although women's economic position was not greatly affected by the industrialization policies of the 1940s and 1950s, certain unintended consequences had an adverse impact on women. The loss of rural employment through mechanization of agriculture and the creation of industrial and service jobs in the cities combined to increase migration to the urban areas.[21] Unfortunately, the number of city jobs was insufficient either to compensate for those lost through mechanization, or to incorporate the even greater number of persons who were previously unemployed but who now sought a new chance in the cities.[22] In an additional complication, those migrating to the cities were not always sufficiently educated or trained to fill what new jobs there were; throughout Mexico the literacy rate was exceedingly low. As late as the 1950s, only one-quarter of the population, male or female, was considered literate.[23]

Men frequently migrated to the cities alone, and many never returned to their families. Abandoned women, as well as those who simply sought a better life, also began to migrate to the urban areas. In time, female migrants outnumbered male.[24] Most of these women had little education and lacked the job skills necessary to find employment in the more modern sectors that were hiring. Unskilled labor was usually heavy labor and was generally denied to women. Like the female migrants of earlier years, the vast majority of these women could find work only as domestic servants or as street peddlers, particularly food vendors. Both occupations had advantages and disadvantages for the women, who, unlike men, often came to the cities as single parents. On the one hand, these occupations allowed women with children to combine work with child care. Additionally, the skills needed were those that women usually acquired as part of their traditional training for the role of wife and mother— food preparation, cooking, cleaning, and child care. On the other hand, these occupations were not usually regulated by individual contracts nor were they covered by the labor codes of the time. As a result, women's employment was unsteady and remuneration minimal.[25]

At the time of the 1950 census, women were still only a small part of the labor force. Of all individuals who were determined to be earning an income in 1950, only 13.6 percent were female. Although the census can be criticized for not adequately accounting for women working in the informal labor sector, such as domestics and street vendors, its findings suggest that only a small proportion of women were gainfully employed.[26] For most women, daily activities were confined to the private domain of the family, and social roles remained limited to those of wife and mother.

Women's Social Status

In the 1950s, males and females still aspired to separate and distinct social roles that drew upon a middle-and upper-class Spanish context. Men remained the undisputed heads of households, the providers of economic necessities, and the primary actors in the public domain. By tradition women were "confined mainly to home, family and Church."[27] Even in their particular domain, women remained under the spiritual and temporal authority of men and were expected to exhibit an uncomplaining and unquestioning obedience to male authority.

Machismo and *marianismo*—terms generally used to describe these traditional roles and attitudes—developed during the era of Spanish colonization.

Machismo is the male "cult of virility" that is characterized by "exaggerated aggressiveness and intransigence in male-to-male interpersonal relationships and arrogance and sexual aggressiveness in male-to-female relationships."[28] Some studies relate the development of such traits to the lack of male power under colonial rule and the consequent need to dispel aggression.[29] To the degree that men continue to feel powerless about altering their condition in life, these studies suggest that attitudes characteristic of *machismo* will persist. *Marianismo* draws its name from the cult of the Virgin Mary, which has been defined as a "cult of feminine spirituality."[30] During colonial rule, the Catholic church taught women to emulate the virtues of the mother of God—patience, perseverance, trust in God, and selflessness. Above all, stress was placed on women's spiritual, as opposed to temporal, role. The Spanish government fostered this perception of women's role through laws and social codes that not only limited women's individual rights, but defined women as subservient to and dependent upon men. There was, however, a second female role possibility, one opposed to *marianismo* and reserved for women who aspired to temporal positions, or who exhibited limited spiritual devotion—that of *la chingada* (the whore) or *la Malinche*. This role (and the term) derives its name and its characteristics from Malinche, the Indian woman who became the mistress of the Spanish conquistador Cortés and who acted as his interpreter and guide while he enslaved the indigenous population.[31]

A "good" woman emulated Mary. She unquestioningly followed the wishes of male authority in the home and in the church. She used her special role to maintain her domestic residence during this life and to prepare a spiritual home for herself and her family in the next. If a woman attempted independence, or if she sought a temporal role within society, she was reviled and damned, as was the mistress of Cortés.[32]

Although the Indian populations did not have the Catholic and Spanish social roles imposed on them as directly during the early colonial period, the political and domestic relations of these societies exhibited a greater degree of patriarchy and sex role stereotyping as the conquering culture fused with local traditions and reinforced existing patriarchial structures.[33]

Neither the Revolution of 1910 nor the constitution of 1917 did much to alter the social perception of women. Although civil marriage was instituted, divorce made available, and women granted rights to alimony and child support upon divorce, the new laws altered the temporal role of the Catholic church more than the role of women.[34] In rural areas, women continued to marry or live in consensual unions as soon as they reached puberty, and in these relationships, a woman was subservient to her husband.[35] In urban areas, as well, marriage and motherhood remained the only socially acceptable role for women. A 1952 study conducted in Mexico City on male and female attitudes toward women's social role found that 91 percent of the men and 90 percent of the women surveyed agreed that "a woman's place is in the home."[36]

In general, however, women's suffrage was not perceived to be socially disruptive. Speaking to this issue in 1958, President Adolfo Ruiz Cortines asserted that women's suffrage would not alter women's role in society. Rather, he claimed; "women will continue to be the principal guardians of their homes as mothers, wives, and daughters."[37] The degree to which the president was or was not prophetic is examined in the following sections.

• WOMEN'S POLITICAL POWER: SUFFRAGE AND BEYOND •

Women's Political Rights

The 1953 constitutional amendment granting Mexican women equal suffrage was reinforced in the 1975 constitution that proclaimed equal rights for men and women under the law.[38] In the three decades since suffrage, although women have been incorporated into political party organizations, have exercised their right to vote, and have won elective office, they have not made major strides toward gaining equal political influence or authority with men. The structural features of the Mexican political system, the limitations of Mexican economic development, and the restricted social roles offered to women have all acted to limit women's equal opportunities to exercise what, by statute, are equal political rights.

Women's Political Influence

Although the Institutional Revolutionary Party (Partido Revolucionario Institucional, or PRI) has been the dominant political party throughout the years since women's suffrage, other parties have participated in electoral politics.[39] To one degree or another, every political party affords women a place in the party organization and puts forth women candidates. Throughout this period, however, the PRI has controlled all national executive positions and has held almost exclusive control of the Senate and Chamber of Deputies, the two houses of the National Assembly. Women's political influence has been conditioned, in great measure, by this fact.

To influence policy, any group in Mexico must have an effect on the PRI, either through the PRI's internal structure, or by posing a viable threat to the PRI's dominant political position. Women, as any other interest group, have had to work within this system. None of the other political parties has ever held a significant degree of national political power, nor have they posed a viable threat to the PRI. As such, women's role in these parties has had little influence on government policy. Further, women have not successfully organized as a separate political force. Because of these factors, women's political influence is examined here solely with regard to the PRI. Although there are no studies that specifically address women's influence within the PRI, an examination of those groups that have influence in the party, as well as their patterns of organization and recruitment, gives some indication of women's political influence.[40]

The PRI has developed what is described as a "corporativist" structure.[41] Specifically, the party has identified various groups in the Mexican society that have distinct and possibly contentious interests. In order to limit the effect of partisan appeals to these groups by other parties, to retard the growth of parties that represent the interests of only one group, and to ensure the exclusive support of these groups for the PRI, official party organizations developed to incorporate each group into the PRI structure and, ostensibly, to guarantee that each group's interest is considered in policy formation. The groups incorporated into the PRI, which closely resemble interest groups at the time of the 1910 revolution, are peasants, organized workers, and the middle and upper classes of professionals, financiers, and commercial interests. The National Peasant Confederation (Confederación Nacional Campesinos, or CNC) is the official PRI peasant organization. Organized labor is represented by the Confederation of Mexican Workers (Confederación de Trabajadores de Mexico, or CTM). The official organ acting as broker for the middle and upper classes is the National Confederation of Popular Organizations (Confederación Nacional de Organizaciones Populares, or CNOP).

Even before suffrage, the PRI and its predecessor, the Party of the Mexican Revolution, had women's action sections in the various official organizations, and independent women's organizations developed loose ties to the party.[42] With suffrage, the PRI attempted to "strengthen its control over the feminine vote" by granting regular membership in the official party organization to women who belonged to each of the identified interest groups and by allowing any women who wanted to organize for women's concerns the right to join the ranks of the CNOP.[43]

However, the recruitment patterns and structures of these organizations have acted to restrict women's ability to influence policy. Women's ability to participate in or be represented by the CTM is limited because women are not well represented in the ranks of organized labor. The CNC, representing peasant interests and based in the rural areas, gives women a limited influence base as well. For example, although a majority of the peasants are landless, those without land are not organized to any significant degree, and within the main groups of organized peasants (the *ejidatarios),* married women have been excluded from participation in group decisions. This leaves the CNOP. But here, too, women are limited in their ability to wield political influence. Only a small number of women are employed in the professions associated with the CNOP, and social attitudes in this sector further inhibit such women from playing a major political role. In the middle class, "social activism" is "not considered

[a] positive asset in a woman."[44] Although upper class women have traditionally been more active outside the home, most often their prominence in political organizations is not a result of work done on behalf of women's causes but is derived "from associated status: they are the wives of men in prominent positions."[45] Women who wish to influence policy on issues of concern to women, although officially welcomed by the CNOP, find themselves isolated and have difficulty mobilizing support for their agendas.

Neither the full population of males nor females is incorporated into the influence structures of the PRI, but given the composition of the groups, one might logically conclude that women would be less likely than men to participate in political activities. The results of a 1958 study conducted in Mexico City support this conclusion. The study found that of those responding to a survey, "about 23 percent of the men and 8 percent of the women said that they were or had been at one time members of a political party. Sixteen percent of the men and only 4 percent of the women reported ever having tried to influence a law or decision of the national or local government."[46]

Patterns of political influence have not altered since suffrage. Influence necessitates affiliation with one of the official party organizations, and women remain less likely than men to be participants in the population groups identified for recruitment into these organizations. As such, women are less able than men to have influence in the structures that affect government policy and must rely on the good graces of the government to look after their interests. Patterns of women's political authority are also conditioned by the dominance of the PRI and the role played by its official influence groups in candidate selection.

Women's Political Authority

Although patterns of women's political authority altered with suffrage, the gains women have made are almost exclusively at the national legislative level, and until 1980 such gains remained limited. By 1976, only 4 percent of the senators and 7 percent of the deputies in the national legislature were female. Something happened in the 1980 elections, however, as women are reported to have won 33 percent of the seats in the combined houses of the National Assembly.[47] Whether this portends a new trend, or is an aberration, remains to be seen.

Although a woman was appointed to the Supreme Court of Mexico in 1961, by 1980 women were still a rarity in the federal judiciary.[48] No women have ever held top positions in the executive branch of government. Even when the executive branch is defined to include "positions in the cabinet, major decentralized agencies and the federal banks," and extended to take into account cabinet level positions "all the way down to the third rank," and director as well as subdirector positions in the various agencies, few women are found. As late as 1976, Camp reports only two women at these levels.[49] Neither has a woman ever been elected governor of a state or mayor of a major city.[50] Similar patterns of political authority or lack of it, are replicated at the village level.[51]

With the exception of the most recent elections, the small number of women in positions of political authority is not surprising when the patterns for recruitment to political office are examined. A 1975 study of such patterns found that 75 percent of all political officials had a university degree, and of this group, more than one-half, or 65 percent, obtained their degree at the National University in Mexico City where early political recruitment occurred in the departments of law and economics and their respective student organizations.[52] As late as 1970, only 1.5 percent of all Mexican males and 0.5 percent of all Mexican females were enrolled at the university level, and less than 20 percent of the university students were female.[53] Of those women attending all universities in 1970, only 13.6 percent were studying law.[54] Although precise figures for the field of economics were not reported, in all the social sciences, only 17.5 percent of the students were female.[55] For the 25 percent of national leaders not recruited out of the university, recruitment usually came through one of the official PRI organizations or, in the case of males, through the military. The recruitment patterns for male and female in those cases were the same.[56]

Limited female participation in positions of political influence and authority stems in large measure from women's low participation rates in those economic and educational sectors that act as recruitment paths to positions of political power. Unfortunately, patterns of women's education and employment have not changed much since the 1950s.

• WOMEN'S ECONOMIC POSITION: SUFFRAGE AND BEYOND •

Women's Economic Rights

Constitutional provisions concerned with women's economic rights have developed in two directions. The first direction concerns male and female equality, and in this regard, both women and men are guaranteed equal rights to minimum wages and collective bargaining. The second trend pertains to the area of protective legislation and certain rights, such as maternity leaves and child-care provisions, that are seen as pertaining only to women. Neither category of law is always enforced, however, nor do the provisions of the law cover all workers equally. For example, rights to collective bargaining and a minimum wage only apply to individuals who are organized into unions or who work in large enterprises. Maternity laws are similarly restricted. When professional women employed in the government were questioned in 1980 about their rights, all felt confident that on the birth of a child, they would be given time off and some degree of monetary compensation for lost wages. However, for the vast majority of women who are not employed by the government or in other regulated positions, rights to maternity leave and monetary compensation are not usually forthcoming.[57] The same is true for protective laws and child-care provisions. Although Mexican law provides equal protection within occupational groups, it allows for unequal protection between occupational groups. Women are more adversely affected than men by such provisions because of their lack of employable skills and their occupational concentrations.

Women's Economic Participation

As industrialization has increased, women have slowly moved into the paid labor force. Women were estimated to be 13.6 percent of the total labor force in 1950; 1980 estimates suggest that women make up 21 percent of the labor force.[58] The percentage of women employed outside the home has also grown. According to the 1960 census, only 16.1 percent of the females of working age were employed. By 1970, the figure had risen to 16.4 percent. Projections made in 1980 suggest that 21 percent of the women over age fifteen were employed.[59]

Young, single women are most affected by the process of industrialization. In examining the relationship between female labor force participation rates and industrialization in Mexico, Lourdes Arizpe concluded: "The level of participation of single females does seem to vary systematically with development levels, while rates for ever-married females remain relatively unaltered by degree of development."[60] According to figures compiled in 1975 by the United Nations Economic Commission for Latin America (ECLA), the labor force participation rates for single women were "several times higher" than those for married women, and at the crucial child-bearing years, from age twenty to age twenty-four, the rates for single women were five times as high as those for married women.[61] This figure takes on added significance when it is understood that, overall, 24 percent of the women in the age group twenty to twenty-four were likely to be economically active, as compared with the overall female average of 16.4 percent.[62]

Any positive effects on women's labor force participation resulting from industrialization tend to be mitigated by women's role as wife and mother. The traditional perception of women's social role limits women's ability to effectively use their economic rights, if married, with the result that single women tend to work in larger numbers than do married women. Despite the fact that industrialization has increased women's labor force participation rates, it has not done much to alter the character of women's occupational distribution.

Women's Occupational Distribution

In Mexico, men and women tend to work in different economic sectors, and within sectors they tend to concentrate their efforts in different occupations. For example, in the 1970s, the agricultural sector employed almost one-half the male, but only 10 percent of the female labor force. In the general area of services, however, the pattern was reversed, with services generating employment for nearly 65 percent of employed women, but only 26 percent of employed men.[63]

In the service sector, male and female employment patterns differ greatly. Although women predominate in services, they concentrate their employment in relatively few occupational categories: over one-quarter are domestic servants[64]; about 15 percent are engaged in sales and white-collar, auxiliary positions, such as office work; and an additional 15 percent are engaged in tertiary services, working in small shops or street vending.[65]

Since the 1940s, both males and females have found greater employment opportunities in manufacturing. However, the opportunities for women have been more restricted than those for men. The overwhelming majority of women who work in manufacturing are concentrated in two areas—food processing and textiles.[66] At the U.S. textile factories that began operating along the Mexican border in the 1970s, for example, between 80 and 90 percent of all employees were female.[67] All were unorganized and thus not specifically covered by many Mexican labor codes.[68]

The percentage of all Mexicans engaged in professional, semiprofessional, or technical fields remained exceedingly low in the 1970s—only 2.2 percent of all workers—but women made up only 17 percent of this group.[69] In the broad classification of lawyers, economists, and social scientists, for example, a 1977 report found that only 11 percent were women.[70] Only in the semiprofessional occupations of teaching and nursing do women predominate. In the mid-1970s, for instance, women were 61 percent of all elementary school teachers. However, as the level of education rose, the percentage of women instructors decreased: Only 20 percent of all secondary teachers and just 13 percent of all university faculty were female.[71]

Industrialization has not created enough jobs, and women have not fared well in a situation of limited employment opportunities. From 1960 to 1970, for example, for every three women brought into the economically active population, five men were incorporated into this group. By 1978, the employment gap between men and women had grown again, with ten men entering the labor force for every three women. Unemployment patterns were almost a mirror image of this phenomenon. For every three men added to the economically inactive category between 1960 and 1970, five women found themselves unemployed. By 1978, for every three males newly categorized as economically inactive, eleven women joined this group.[72]

Even when women join the labor force, they tend to enter occupations that offer even lower remuneration than the minimal wages offered to men, and they remain in lower paying positions.

Women's Remuneration

Although studies comparing male and female wages are not available, either in general or in occupational categories, other information suggests that women's remuneration is generally less than men's. For example, in the service sector where women predominate, surveys estimate that about one-half of the jobs are not covered by labor legislation, social security regulations, or protective laws.[73] In the 1970s, although the majority of Mexican workers were not fully covered by such legislation, in all categories of employment 72 percent of employed women, as opposed to 53 percent of employed men, "received less than the official minimum salary" guaranteed by law.[74]

Women's Education and Training

Projections in 1980 suggest that approximately 84 percent of Mexican women are literate. The same study reports that 71 percent of the females age five to nineteen were enrolled in school.[75] This percentage is misleading, however, as most studies indicate that the percentage of females enrolled in school drops dramatically as education levels rise. In 1977, for example, government statistics revealed that only one-third of the secondary students and 27 percent of the university students were female.[76]

Even when females are educated, however, their schooling socializes them to aspire to different roles than males. From elementary school texts, little boys learn that they must provide for the family through some type of employment; little girls are taught that a woman's role is that of wife and mother. The skills needed to perform these different roles are taught to each sex, often at separate schools.[77] Although the vast majority of children who finish elementary school do not go on to secondary school, girls are less likely than boys to continue their education because the skills needed for homemaking can better be learned outside the classroom. Even those few women who continue their studies through to the university level tend to drop out at a much higher rate than men, and they study in fields that allow them to work at something interesting prior to marriage. In general, they do not study in preparation for a career.[78]

Even though women have the same legal rights as men to education and training, and to most occupations, the dominant attitude concerning proper male and female social roles acts to inhibit women's equal benefit from such rights, and this, in turn, adversely affects the possibilities for women to increase their economic position and political power.

• WOMEN'S SOCIAL STATUS: SUFFRAGE AND BEYOND •

Women's Social Rights

Under Article 2 of the 1975 civil code, men and women have the same legal rights. In the area of marriage rights, and with regard to control over maternity, however, women's rights are not always the same as men's. Even when they are, women's ability to exercise their rights is often limited by material and attitudinal constraints. Although males and females can both enter into marriage at eighteen years of age, and neither can be forced into marriage against his or her will, under Article 148 of the civil code, a girl may marry at age fourteen if she has the approval of her father and/or grandfather. Her mother has no right to give or withhold consent. Many young girls, especially those in rural areas, enter into marriage at this young age—the society continues to condition girls to view marriage and maternity as their primary purposes in life.[79]

The civil code is not as specific regarding relations within marriage, but particular transgressions on the part of either husband or wife are spelled out as grounds for divorce in Article 267: Adultery on the part of either party, prostitution (almost exclusively considered to be a female crime), corruption by the husband of the wife or children, violence against the wife, absence of either party from the home for more than six months "without good cause."[80]

Although Article 4 of the constitution gives husband and wife equal rights to decide on family size, social conditioning has made men reluctant to consider family planning, and material as well as cultural constraints limit women's ability to exercise such options. The number of children a man has is seen as a measure of his virility and is an important part of his social standing. Only limited sex education and birth control information are available through the schools.[81] Such information is available in health clinics, but health services for the poor are generally overcrowded and understaffed in cities, available in limited numbers in the countryside, and in both areas the price of contraceptives is generally beyond the means of the poor majority.[82]

The Catholic church and the general social attitude toward male and female sexuality also restrict women's opportunity to exercise choice in determining maternity. According to official Catholic doctrine, an individual who practices artificial methods of birth control faces the possibility of eternal damnation.[83] In general society, a woman's social identity derives from her home and children. If a woman does not have children, she is considered less of a woman. According to a female social anthropologist from Mexico, the fact that most doctors are male combines with such attitudes to further inhibit a woman's choice in the matter of children and birth control. "A woman is supposed to be the property of one man, her husband. If she goes to a clinic, the doctor is going to see her. The husband won't let her go . . . and she, too, is reluctant."[84]

Despite the fact that the Mexican government has officially given its support to the concept of family planning, it has not developed policies to alter the material or attitudinal factors that restrict women's utilization of their family planning rights. Neither has the law granted contraceptive rights to single individuals.[85]

Recognition of Women's Dual Social Role

In Mexico, child-care services are handled in one of three ways: through an extended family relationship in which a female relative or an older child assumes the responsibility for young children; through use of domestic servants; and through organized government or private facilities. The majority of women who work outside the home cannot afford domestic help or private facilities and are not eligible for government facilities. Few low-cost government facilities are available, and they usually are found only in the major cities.[86] A study undertaken in the late 1970s of women working in the textile factories of Juárez is instructive in this regard. Even though more than 33,000 women were employed in the factories, only two government-assisted child-care centers, which served 800 children, were available.[87] For wealthier women, working or not, cheap and readily available domestic help usually takes care of the children. Ironically, many of these domestic servants must leave their own young children in the care of older children or other relatives in order to provide such a service.

Because it is generally accepted that women will give up employment upon marriage and motherhood, few resources are allocated to child-care facilities. Because professional women who may have a modicum of political influence can usually afford domestic help, or are eligible for government-assisted facilities, they exert little pressure on the government to alter the present situation. The women who would benefit from such alterations are without sufficient influence on policy. For the majority of women in both groups, the media has acted in concert with other social institutions—the church, the schools, the family—to reinforce the contention that women's primary social function should be that of wife and mother.

In all socioeconomic classes, the role to which women are conditioned to aspire is that of the person responsible for rearing the children and maintaining the home. God and her husband will provide her with the children, and her husband, with the help of God, will provide her with the home and the money to maintain it. But she alone has the responsibility for the labor and devotion required to maintain home and family.

Women's Social Identity

The distinctly different social identities of men and women in Mexico has been well summarized by Sanders: "The man, from his youth on, is expected to act with independence in his outside relationships and with domination at home. The female, in contrast, is expected to restrict her outside contacts and submit to male judgement in all disputed matters."[88] According to studies conducted in the 1970s, "Women believe that man's ideal woman would be traditionally submissive and place home and family above achieving outside the home."[89] Because women are socially conditioned to expect and desire marriage, they attempt to present a demeanor that will attract a husband. The media is especially adept at portraying this message and in defining those traits that will allow a woman to gain a good husband—passivity, dependence, domesticity.

In a study of Latin American and Mexican fiction, Cornelia Butler Flora found that magazine heroines, "regardless of class, tend[ed] to be either proud and arrogant—and to be put in their place by a strong male—or to be gentle and self-sacrificing, passively awaiting the adored male." In the same study, Flora found that men were four to five times more likely than women to initiate the solutions to problems posed in the stories, and women's dependence on men was financial as well as psychological. Less than 50 percent of the heroines of any socioeconomic class were employed, and once women married, less than 15 percent continued to work outside the home.[90]

The images presented on television in the 1970s were similar to those Flora found in magazine fiction. The only major difference was that one-third of all television programming, in particular film, drama, and comedy, was imported from the United States.[91] Although the sexual roles portrayed in programs imported from the United States were not always the same as those offered in Mexican productions, the differences were not necessarily of the type that would engender greater social equality for women. Even when women were portrayed as independent characters, the U.S. programs tended to stress women's sexuality, not their mental capacities.[92] Throughout the Mexican media, whether domestically produced or imported, a clear message to women emerged: Women survive and are made happy when they depend on men. Without alternative role models, women are conditioned to view such a circumscribed role as the norm.

• SUMMARY •

Although the political economy of Mexico differs somewhat from that of the United States, the general thrust of the strategy for women's equality is conditioned by a similar logic—industrialization, economic growth, and equal political rights will positively affect the social mobility of women and, over time, will lead to women's social equality through changes in their level of political power, economic position, and social status. In the Mexican case, equal rights and industrial growth have not combined in a way that affords women either social mobility or social equality.

For the most part, neither the process of industrialization and economic growth, nor the granting of equal political rights, has changed the Mexican perception of women's social role. Women's social role is still restricted to that of wife and mother, and women's economic position remains constrained by this perception. It limits the employment opportunities available to women and thus inhibits greater social mobility for women in general.

Women are not socialized to aspire to public roles, nor are they educated and trained to have the skills such roles require. Neither is society prepared to view public participation as a proper role for women. As a result, most women do not choose to have a career outside the home, and when economic conditions necessitate taking a job, women find that their training has ill prepared them to compete equally with men for the jobs that would afford some economic or social prestige. Employed women tend to remain trapped in the lowest paying sectors of the economy, with little chance for economic advancement or social mobility.

Because the society does not view women as having a public as well as domestic role, few attempts have been made to supply women with a sufficient level of support services when they do work. Although child-care and maternity benefits have been recognized by law, they are not generally available in those sectors of the economy where women tend to seek and gain employment.

The granting of equal political rights has not made any significant change in women's access to political power either. Since suffrage, women have not generally assumed a large number of the politically authoritative positions, nor have they gained a significant degree of political influence. As in the case of the United States, the political power of Mexican women is constrained by their lack of participation in those sectors of public life that are either viewed as preparatory paths to political office or have been judged as legitimate arenas for the exercise of political influence.

The liberal/capitalist and Marxist logics offer distinctly different explanations for this lack of progress. In the liberal/capitalist logic, women's lack of social mobility and limited social equality are explained by two factors. First, the degree of industrialization and economic growth found in Mexico is presently inadequate. Second, the period of time since women's suffrage is too short to bring forth significant changes in women's political power and influence that might positively affect women's economic position or social status. In time, however, with continued industrialization and greater economic growth, more employment opportunities will arise, and a greater need for female labor will develop. In order to ensure this labor, a greater amount of public revenues will be allocated to expand the network of support services for women. As women are increasingly drawn into public life, they will also begin to participate more fully in those economic sectors affording greater access to political power and influence.

To the extent that more time and greater economic growth have allowed women in the United States to achieve greater economic participation and a broader choice of social roles, such a perspective has validity. But, if the U.S. experience is illustrative of this logic, certain qualifications must be made as well. The limited gains women in the United States have made since 1920 occurred during a period of time in which the United States was, for the most part, experiencing great domestic industrial expansion and international economic preeminence. Is the same degree of economic growth a possibility for Mexico during the next few decades? Even if the long-range projections are positive in this regard, the question remains: Would women in Mexico necessarily be any better off in fifty years, say, than women are presently in the United States? In other words, would the effects of equal political rights and industrialization give women in Mexico any greater degree of social mobility than they have given women in the United States? Or would women in Mexico find themselves, like women in the United States, with differential and unequal access to the political, economic, and social relations of the nation?

A Marxist logic would agree that some women in Mexico might well benefit from the process of capitalist industrialization and liberal democracy. However, as long as the political economy of Mexico remains essentially capitalist, this logic argues that those benefits will remain limited and be confined to a small segment of the population. Mexico's opportunities for substantial economic growth and broader social equality are constrained by its position in the capitalist world economy.

In order to be competitive and advance in the current system of global economic relations, Mexico must exploit its comparative advantage—cheap labor and raw materials—as well as employ modern methods of industrial production that do not require large inputs of human labor. Although women could offer an abundant source of cheap labor, and greater opportunities for female employment might arise, the political and economic costs of fully utilizing this labor would be great. Mexico's political stability has rested on satisfying those primarily male groups that form the base of political influence in the PRI. Unless the economic concerns of these groups are satisfied, attempts to promote greater opportunities for women could prove politically disruptive. Additionally, if either private employers or the government acted to provide the services necessary to support greater numbers of employed women, women would lose any comparative advantage they might have over men in the labor force because the cost of women's employment (wages and benefits) would increase.

Only if the economy expands greatly, and expands in a manner that creates increasingly large numbers of jobs, could both groups be satisfied. Unfortunately, although reliance on more modern forms of production might help economic growth, such techniques would have an adverse effect on employment opportunities, as fewer, but more highly trained workers, would be required.

Under such conditions, women would be less likely to successfully compete with men for the limited number of jobs available, unless an altered perception of women's social role generated changes in women's education and training. Such a change is not impossible, but given the present sexual composition of politically influential groups, it seems unlikely.

As implemented in the United States and Mexico, the liberal/capitalist strategy for women's equality has not provided women with the equal opportunities necessary for greater social mobility. As a result, each nation demonstrates only limited movement toward greater equality for women in the areas of political power, economic position, or social status. However, a comparison of the condition and status of women in both nations suggests that some positive changes do occur as industrialization and economic growth proceed. The question still remains, however, whether or not such a strategy is sufficient to ensure equality for women in the long run. Another question remains as well. Does the Marxist logic offer a strategy for women's equality that is any better?

• CHAPTER FOUR •
Equality Creates a Double Burden: Women in the Soviet Union

The first attempt at implementing a Marxist strategy for women's equality began in October 1917 in Russia. Although Russia began to industrialize in the latter half of the nineteenth century, and women were incorporated into the industrial labor force in growing numbers, research suggests that by 1917 less than 15 percent of the population lived in urban centers, was involved in industrial activities, or was affected in any way by the political or social norms that characterized European Russia.[1] The peasantry, attached to traditional methods of agricultural production and ruled by customary law, comprised the overwhelming majority of the population. Consequently, with the Bolshevik seizure of power in 1917, there were two societies targeted for transformations: one more urban and modern, and one more rural and traditional.

The Marxist strategy for women's equality in Russia was thus twofold: The state would grant women equal legal rights, develop institutions that would afford women opportunities for equal treatment, and resocialize the society to new conceptions of women's and men's roles. In addition, an economic base capable of generating a domestic product sufficient to allow all this would also have to emerge. Thus, the central question of this chapter— to what extent has a Marxist strategy allowed women to attain economic, political, and social equality in the Soviet Union?— must be augmented by a second question: To what extent, and in what ways, have the Soviet needs for economic growth affected issues of women's equality? In other words, have women's needs been given equal attention, or have questions of economic growth eclipsed women's concerns?

In order to assess changes in women's relative equality since the revolution, however, it is necessary to begin with a general description of women's condition prior to the October Revolution.

• THE ROAD TO REVOLUTION: 1860–1917 •

Women's Political Power
Until 1917, women in Russia were without equal political rights. Although a few women, such as Catherine the Great, held the reins of political power

eighteenth century, most women were without legal rights to citizenship and possessed less than equal civil rights. Until 1861, the rights of citizenship were only granted to those who performed government service or to those who paid taxes.[2] Women could not qualify for citizenship through government service, as both military and civilian government positions were limited to men. Although women could hold property, their access to property was greatly limited by discriminatory inheritance laws, inequitable family codes, and the fact that opportunities for women to acquire money or property in their own right were almost nonexistent.

In the peasantry, neither males nor females had legal status until 1861; both were bound to the land under feudal arrangements. However, although peasant men and women were equally deprived of citizenship and other legal rights, custom and tradition dictated that males dominated in all social and familial relations. According to customary law, a woman was the property not only of the landlord, but also of the male with whom she resided—father, husband, brother, brother-in-law. In all social and domestic relations, his word was law. If a woman disobeyed the wishes of the man to whom she belonged, she could expect and usually received direct, physical punishment. In the countryside, there was "no penal law for killing a wife or slave, if it happen[ed] upon correction."[3]

It was only with the freeing of the serfs in 1861, and the consequent reforms in local governance, that issues of women's legal rights began to emerge. Coincident with the emancipation of the serfs, limited local suffrage dependent on property rights was granted. However, as customary law excluded women from inheriting peasant land—lands went to the male head of the household—and the inheritance legislation that covered the remainder of the country limited a wife's claim to what she brought into a marriage and a daughter's to one-fourteenth of her father's land, women were effectively excluded even from limited local suffrage.[4]

When the first representative national assembly, the Duma, was organized as an advisory body to the tsarist government in 1905, suffrage was again dependent on property rights. However, even those women who had sufficient property to vote in elections could not do so as women. Women "had to cast their vote through male relatives. In the absence of such relatives, they were disenfranchised."[5]

Although women were without political rights, they did attempt to influence government policies through their own organizations and through membership in other political groups. During the late nineteenth century, women's groups began to develop and organize around two issues: women's suffrage and the alleviation of the worst excesses of early industrialization and urban poverty.[6] With the creation of the Duma, two distinct factions emerged in the women's movement. One faction, represented by the All-Russian League for Women's Equality, directed their organizational efforts at issues of universal suffrage and socioeconomic reforms. The other faction developed from within the Bolsheviks, who tied the issues of women's equality to the need for more radical changes in the entire social order. Whereas the first faction was composed mainly of progressive, educated women who organized conferences in an attempt to educate politicians, intellectuals, and working women regarding the necessity for legal reforms, the latter stressed organizational efforts among male and female factory workers in an attempt to link the issues of women's rights and women's equality to the need for socialist revolution. Although each faction othe Bolshevik party also employed its own propaganda developed *zhenotdyely,* or women's sections, within the party structure to raise what was termed "the women's question" in party discussion and to incorporate women into party activities.[7]

Until the October Revolution, neither the liberal nor the Marxist factions secured changes in women's political status. However, in 1912, the Bolsheviks did succeed in pushing a social insurance law through the Duma that improved working conditions for some women and gave recognition to women's dual roles in production and reproduction. Less than 9 percent of the women workers were covered by this social insurance (it only dealt with workers in heavy industry), but worker's sick benefit societies were instituted. Women had full voting rights in the election of worker's representatives, and a maternity leave of six weeks—at varying levels of compensation—was instituted under the jurisdiction of these sick benefit societies.[8]

In general, however, women's economic position, like women's political status, was restricted and inequitable prior to 1917.

Women's Economic Position

Although the emancipation of the serfs did not measurably change women's political power, when combined with the beginning of industrialization, emancipation did have an effect on women's economic position. Once freed from agricultural servitude, a portion of the peasantry in the Western or European areas of Russia began a slow migration to the developing urban centers. There, with other propertyless people, they were employed in the newly developed industries. Women as well as men joined the ranks of industrial labor. Information on the period 1860-1890 is scarce, but official census data show that "women worked only rarely and in insignificant numbers" in industries until 1860, although in certain industries, such as textiles and tobacco, and in particular cities, like St. Petersburg, women were becoming a factor in industrial labor.[9] By the census of 1897, there were only 3 million women working for wages in Russia: "Roughly 50 percent were employed as domestic servants, 25 percent as agricultural laborers, 13 percent in industry, and 4 percent in education and health."[10]

Although industrialization was minimal during the first two decades of the twentieth century, women's participation in industrial labor continued to grow, and the percentage of women employed in professions increased. By 1913, one-third of the industrial labor force was female. By the end of the Russian involvement in World War I, the need for female labor to replace male conscripts had increased the female component in industrial labor to 40 percent of the total.[11]

Although women increasingly joined the ranks of wage laborers, their jobs remained concentrated in the lowest paying sectors of the economy—domestic service and light industrial production such as textiles and tobacco.[12] Throughout Russia, women's wages averaged from one-half to two-thirds the wages of male workers during the first decades of the twentieth century. Even in the same industries and with the same level of skill, women were paid less than men. Commenting on increased female wage labor during the early 1900s, government factory inspectors concluded that "substitution of women for men where possible is a positive preference on the part of factory administrators [because] the substitution of female for male labor allows the factory to economize on wages."[13]

Poorly paid industrial labor was the only means of survival open to most urban women. Although 1913 census data show that the country had 2,800 women doctors—fully 10 percent of all practicing Russian physicians—and 8 percent of all teachers were female, education and training for entrance into better paid positions were limited.[14] Before 1917, education was a luxury enjoyed by a very small segment of the population—only 10 percent of school-age children were enrolled in any type of education. Schooling, even for this group, usually stopped by the second or third grade.[15] Most of the population was illiterate; female illiteracy overshadowed male illiteracy by a factor of two to one, and illiteracy in the countryside was proportionally greater than in the urban areas.[16] The last prerevolutionary census reported that 83 percent of all women were illiterate.[17]

Even for those with a basic education, there were few opportunities for advanced training. By 1910, secondary education was available to only one out of 400 males and one out of 300 females. Although girls completed secondary school in larger numbers than boys, the education of boys and girls was segregated. The curriculum for a girl was not designed to prepare her for entry into the labor market, but rather "to prepare her for a vocation as wife and mother in an aristocratic household." Beginning in 1870, women were allowed into universities, but women's education involved "separate women's courses and institutions," and most women were limited in their study to the fields of pedagogy and medicine.[18]

For both men and women, educational opportunities were limited, and for women the choices within those limited opportunities were few. Even with these drawbacks, however, women were beginning to actively participate in what education was available. By 1916, "women constituted 30,000, or almost a quarter of the 125,000 students in higher education."[19]

Women's Social Status

The prerevolutionary social identity of women varied. Although women's traditional role was questioned and somewhat altered in the more urban, industrial areas, in the vast rural areas, tradition continued to dominate.

Among the peasantry, age-old traditions and religion dominated and combined to severely limit women's social role and women's rights. Two proverbs common in the countryside best summarize the social identity of women at this time: "A hen is not a bird, and a woman is not a person,"[20] and "I thought I saw two people, but it was only a man and his wife."[21] Not only were women not the equals of men, they were not even considered people. That a woman's life was bound by her duties to husband and home is suggested by another proverb: "The woman's road— threshold to stove."[22]; This traditional perception of women was reinforced by the official religion of much of European Russia—Russian Orthodoxy—where, according to canonical law, "man was considered to be divinely ordained to rule over woman, reducing the woman's positions to that of a man's charge, if not property."[23]

A father's rule over his daughter was absolute and could only be broken at the time of marriage, whereupon the rights over a woman passed to her husband. In marriage, women's rights and duties were defined in light of male rights: women were morally obligated to obey their husband's wishes, a wife had to reside with the husband no matter where he moved, children were the sole property of the man. If a marriage was to be dissolved, only males could institute divorce proceedings, and the only acceptable grounds were adultery on the part of the wife. "Men's adultery was not even listed among the transgressions in Orthodox canon laws."[24]

In those areas of European Russia under more direct tsarist influence, some changes in women's social status came into being during the latter part of the nineteenth century. By law, "husbands were forbidden now—for the first time—to beat or mutilate their wives." However, by law, the husband remained the head of the family with all rights over both wife and children. Only religious marriage was recognized, and ecclesiastical laws governed women's domestic rights and duties in the same manner as they did in the countryside. Although women had the right to education and employment, under tsarist law a woman's public rights were not automatically guaranteed. The permission of the male head of household was necessary for a woman to travel, to receive an education, or to seek employment.[25]

Throughout Russia, women were not persons in their own right; rather, they were appendages of men who made all public and private decisions for them. Such legal arrangements not only defined women as second-class citizens and deprived women of a separate legal identity, but they also combined to restrict a woman's ability to alter her socioeconomic or political status. As women were beginning to venture into the public arenas of education and economic production, their ability to do so was circumscribed by male prerogatives over such activities. Without political rights and with limited access to education or employment opportunities, women's ability to influence policies that affected their lives was marginal.

• WOMEN'S POLITICAL POWER: THE REVOLUTION AND BEYOND •

Women's Legal Rights

Immediately upon seizing power in 1917, the provisional government declared that women were to have full equality with men in all areas of law. Decrees were promulgated giving women equal political and economic rights and affording women equality in family law. The regime not only decreed equal rights for women, but declared its intention to develop policies meant to go "beyond the elimination of legal impediments to sexual equality and the mere promulgation of equal rights [by adopting] measures that would guarantee their exercise in practice."[26] Women's ability to participate equally in and benefit from the new Soviet society was seen as contingent upon three factors. The first was the transformation of all social relations—economic, political, and cultural—from capitalist to socialist forms. The ability of the society to effectively incorporate women into the social life of the nation would also be conditioned by the ability of the nation to provide women with the services necessary to free them from domestic labors. This, in turn, would be affected by the manner in which male and female social roles were defined. All three factors would be dependent on ideological and material factors: the commitment of the government and the level of economic development. Both commitment and level of development have varied over time.

What has not changed in any dramatic manner is the law. The early decrees of the provisional government concerning women's legal equality have been reflected throughout successive Soviet constitutions, at both national and republic levels. Articles 34, 35, and 53 of the 1977 constitution provide a good summary of women's legal equality as presently defined:

Article 34: Citizens of the USSR are equal before the law, without distinction of origin, social or property status, race or nationality, sex, education, language, attitude to religion, type and nature of occupation, domicile, or other status.
Article 35: Women and men have equal rights in the USSR. Exercise of these rights is ensured by according women equal access with men to educational and vocational and professional training, equal opportunities in employment, remuneration, and promotion, and in social and political, and cultural activity, by providing conditions enabling mothers to work; by legal protection, and material and moral support for mothers and children, including paid leaves and other benefits for expectant mothers and a gradual reduction of working time for mothers with small children.
Article 53: Marriage is based on the free consent of the woman and the man; spouses are completely equal in their family relations.[27]

However, although decrees and successive laws could (and did) grant women political equality and legislate equal opportunities for women, change did not come about overnight. Great progress has been made since 1917, but women's struggle for equality is still unfinished.

Women's Political Influence

Women's political influence has changed as the political structure of the government and patterns of influence have altered during successive decades. When the Bolsheviks seized power, the overwhelming majority of people were not active participants in the revolution. Neither was there a tradition of popular participation in government. Further, those opposed to the Bolsheviks took up arms, and a civil war ensued. The power of the new government was limited both in the areas under its jurisdiction and in the support needed to enact its policies. In order to organize women in support of the new government, educate them as to their new rights and duties as citizens as well as develop and organize female input into policy decisions, the new government reorganized and expanded the *zhenotdyely*.

In 1917, Lenin signed a decree authorizing payment to women who were already active in the party so they could devote full time to organizing other women. The original *zhenotdyel* organizers focused their attention primarily on urban, working women and the issues that affected them. They held meetings and conferences to discern the particular needs of working women and to educate all women to their new rights. Armed with this information, women participated in the discussions and drafts of state decrees and helped to determine state budget allocations.[28] By 1919, *zhenotdyel* branches were an integral part of all areas of the party structure, and they operated at all levels.[29] At this juncture, the focus of the *zhenotdyel* activities began to reach beyond the confines of the urban areas.

In Central Asia and throughout the rural areas of the Soviet Union, *zhenotdyel* organizers stressed a two-pronged attack against women's inequality that challenged women's private as well as public roles. Through their programs, the organizers "led an assault on patriarchal family structures and roles" and attempted to "integrate women into the larger political community" that was developing. Such activities did not go unchallenged, however. According to Lapidus, in Central Asia male resistance to such changes was particularly strong and "so endangered other regime priorities that [the *zhenotdyel* campaigns] were abandoned in favor of more patient, incremental, and comprehensive strategies" that stressed alterations in women's public roles rather than presenting a direct challenge to familial structures.[30]

Through literacy campaigns, women were taught how to read and made more aware of their rights. The commitment of the new government to these efforts was reflected in the number of women's periodicals funded and produced by the party. By 1927, there were eighteen women's periodicals with a direct circulation of 386,000.[31] Once made aware of their rights, women were organized into political groups where they were given various responsibilities: educating other women, helping to set up new governing institutions, organizing and constructing the communal institutions for child care, cooking, and other traditionally "female" functions that would free women for other activities in their communities, and training women for jobs in agriculture and industry.

In all areas where the *zhenotdyel* operated, women elected delegates (approximately one delegate per thirty-five women) to represent their needs and interests at political assemblies. Delegates from lower levels would elect from among their number delegates to higher assemblies, and so on. By 1928, approximately 2.5 million women were participating in such delegate assemblies, representing the interests of millions of other women.[32] These assemblies devised programs to serve the needs of their female constituents. They also pressured the government to allocate scarce resources to services that would positively affect women and put the weight of its authority behind resocialization efforts aimed at freeing women from the traditions that bound them to home and husband. The effectiveness of such endeavors can be ascertained by the degree to which women became incorporated into village and urban life during the 1920s.

The *zhenotdyel* not only helped to "integrate women into the larger political community through its programs" and focus government attention on the condition and status of women throughout the nation, but perhaps most importantly, it "tended to heighten the consciousness of women as women, to encourage them to take an active part in their own liberation, and to defend the distinctive needs of a female constituency."[33] This latter function grew in importance when, during a reorganization of the Central Committee Secretariat in 1930, the *zhenotdyel* was disbanded as a separate organization, and women's sections were set up within the party organization. Since then, women's political influence can best be evaluated through an examination of women's role in these organizations and the policies these bodies advocate and encourage concerning the needs of women.

In all party organizations, women's sections have remained active. In those nonparty groups active in policy advocacy and policy implementation, women have formed a large proportion of the membership. In discussing women's recent role in policy advocacy and policy implementation, Hough has commented:

> Women are extremely well represented among Soviet professionals normally involved in policy advocacy and analysis as part of their vocation. For example, in 1970 women constituted 43 percent of *vuz* (college) teachers, 40 percent of Soviet scientists, 45 percent of Soviet journalists and writers, and 82 percent of economists and planners. Moreover, they were 32 percent of the leaders of organs of state administration, party, Komsomol, trade union, and other public organizations, and their structural subdivisions.[34]

In other words, women have remained in those organizations that have some degree of political influence, although their numbers are not always equal to men's, and women's issues now have to compete with other issues of importance for position on the group agenda. Women have also made progress in most areas of political authority, and although not always represented in equal numbers with men, they have had an influence in policy determination.

Women's Political Authority

It is impossible to assess the number of women who held positions of political authority in October 1917. However, in August of the same year, a survey of delegates to the 6th Party Congress (Bolshevik) was conducted. Of the delegates who responded to the survey, only 6 percent, a total of 10 out of 171, were identified as women.[35] Given Lenin's urging during the elections of 1920 that the people of Moscow "Elect women workers! Both Communist and non-party women—more, more women!" it is safe to assume that women's participation in positions of political

In 1922, women made up only 1 percent of those elected to village soviets and 6 percent of the members elected to city soviets—the local organs of political authority. The Komsomol (Young Communist League) membership was approximately 15 percent female, and the percentage of female Communist party members was only 7.8.[37] In 1921, there were no women on the Central Committee of the Communist party, the organ responsible for directing overall government policy. By the middle of the 1920s, and due in great measure to the organizing efforts of the *zhenotdyel,* the number of women elected to local soviets began to rise. In 1926, the percentage of women elected to rural and urban soviets had risen to 10 percent and 18 percent respectively, and in 1927 women were 13.1 percent of the membership of the Communist party and 21.3 percent of all Komsomol members.[38]

The number of women elected to local soviets has grown dramatically since the 1920s. By 1975, women represented 48.1 percent of the members elected to local soviets. Although females were not elected in equal numbers to regional, state, or national office, by the mid-1970s the percentage of women elected to positions of authority at these levels had also grown dramatically. In 1975, 31.4 percent of the Supreme Soviet (similar to a national assembly) was female. In the same year, 35.4 percent of the Supreme Soviet of Union Republics and 39.1 percent of the Supreme Soviet of the Autonomous Republics (in structural and electoral policies these soviets are somewhat analogous to a bicameral U.S. state legislature) were female, and 44.9 percent of the *oblast,* or regional soviets, were female.[39] A 1984 survey indicates that figures remain nearly the same.[40]

In the republic, regional, and local soviets, the national average of women elected as deputies seems to be quite steady over time, with the percentage of women elected to local soviets, for example, ranging from a low of 44.8 percent to a high of 49.4 percent. The similarity in sexual composition of the deputies elected to soviets at comparable levels and across diverse ethnic areas has suggested to some authors that "the selection of delegates is guided by norms for sexual composition."[41]

In 1975, women also held significant, though not always equal, authoritative positions in the various republics of the Soviet Union. For example, in the twenty autonomous republics, women held the position of Chairman of the Presidium of the Supreme Soviet in five, and in more than half of the fifteen Union Republics, women were represented in substantial numbers in the Republic Council of Ministers.[42] In the judiciary, women are also a large, though not always equal, force. In the mid-1970s, almost one-third of the judges and one-half of the people's assessors—auxiliary judges who are elected to represent local areas interests and who serve alongside regular judges— were women.[43]

It is in the Communist party, and at the highest echelons of the party, that women remain without equal political authority. Although the percentage of female party members increased from less than 10 percent to 23 percent between 1920 and

1975, women have never represented more than 4.2 percent of the membership of the Central Committee of the Communist party in the Soviet Union.[44] In 1984, no woman sat on the Central Committee.[45] At the Komsomol level, there is greater female participation—about 50 percent of the membership and one-third of the elected officers of the organization were female in 1975.[46]

These statistics suggest that as women begin to grow older and assume family and job responsibilities, and as the level of government and party activity increases, fewer women are represented in positions of political authority. Because both party work and elective office require a great deal of time, and many elected positions are not remunerated, women's responsibilities at work and at home act to effectively preclude equal female participation in Soviet political life. Interviews with Soviet women reinforce this conclusion: Having little free time, women are not as active as men in voluntary political activities, and "many women nominated during elections refuse to be active candidates" because of the time involved in such activities.[47]

Although women have equal political rights, their ability to fully utilize these rights in order to attain equal political authority is constrained by specific economic and social factors.

• **WOMEN'S ECONOMIC POSITION: REVOLUTION AND BEYOND** •

Women's Economic Rights

The earliest decrees issued under Lenin's signature had an effect on women's economic position. The Decree on Land, proclaimed in 1917, gave women equal rights to own property. The new social security proclamations provided women with a paid maternity leave of fifty-six days prior to and fifty-six days after birth. Minimum wage rates for male and female alike were established, and the provisions of the decree on pay were based on "the principle of equal remuneration for equal work."[48] Although on paper women were to receive equal treatment with men, the economic chaos created by the civil war had a disruptive effect on all workers and a particularly adverse effect on working women.

Because of the economic disruptions, many enterprises began laying off workers. Women most often bore the brunt of the layoffs, and the young government quickly responded to this problem. In April 1918, for example, the Petrograd Council of Trade Unions addressed the following appeal to all workers and to all factory committees:

> The question of how to combat unemployment has come sharply before the unions. In many factories and shops the question is being solved very simply . . . fire the women and put men in their place. With the transfer of power to the Soviets, the working class is given a chance to reorganize our national

economy on a new basis. . . . The only effective measure against unemployment is the restoration of the productive powers of the country, reorganizing on a socialist basis. During the time of crisis, with the cutting down of workers in factories and shops, we must approach the question of dismissal with the greatest care. We must decide each case individually. There can be no question of whether the worker is a man or a woman, but simply the degree of need. . . . Only such an attitude will make it possible for us to retain women in our organization and prevent a split in the army of workers.[49]

Government policies were soon developed that not only offered protection to women who were already employed, but encouraged greater female employment. In order to increase the number of women employed, laws were instituted that reserved for women a particular percentage of positions in various industries and minimum quotas for women in technical training institutes. Additional laws proclaimed certain occupations reserved exclusively for women, some exclusively for men, and certain others to be reserved predominantly for women.[50]

The philosophical rationale for such protective legislation was twofold: biological and sociological. Physically, certain tasks were viewed as potentially harmful to pregnant women and their potential offspring. These tasks were legally denied to women, at least until such time as technological adaptations made them safe. Reserving particular jobs for women was viewed as an incentive in drawing women into particular occupations. If an occupation was deemed a "woman's" occupation, government officials felt traditional social attitudes towards female employment outside the home might be mitigated.[51] Although the philosophy behind such protective legislation has remained, technological developments and the requirements of industrialization have altered the biological rationale, and recently the need to gain greater sexual balance in certain occupations and the near total involvement of most women of working age in the labor force have altered the sociological requirements.

The majority of early legislation did not have great impact on the four-fifths of the female population that lived in the countryside, however. Until 1929, Soviet laws that regulated property, wages, and working conditions, were not really enforced in rural areas. It was not until the 1930s, and the period of collectivization, that rural women gained equal rights with men in practice as well as in legal theory. With collectivization, women received equal training for various occupations, equal wages for their work, and, for the first time, received those wages directly and not in the form of a family wage. In addition, the maternity benefits afforded in industry were extended to rural women with the advent of collective farms. Interestingly enough, however, the concept of protective legislation had little bearing on the heavy tasks women undertook in the countryside. It was only with the appearance of mechanization that women's heavy labors were mitigated.

Women's economic rights as declared in earlier periods, as well as the philosophy behind them, have prevailed. Maternity leaves now cover all working women. By the 1970s, not only did women receive their full average pay for the leave period, but legislation passed that gave women partial payment if they chose to remain off the job for the entire first year after childbirth. In addition, a woman's leave would not affect her seniority or other benefits.[52]

Protective legislation is still in effect, although the major rationale is now biological. In accordance with various International Labor Organization conventions, women may not be employed in certain occupations considered hazardous to a woman's health or harmful in cases of pregnancy.[53] Additionally, even if a woman's regular job is not proscribed, but on becoming pregnant a physician determines that her physical well-being and that of the fetus necessitate lighter work, a woman can receive a transfer to another, more compatible job while continuing to draw her previous pay.[54] Whenever protective laws are put into effect, and women are excluded from occupations, Soviet law provides that those women so affected change to other positions "without loss of income."[55] The labor codes also forbid discrimination against women because of pregnancy, and this prohibition covers hiring and firing as well as pay reductions due to pregnancy or the needs a mother might have for nursing. In addition to their own sick leave, women in the Soviet Union are also given paid leaves to take care of sick children.[56]

The philosophy underlying all of these laws is quite simple. Women are viewed as important members of society. Women benefit from their ability to participate in social production, and society benefits from their labors. In order to assure women's active participation in production, the additional costs such measures necessitate are borne by the full society. In order to assure compliance with the laws, the responsibility for compliance is vested with local organs of the various trade unions.

In the trade unions, women have made tremendous gains since 1917. Not only has membership in trade unions grown to encompass nearly all workers, but the percentage of women in these groups has grown dramatically. Whereas in 1922 the majority of workers were not members of trade unions, and of those who were only a little less than 28 percent were women, by 1975, with nearly universal membership, women constituted half of all trade union members. In the central committees of the various trade unions, women were 44.8 percent of the elected officials.[57] In the All-Union Central Council of Trade Unions (something akin to a combination of the joint executive committees of the AFL-CIO, the Teamsters, and Longshoremen's Unions in the United States), 34.5 percent of the officials are women.[58]

With regard to economic rights, then, it could be said that women have equal rights to employment. Where protective legislation does limit women's equal choice of occupation, the official rationale cites international guidelines concerning the potential hazard to women engaged in these occupations. Although some studies suggest that the modifications in protective legislation have been slow to keep up with technological changes and are not always based on up-to-date scientific information, such legislation has not adversely affected women's participation in economic production.[59] It has, however, made some difference in women's occupational distribution.

Women's Economic Participation

By the end of the 1920s, rapid industrialization created greater demands for labor. Between 1922 and 1928, the number of women employed almost doubled. During the collectivization of agriculture in the 1930s, women's percentage of the labor force grew again. Just prior to the Soviet entrance into World War II, women were 41.6 percent of all those employed.[60] Although the devastation of Soviet males during World War II pushed the female proportion of the labor force to 56 percent in 1945, by 1980 it corresponded almost exactly to the percentage of the population that was female—49 percent.[61]

Although earlier estimates regarding the age and marital patterns of working women are problematic,[62] it is clear that by 1940 the majority of women in all age groups were working, and Lapidus reports that aggregate data since 1959 show the overwhelming majority of women gainfully employed. The percentage of the female population that is employed increased for all age groups except for the age cohorts sixteen to nineteen, and those over fifty-five. Although the data are not broken down into categories of married or single women, or mothers and those without children, the large proportion of the female population that is economically active in the age cohorts twenty to twenty-nine and thirty to thirty-nine suggests that married women and women with children commonly seek employment and, once employed, remain in the work force. The decline in labor force participation rates for ages sixteen to nineteen during the years 1959 to 1970 reflects an increase in the number of women attending school full time. Similarly, the decline in the participation of women over fifty-five years of age is explained by the fact that during this time period the retirement age for women was lowered to age fifty-five.[63] Although more recent data are not available in corresponding form, in 1980, 71 percent of all women between the ages of fifteen and sixty-four were employed.[64]

The fact that women have entered the labor force in large numbers might well be due to the needs of a growing industrial economy and the devastation of the male population during World War II. However, the extremely high participation rate of women during the childbearing years cannot be explained by such factors alone. Women's rights to maternity and child-care benefits as well as other auxiliary domestic services are usually considered instrumental in allowing such a large number of women to work. The fact that most women work, and do so in increasing numbers, does not, however, guarantee that women have an equal economic position in Soviet society. Occupational distributions and remuneration patterns shed additional light on a woman's economic position.

Women's Occupational Distribution

Just prior to the revolution, women who worked in urban areas were fairly evenly split between those who toiled as domestic servants and those who labored in light industry. Only a small percentage was employed in nonmanual or professional occupations. In the rural areas, women overwhelmingly concentrated their activity in agricultural labor. The combination of industrialization and agricultural collectivization with greater economic rights and educational opportunities dramatically altered women's occupational distribution. Although males and females in the Soviet Union are not equally distributed among the variety of occupations and professions enumerated in census data, women are presently in a greater number of occupations and, in many instances, in the most prestigious.

In 1926, more than 90 percent of the women and nearly 80 percent of the men in the Soviet Union were still engaged in agricultural labor. By the end of the first decade of collectivization, the figures were 73.1 percent and 51.5 percent for females and males respectively. With the policies of rapid industrialization, changes came about in urban areas as well, so that by 1940 women were a significant portion of the labor force in nearly all economic sectors.[65]

Although sex stereotyping of occupations still remains, both across as well as within economic sectors, women seem to predominate in both the higher as well as lower status positions. Women predominate in light industry and service occupations—jobs that until recently have not held much prestige and have not been viewed by the government as areas of priority, and women also predominate in professions that rank highest in prestige. The results of surveys on occupational status taken during the early 1970s indicate that the status ranking for occupations is as follows: medicine, college teaching, civil and mechanical engineering, and secondary school teaching.[66] By the middle of the 1970s, women were 49 percent of all engineers, held 50 percent of the assistant professorships at the university level as well as 25 percent of the associate professorships and 22 percent of what would rank as full professorships in the United States, and were 75 percent of the secondary school teachers.[67]

The fact that women began to gain parity in engineering during the 1970s is especially important because a degree in engineering "is almost a prerequisite for advancement to positions of responsibility in Soviet industry." In the early 1940s, when the industrial directors of the late 1960s and early 1970s were beginning their careers, only a small proportion of all engineers were women, and the small proportion of women industrial managers—16 percent in 1970—reflects women's lack of training in this key area.[68]

In medicine, where women comprise 75 percent of the professional personnel (physicians are included in this category), 73 percent of divisional heads of medical establishments and laboratory chiefs in 1975 were women. In the same year, close to 60 percent of the heads of individual medical establishments, deputy chiefs, and head physicians were female. In the area of industrial production, the overall average of women directors and administrators does vary between industries and seems to be conditioned in large measure by the percentage of females employed in a particular industry, as well as by women's previous education and training. For example, in 1973, in areas of heavy industry, women were only 9 percent of enterprise directors. But, in the area of economic planning, where women dominate the field, 86 percent of those in administrative positions were women. No breakdown in the available sources gives the proportion of women in administrative positions in all areas of the economy combined. The best estimates range from 16 to 26 percent outside of government and 32 percent in the government bureaucracy.[69]

Because women do not seem to be evenly distributed among all categories of employment, but rather they cluster at either the highest or lowest levels of occupational status, the remuneration women receive is a very important indicator of their economic position in the Soviet Union.

Women's Remuneration

Soon after the revolution, the Soviet government set up a nationwide pay scale. Wage rates were set for each economic sector, and within sectors an individual's pay was determined by level of skill—set through qualification examinations—and length of service. The purpose of this policy was twofold. First, by setting different pay rates for different sectors of the economy, government leaders hoped pay incentives would attract labor to those areas that at any given time were deemed a national priority. This would facilitate economic growth. Second, by pegging an individual's wages to her or his skill classification, the government hoped to eliminate the discrimination that might arise, for instance, between men and women. This would facilitate equality.

During the mid-1920s, women's wages in all industries have been estimated at about 70 percent of men's wages, and in agricultural areas where women worked for wages, their salaries were about 77 percent of those earned by men.[70] Because the government placed a major emphasis on heavy industry from the mid-1920s through the late 1960s, and because both protective laws and socialization limited women's entrance into these fields, women's average remuneration in industry in the mid-1960s remained about 70 percent of men's. In light industry, however, women's wages had gained near parity with men's. In a study conducted during the mid-1960s in the light industries of Kiev, "women's wages reportedly ranged from 83-90 percent of men's."[71]

Overall, women's remuneration as compared with men's has advanced toward greater parity since a major effort began in the early 1970s to devote more attention to those areas of the economy in which women predominated—light industry, consumer goods, and the service sector.[72] Whereas in the late 1960s women's average salaries were only 75 percent of men's,[73] by 1974 a Western study of Soviet wage rates estimated that "per capita female income in the USSR was roughly 87 percent that of males."[74]

In the Soviet Union wages are not the only kind of remuneration that must be considered. For instance, teachers receive a monthly bonus for correcting written work, and this is not calculated as part of their wage. Engineers and technicians receive bonuses as well, which add substantially to their income. Because the work week for teachers and physicians is considerably shorter than that for other occupations, consulting work is often an additional source of income not counted in regular wage statistics. Additionally, teachers and all medical personnel working in rural areas receive free apartments and utilities.[75] Not only are women between 70 and 75 percent of all teachers, doctors, dentists, and other medical personnel, but by the mid-1970s nearly half of all engineers and close to 80 percent of all technicians were women.[76] Thus, if these additional prerequisites are added to the calculations of remuneration, the average wage differential of 13 percent between women and men lessens.

Even without this calculation, recent policy trends should result in an improvement in women's relative remuneration. The shift in economic priorities toward the service sector has led to increased wage rates in this female-dominated area, thus lessening the differential between sectors. As greater emphasis is placed on developing the service sector, the home and child-care burdens that still fall predominantly on the shoulders of women may be lessened. If this occurs, women will have more free time to pursue additional training, upgrade their job classifications, and, as a result, increase their earning capabilities.[77]

Women's Education and Training

As a result of limited economic resources and the drain on finances caused by the civil war, "educational claims on the central budget [were relegated] to low priority" during the early years of Soviet power.[78] However, beginning with the drive for industrialization in 1928, education became a priority because it was viewed as an important accompaniment to the development of an industrial society. Compulsory education for both sexes in a single, nationwide system became a reality, and in higher educational establishments and in schools that offered technical training, minimum quotas for female enrollment were set to encourage women to seek higher education and acquire skills in nontraditional fields. As a result, by 1937, the percentage of women enrolled in higher education had risen from the 1927 figure of 28 percent to 43 percent,[79] and by 1940 women constituted more than one-half of the students studying in specialized secondary schools—where a particular skill as well as a regular academic curriculum is offered.[80]

At the level of vocational schools, which emphasize manual arts and offer a less comprehensive academic program, women were less visible; they were less than 10 percent of the enrolled students until the 1950s. By 1974, women still constituted only 33 percent of the students in vocational schools but were 55 percent of those attending technical schools, which, like vocational schools, offered training in skilled trades but combined this training with a regular secondary school curriculum. At specialized secondary schools, which gave children the opportunity to train in particular skills and to prepare for college, women were more than 50 percent of the student body.[81]

At the university level, women's enrollment was equal to men's both at entrance and at graduation by the early 1970s but diminished at the graduate level where, during the same years, women only received approximately one-third of the Candidate of Science degrees—the equivalent of the American Ph.D. In the Soviet Union, there is no degree equivalent to a Master of Arts. The Soviets do have a special degree, the Doctor of Science, which has no similarity to any degree offered in the United States. It is awarded to those individuals, both in and out of academia, who have made outstanding research contributions in their field. In 1974, 20 percent of these degrees were awarded to women.[82]

The areas of specialization in which women receive their training have also become more diversified. According to reports cited by Lapidus, by 1975 women made up 40 percent of those specializing in industry, construction, transportation, and communications, 33 percent of all agricultural students, 72 percent of those preparing for careers in law and economics, 56 percent of all students in public health, physical culture and sports, and 68 percent of education, art, and cinematography students.[83] As all students are guaranteed employment in their field of study after graduation, what a woman studies is an important indicator of where she will be working in the near future.

Women's equality in education seems to fall apart in two specific areas, however. First, boys still tend to enter the more skilled craft specialties in technical and vocational schools.[84] Second, although all workers are encouraged to upgrade their classifications through study, and workers are "entitled to paid leaves for taking examinations and preparing for their diploma theses and to days off" to attend special classes, men take greater advantage of these opportunities than do women.[85]

In a society that determines wages not only by sector but by level of education and skill, the areas where women train as well as the degree to which they continue to upgrade their skill are major determinants in women's economic position. Although educational policy does not preclude women from entering any field of study except for those that specifically prepare students for occupations excluded by protective legislation, and although admissions policies actively seek to equalize male/female enrollments in all areas of study and specialization, a woman's lack of free time for classification upgrading and the socialization of males and females to particular roles act as hindrances to women's educational and, thus, economic opportunities.[86]

• WOMEN'S SOCIAL STATUS:
REVOLUTION AND BEYOND •

Women's Social Rights

Immediately after the revolution, ecclesiastical control of marriage was replaced by civil registration, which gave equal rights to husband and wife in marriage as well as equal rights in the dissolution of marriage. In a decree dated December 28, 1917, procreation was proclaimed a social function, with a woman's rights in childbearing and the state's responsibilities for child maintenance spelled out. The purpose of the first family code instituted in 1918 was twofold: to reshape the relationship between women and men in marriage and to alter the relationship between family and society. The designers of the code hoped that "by granting new economic rights and responsibilities to women and by creating new social conditions to facilitate their exercise, the foundations of female subordination" in the family would be challenged, and women would become more active participants in the society.[87] For example, the family's former function as an economic unit was weakened through changes in property and inheritance laws that gave women equal rights with men. In this way, it was hoped that women would not have to remain in a social relationship simply because of economic necessity.

Although childbearing was recognized as a uniquely female function, the burdens of childrearing were not the sole responsibility of either parent. Responsibilities such as child care and education were deemed to be a social responsibility, and the financial responsibilities associated with these activities were assumed by publicly supported institutions. Each parent retained responsibility for the personal maintenance of all her or his children, however, and even in the case of divorce, the party that no longer resided with the child was held financially responsible for support, which could claim up to one-third of that parent's income.

The basic provisions of the 1918 family code have been retained until the present, with the following exceptions. Under the 1926 revisions, a spouse who was disabled or otherwise unable to work could claim support for one year following a divorce, and unregistered as well as registered unions were included under the provisions of code.[88] The changes wrought by the family edict of 1944 came about as an immediate consequence of the World War II—a declining birthrate, a large number of children resulting from rape in the occupied areas, and a devastated male population. In order to stimulate the birthrate and provide for greater family stability under these circumstances, divorce proceedings were made more difficult.[89] So as not to stigmatize those children born out of wedlock, or their mothers, paternity rights were limited solely to registered unions, and the state took full responsibility for the costs that paternity would have conferred on any male.[90]

By the mid-1950s, due to pressure from women and a changed social circumstance, the restrictions on divorce and paternity claims were removed from the code, although the state still assumed financial responsibility for any children whose mothers did not wish to declare paternity.[91] The only other modification in the family codes came about in 1967, when all child-support allotments were automatically garnisheed from the salary of the financially responsible parent and sent directly to the parent with whom the child resided.[92]

A woman's legal right to control her maternity also appeared early in Soviet legislation, although without full governmental or societal support. Abortion was legalized in 1920,[93] and in 1925 the dissemination of birth control information was endorsed by the government.[94] However, as William Mandel illustrates, the material conditions of the time severely restricted full exercise of these rights: "With virtually no doctors in the countryside, abortion was solely an urban phenomenon. With hardly any rubber industry in the days of the condom, birth control was nearly impossible."[95] But even as the material constraints lessened, so too did support for these services. Once he'd consolidated his power, Stalin drew on the dissension caused by previous birth control laws and in 1936 banned nontherapeutic abortions. Although other methods of birth control were still available, it was not until 1955 that abortions were once again a legal right for women.[96] Sex education is not presently part of the school curriculum, but birth control information and educational materials are available at the women's clinics that operate nationwide on a neighborhood basis.[97]

Despite the fact that the provisions of the earlier family codes were not immediately enforceable in the vast rural areas, by the 1930s fairly comprehensive enforcement was the norm. Except for a twenty-year period under Stalin, a woman's right to control her own maternity has been recognized. The establishment of comprehensive, institutional arrangements to free women from the traditional burdens of childbearing and auxiliary household functions was not as easily forthcoming. Neither have attitudes toward female and male social roles altered sufficiently. As such, although women have been granted equal rights within the family, insufficient material support structures and limited attitudinal change are still the norm. These conditions, when combined with women's special role in childbearing, act to create a double burden for Soviet women.

Recognition of Women's Dual Social Role

Recognition of women's dual social role was an instrumental part of the Bolshevik program for women's equality even prior to the Russian Revolution. As early as 1903, a system of publicly funded child-care facilities was "explicitly included in the Party Program."[98] In 1917, the new government dismantled the extremely limited system of private, urban kindergartens that existed prior to the revolution and immediately established a section for preschool education under the Commissariat of Enlightenment.[99] Working with the Commissariat and the party, the *zhenotdyel* began organizing women to develop child-care facilities under government sponsorship. By 1927, 2,100 facilities served 107,500 children.[100]

A lack of resources in the early decades, and later a limited commitment to utilize what resources were available for child care, limited the growth of these facilities. Although the increase in child-care facilities is impressive, 1973 figures reveal facilities sufficient to accommodate only 50 percent of the urban and 30 percent of the rural children of preschool age.[101] The allocations for child care in the central budget for the 1975-1980 Five Year Plan were a tremendous increase over past years, however. Not only would these allocations increase the percentage of all children attending organized child care, but at the level of children three to six years of age, the percentage attending kindergartens would increase from the 1975 level of 60 percent to an all time high of 80 percent.[102]

The system of child care in the Soviet Union is coordinated by the ministries of health and education. As a result, child care is concerned with the physical and mental development of children, not with what is commonly termed "babysitting." Additionally, the services of all preschool facilities include three hot meals. When combined with the main luncheon meals provided at reduced cost in most workplaces, such services act to reduce the time spent on meal preparation at home. Fees for child care are prorated on a sliding scale—about 10 percent of the average per capita income of each worker in a family—but never exceed one-fifth of the cost of care.[103]

In addition to nursery and kindergarten, other child-care arrangements are offered, although they, too, are insufficient to satisfy demand. A limited number of boarding schools, where children remain for five days a week, are available to parents whose occupations necessitate travel or which place other impediments in the way of quality home care. On-campus, after-school activities and the facilities of the "children's palaces" provide supervision for children enrolled in elementary school, although, once again, their numbers are not always sufficient. During the summer vacation, Young Pioneer camps and local trade union resort areas attempt to provide the children of working parents with supervised activities. Expansion of these services is planned, but no definite information is available as to the amount of money allocated for expansion or the number of children that will be accommodated.

Auxiliary and surrogate household services have emerged, although they, too, have been similarly slow to develop. The first factory kitchens built to provide workers with reduced-price hot meals opened in 1925, and this service was provided to 70 percent of the workers "in the main branches of industry" by 1932.[104] However, it was not until World War II and the pressing need for female labor that such services began to reach workers in all sectors of the economy. By the 1970s, each educational institution and each work establishment had such facilities.[105] Although the priorities of industrialization limited the production of individual consumer goods, such as automatic washing machines, until the early 1970s, a large service industry developed to fill the gap. For example, a survey of the Moscow area conducted in the 1970s found that nearly 80 percent of women contacted sent their washing out to a laundry.[106] However, even in the late 1960s, the availability of public laundries and other services was not yet consistent throughout the country.[107]

One problem that has hampered the development of these services is the prevailing attitude that such services are primarily for the benefit of women. As a result of this perception, these services are not always considered a key component in national development plans. This attitude has placed a tremendous burden on working women, and it forces them to work a double shift—work at home on top of work outside the home. The traditional attitude that household maintenance activities are women's jobs is reinforced by a lack of government commitment to the development of surrogate domestic services. The social emancipation of Soviet women has been hindered as a result.

Women's Social Identity

In the Soviet Union, a lack of change in women's social identity is not really the cause of women's problems. Rather, the problem lies in a lack of any corresponding change in the social perception of men's roles. Since the 1920s, women's social identity has expanded to encompass public as well as domestic roles. A review of Soviet literature during the 1920s indicates that "the impact of the *zhenotdyel* on public consciousness was even more dramatic" than anticipated.[108] Numerous women's journals and a popular novel series, *Library of Women Workers and Peasants,* portrayed women in a variety of roles. In the general press as well, women's new roles as worker and social equal were given prominent play.[109] The hard-working factory or peasant woman helping to build socialism remained the dominant theme until World War II when the image of the Soviet woman was additionally imbued with the theme of women's great wartime sacrifices and with a cult of motherhood.[110] Studies conducted in the 1970s indicate that the Soviet media and educational institutions continue to portray women in the dual roles of mother and worker.[111] Furthermore, all studies of Soviet media concur that sexual tfemale body, whether in books, films, or magexploitation of azines, is nonexistent.[112]

Conspicuously absent from most media portrayals of men, however, is any depiction of men as workers *and* fathers.[113] Although all forms of media appear to make a conscious effort to show women and men in all areas of public life, in the domestic sphere the media present only limited portrayals of men. This lack of male role resocialization has had a dramatic effect on women's daily lives. Even though studies show that nearly 60 percent of younger Soviet men believe both partners in a marriage should have equal household responsibilities, in most households men contribute far less time to household chores than do women.[114]

A Soviet analysis of survey data compiled between 1969 and 1974 concluded that only 50 percent of men helped with child care or dishwashing, only one-third shared cooking, housecleaning, and shopping chores, and less than 20 percent regularly did the washing or took responsibility for bringing clothes to the laundry.[115] There is, however, one trend that is cause for some hope. Although the overwhelming majority of husbands who are more than fifty years old do very little housework, a much greater proportion of younger husbands share household responsibilities. Of those men who take an equal responsibility for household duties, the overwhelming majority received their early role socialization in state-sponsored, child-care facilities where every student, boy and girl alike, is taught how to care for and clean up after him or herself.[116]

As the percentage of children enrolled in child-care facilities increases, the possibility arises that both males and females will consider household tasks a joint responsibility. However, until such time as attitudes change and additional social services become a priority, women in the Soviet Union will continue to work a double shift. As a result, the time women have available to spend on political activities, educational improvements, or relaxation will be more limited than for men, and the social emancipation of Soviet women will remain incomplete.

• SUMMARY •

A Marxist strategy for women's equality is a threefold process of social reorganization. In addition to legislation allowing for equal rights, the strategy argues for social control of production, accumulation, and the reallocation of surplus value in order to provide direction for an expanded economic base and allow for the provision of social needs as opposed to private wants. Second, the society must recognize women's dual social role in production and reproduction and reallocate a proportion of the surplus value accumulated through production toward the provision of material services that would allow women an equal opportunity to participate in and benefit from all social relations. In particular, the strategy calls for the development of laws and institutional arrangements that would lift from women the private burdens associated with maternity, childbearing, and the auxiliary domestic functions usually connected with a woman's family responsibilities and place the responsibility for providing such services on the society as a whole. Finally, in addition to changes in the material condition of social relations, and in part resulting from such changes, a Marxist strategy calls for a transformation in attitudes toward male/female social roles.

Simply put, a Marxist strategy for women's equality views attitudinal changes as preconditioned by material changes in social relations. Once the material conditions allowing for women's equal opportunity emerge, women should begin to participate more equally in and benefit more equally from public and private relations. Over time, the social perception of sexual roles will alter to reflect these new realities, and women will attain social equality with men.

Although the Soviet Union has socialized the processes of production, accumulation, and reallocation and has recognized women's dual social role in production and reproduction, the provision of material supports for women's equal opportunity has not been sufficient to fully transform either the material conditions of women's social relations or the social attitudes toward male and female roles. Although women in the Soviet Union have increased their participation in public affairs, and their economic position, political power, and social status have improved considerably, Soviet women have made such gains by assuming a double burden. Looking at the transformation of the Soviet society since 1917, it would seem that concern for women's equal opportunity and social equality have often been overshadowed by policies initiated to facilitate industrialization and economic growth. Policies that limit the development of support services have forced women to assume a disproportionate share of the social cost of development as they assume individual responsibilities for both productive and reproductive services. This assumption of a double role for women tends to reinforce traditional sexual roles in the home and limits women's ability to fully participate in economic and political activities, thereby limiting their opportunity to achieve social equality.

Such an analysis of the Soviet attempt at a Marxist strategy for women's equality is not meant to dismiss the extraordinary progress Soviet women have made since 1917. Neither is the analysis meant to dismiss the Marxist strategy for women's equality. Rather, what the analysis attempts to point out are the constraints imposed on this strategy when it is employed in a society that often must choose between efficient economic growth and greater social equity.

Since the Bolshevik Revolution, Soviet women have made impressive strides toward social equality. In the economic realm, not only have women's economic participation rates gained parity with those of men, but women tend to be employed in most all occupational sectors, including the most prestigious. Further, women's remuneration has moved toward greater parity with men's. However, although women tend to attain an equal level of education and to be trained for a variety of professions, once employed, women do not tend to upgrade their classification or skill level through further, on-the-job study to the same degree that men do. This limits women's chances for advancement in their field of employment and reduces their earning potential. Traditional social attitudes concerning male and female family roles and insufficient networks of support services also restrict women's advancement toward equal political power.

Women are fairly equally represented in local and regional soviets, at the republic level, and in the judiciary. However, at the national level, and particularly in the Communist party and its highest echelons, the percentage of women in positions of political authority diminishes. In the Soviet Union, election to office and membership in the party require that a candidate be highly active in voluntary activities. Because domestic responsibilities place constraints on women's free time that are not placed on men's, women have less time than men to devote to these activities, and consequently, the number of women who seek or gain higher office and party membership is less than that of men. Again, traditional social attitudes toward sexual roles have combined with a lack of support services to impede women's progress toward greater equality.

The social perception of women has altered greatly. Women are portrayed in all media as having both a public as well as a domestic role. There has not been however, a corresponding attempt at resocialization of the male social role. When combined with a limited network of support systems designed to transform child care and other auxiliary domestic functions from an individual, private responsibility to a social one, the social perception of dual roles for women but only public roles for men has led women to assume a double burden in Soviet society.

Again, this is not to dismiss the efforts Soviet society has made toward developing the material supports necessary for women's equality. Maternity benefits are impressive and are a major factor in facilitating greater equality in the realm of public production. Similarly, the development of child-care centers has done much to allow women to partake of public as well as domestic roles. However, child care and other surrogate domestic services have been slow to develop, and their development and expansion seem to have been hampered in large measure by two factors. First, it would seem that such services were not given the same priority as the demands of industrialization and economic growth. Historically, unless support services were seen as directly augmenting these economic goals, helping to politically consolidate the transition to socialism, or, at a minimum, not adversely affecting either political or economic goals, sufficient resources were not allocated to their development or expansion. Second, the extent to which men are not perceived as having a domestic role and thus don't consider themselves beneficiaries of these services and programs has made it easier to view such services as less than a national priority. Additionally, as women assume both public and domestic roles without sufficient material supports, a delay in the provision of such services can be rationalized until greater surplus is accumulated. Such a delay tends to reinforce traditional sex-role stereotypes rather than transform them, and it limits women's opportunity to advance toward greater economic, political, and social equality.

A Marxist analysis of the Soviet attempt at bringing forth women's equality might well argue that rather than disproving the Marxist strategy, the Soviet case simply demonstrates a Marxist logic. Where women's dual role in production and reproduction have been recognized, and where support services have been provided, women have tended toward greater equality. Further, without sufficient transformation in the material conditions of social life, in what men and women do and how they do it, traditional social attitudes toward sexual roles will be reinforced. Changes in attitude, a Marxist logic argues, can only come about when the material conditions from which these attitudes emerge are, themselves, transformed. Finally, the Soviet case demonstrates the problems that result from a trade-off between the needs of economic efficiency and those of social equality and only reinforces the need for socialism if women are to attain general social equality.

The provision of a network of services to eliminate women's double burden is costly. Yet to allow women equal opportunity in any real sense, resources must be allocated toward equity at some cost to efficiency. To expect such an allocation of resources to occur in a system of private profit is inconceivable in a Marxist framework. Not already having the material resources available for reallocation, nor possessing large amounts of available surplus so as to promote social equality while at the same time maintaining economic growth, a less-developed socialist state of necessity has to engender industrialization and economic growth at the same time as it promotes greater social equality. In this process, neither the material well-being of the society nor a more equitable distribution of social benefits occurs as quickly as would be the case if only one goal or the other were attempted; but each proceeds forward and together they augment the overall social benefit received by all segments of the society.

A liberal/capitalist logic offers a drastically different analysis of the Soviet case. Although admitting to the benefits Soviet women have gained since 1917, such an analysis explains women's increased economic activity as the result of the process of industrialization—something that may occur in either a socialist or capitalist economic system. That women in the Soviet Union have made such gains only at the expense of assuming a double burden provokes a more complex explanation, incorporating both a pluralist/democratic as well as a capitalist logic.

Viewed from a capitalist perspective, the Soviet model of production—one of centralized planning, allocation, and reallocation—is both inefficient and incapable of easily responding to consumer demand. Both of these flaws limit the Soviet Union's ability to provide sufficient services for women. Soviet productive capacity is viewed as inefficient and rigid because decisions concerning production are made according to perceived need rather than general consumer demand. Likewise, Soviet reallocation policy hinders productivity because productive surplus is funneled into nonproductive social programs rather than reinvested in areas that would provide a greater product to be divided later. As a consequence, the Soviet economy has restrained its productive potential and does not presently have sufficient surplus for those services that would lessen women's double burden. In other words, the capitalist logician argues that had Soviet planners given more attention to efficiency and less to equity, the general condition of women—in absolute if not relative terms—would be far greater today.

A liberal/democratic or pluralist logic focuses on why the Soviet system of political relations precludes women from organizing as a distinct group to pressure for different allocative policies. In the USSR decisionmaking powers are not contained in the governmental bodies to which women are so generously elected. Rather, policy decisions emanate from precisely that group where women's participation is rare—the Communist party and its Central Committee. The manner in which strategic policy decisions are made in the Central Committee further dilutes women's ability to pressure the government to serve their needs and interests. Policy guidelines are conditioned by organized, official pressure groups, but women are not organized as a group. Rather, they are represented in a variety of groups where issues of concern to women must compete with other issues of concern to the group. Women in the Soviet Union, such logic argues, cannot expect to place greater pressures on the political system to serve their needs; to obtain greater political power, women would have to alter the political system, or at least their position in it.

Both the Marxist and liberal/capitalist logics agree that although women in the Soviet Union have made impressive gains since the October Revolution, they have yet to obtain equality with men. However, whereas a Marxist analysis of the Soviet case assumes the possibility of women's equality in the Soviet Union, a liberal/capitalist analysis precludes such movement in the context of the existing political economy. The Cuban case sheds further light on this debate.

• CHAPTER FIVE •
The Revolution in the Revolution: Women in Cuba

Social revolution is a transformational process that affects all of a society's relations and institutions. Such a process began in Cuba on January 1, 1959, and is still proceeding as the society moves to create a socialist political economy and the institutions and relations that will augment it. Any careful reading of Cuban history would suggest, however, that the struggle to improve the condition and status of women has been a long one. As early as 1869, during meetings organized to foment rebellion against Spain, Anna Betancourt argued that in any independent Cuban government women should be granted equal rights with men. Although Cuba gained independence from Spain at the turn of the century and women were granted suffrage in 1934 and equal civil rights in 1940, significant changes for women did not occur until the triumph of the Cuban Revolution in 1959. The degree to which the revolution has affected women's status becomes clear when examined against a historic backdrop of those forces that previously conditioned Cuban society and women's role in it.

• FROM INDEPENDENCE TO REVOLUTION: 1900-1959 •

Women's Political Power

Although Cuba attained its independence from Spain in 1898, for the majority of the population the early decades of the twentieth century brought little change in political power relations. Initially, Spanish rule was replaced by U.S. political and military domination, and although the new Cuban constitution guaranteed male suffrage, Cuban policy was more often dictated by U.S. interests than Cuban needs.[1] In the statutes of the first constitution, women's political and legal rights remained similar to those defined under the previous Spanish civil codes. Women were disenfranchised and without legal standing, being represented in all public affairs by a male relation.[2] It was not until 1934 that women were granted suffrage, and not until the constitution of 1940 was discrimination on the basis of sex legally prohibited.

Prior to 1959, however, the promises of the 1940 constitution went unrealized, remaining "more an indication of aspiration than of the reality."[3] Although women had equal rights to vote and hold office, women seldom ran for office, and few were elected. Figures on the proportion of female delegates elected to the Cuban House of Representatives during the 1940s and 1950s, for example, show few women in positions of political authority. In 1946, women were 3.4 percent of all delegates; in 1948, 4.4 percent; by 1954, only 2.3 percent. Nor did women tend to be appointed to policymaking positions at the national or local levels.[4] Research on this period of Cuban history suggests that women's equal political rights were constrained by (1) a corporatist political structure whose avenues of influence and power effectively excluded most women; (2) limited economic mobility due to a stagnant economy and limited nationwide employment opportunities; and (3) traditional sex-role stereotyping.

Even though there was no predominant political party, and governments changed often, politically influential groups and institutionalized access for these oa limited set of socioeconomic interests. The competing interest groups fegroups to Cuba's decisionmaking structures were clearly defined and reflected ll into four elite categories: organized labor, which represented only a small proportion of workers; large sugar plantation owners and sugar mill operators; commercial and banking interests; and the military. Within this set of political relations, the role of the Cuban government was to act "as a broker among competing bureaucracies captured by organized interest groups."[5] To the extent that any president or government was either unable or unwilling to act as broker, the military used its prerogative to remove or take over the government.

The majority of Cubans were without organized and institutionalized political influence. In the rural areas, for example, neither peasants nor the overwhelming majority of workers in the sugar industry were represented by organized labor, although their needs and interests were most often in direct conflict with those of the plantation and mill owners who did have influence. In urban areas, only a small proportion of the population fell under the jurisdiction of organized labor or held commercial or banking power. In all of these groups, women's influence was even more restricted. Not only did women play a limited role in the labor force prior to 1959, but the social perception of women further constrained opportunities for their political involvement.

Women's Economic Position

In prerevolutionary Cuba, women's economic position must be examined with respect to two issues: (1) the effects of class and race as they emerged from the Spanish colonial tradition, and (2) the employment opportunities generated as a result of the character of Cuban economic development. In the Spanish tradition, upper- and middle-class Spanish women did not work; they were either married or preparing for marriage, and in neither case was it appropriate for a woman to engage in physical labor. However, women in a lower socioeconomic position—earlier in Cuban history the African female slaves and later the emancipated black women as well as lower-class white women—did work. Generally, these women performed domestic duties for wealthier white women. Although only a minuscule number of women were employed during the early decades of Cuban independence, close to three-quarters of these women were black, and most continued to be engaged as domestics, laundresses, and tobacco plantation workers. In the 1930s, women represented only 6 percent of the labor force. By 1943, women had moved to more than 10 percent of the labor force, remaining at that level until the last prerevolutionary census in 1953.[6]

Although greater economic rights for both men and women were incorporated into the 1940 constitution—minimum wages, equal pay for equal work, and paid maternity leaves—the economic structure of Cuba offered few employment opportunities for either sex, and economic rights, like the suffrage provisions of this document, were more aspiration than reality. In general, the economy of Cuba prior to the revolution allowed for few employment opportunities except in seasonal employment, the service sector, and the tourist industry.[7] These circumstances as well as the social perception of women as participants in the private as opposed to public sphere of social life limited women's economic participation rates and occupational distribution patterns. Women were viewed as simply a labor reserve and when employed, worked primarily in the lowest wage sectors, most often in the service industries that were not protected by labor legislation.

However, even in factories covered by minimum and equal wage provisions, such as textiles and tobacco, women were usually placed in different and lower paying job categories than men. Commenting on the inequitable condition of women workers in Cuba prior to the revolution, Vilma Espin, the head of the Cuban Women's Federation and a member of the Central Committee of the Communist party of Cuba, has stated:

> This situation could be seen concretely in the case of the female textile workers, especially in the clothes-making branch of the industry, where the work was almost completely done by women. These workers were paid low wages, since those from the city were supposed to be earning a daily minimum of $3.30, and those from the countryside were supposed to be paid $3.10, yet they were paid only $1.50 a day. They had to work more than eight hours, and to get around the social security laws only half of the employees were listed on the books. It is important to point out that in the Ariguanabo textile factory no women were admitted after 1940 so that the employers would not have to comply with the constitutional provisions which favored women."[8]

In the mid-1950s, more than one-quarter of all employed women worked as household domestics; their salaries ranged from $8 to $20 a month. Outside of domestic service, clerk typist was the largest category of work for women. But this form of employment was limited to those women who had an education. Most women were without sufficient education and found themselves limited to domestic service or work in the cabarets and gambling casinos as hostesses and performers.[9]

In general, the prerevolutionary economy did not rely heavily on an educated work force. In 1953, between 20 and 25 percent of the Cuban population was estimated to be illiterate.[10] In the rural areas, illiteracy figures came close to 40 percent.[11] Although girls were more likely than boys to have some primary education, by secondary level only a small percentage of all Cuban children were enrolled in school, and boys greatly outnumbered girls. Few Cubans had any university education prior to the revolution, but at this level as well, males greatly outnumbered females. Formal education was not viewed as a necessity for women in prerevolutionary Cuba. Those women who out of necessity had to work outside the home had little practical use for formal education because the areas of employment open to them required little if any schooling. Similarly, middle- and upper-class women could better prepare for marriage at home. Of those women who did receive more advanced, formal educations, few studied for careers outside the home. Rather, most were educated in the graces that would allow them to be good wives and mothers. For women who trained for employment as primary school teachers, pharmacists, or secretaries, the consensus in the literature suggests that many bowed to social convention and relinquished such careers once married.[12]

Women's Social Status

The social status of women in prerevolutionary Cuba was conditioned by Spanish tradition, slavery, and toward the end of that era, by a U.S. tourist perception of women. From Spain, Cuba received the traditional social and sexual dichotomy of male and female. A woman's place was in the *casa* (house), and a man's domain was in the *calle* (street). A "good" woman of the upper class was virginal before marriage and faithful to her husband after. A man, on the other hand, was expected to demonstrate his virility both at home and outside the home—in the latter case with women who were of a lower class and who, out of necessity, had left the protection of the *casa* for employment in the public arena, the *calle*. The sexual standards of employed women were presumed to be different from those of the "good" woman. In fact, women who left the protection of the home to seek employment for whatever reason were often expected to provide an outlet for male virility.

With the extermination of the Indian population in Cuba, slaves were imported from Africa to work on the plantations, and African traditions and a slave culture mixed with Spanish customs. Slavery allowed for the perpetuation of the upper-class male and female roles and provided an additional outlet for Spanish male virility—slave women were expected, in addition to engaging in physical labor, to sexually service their Spanish masters. The African males who arrived from the Congo and Nigeria also brought with them the *Abakva*, a secret society of men that held women inferior.[13] By the time of emancipation in the mid-1800s, a culture of male supremacy had developed that defined women's social role according to color and class and placed women in distinct "good" and "bad" categories according to a woman's role in the *casa* or the *calle* and, correspondingly, her assumed sexual conduct.

Until 1940, the Spanish civil codes and the first Cuban constitution reinforced these social attitudes toward women. Under Spanish rule, a man was defined as the head of the household, and by law a woman had to "obey" the wishes and dictates of the father, husband, brother, or son. A woman could not even engage in financial transactions without male permission. Although independence from Spain brought a legal separation between the state and the Catholic church, the dictates of the church concerning marriage and divorce were incorporated into the constitution. The only grounds for divorce were adultery on the part of the wife and adultery that led to public scandal on the part of the husband.[14] Although the constitution of 1940 removed the most pernicious remnants of the civil codes and granted women equal civil rights, the full exercise of those social and familial rights was constrained by material and cultural conditions. Before the transformation begun in 1959, the Cuban economy allowed women few options for support other than through marriage, and the Cuban culture reinforced a view of women's place as restricted to the home and centered on the family.

Beginning in the 1930s and increasingly after World War II, the influx of tourists from the United States had an impact on the social perception of Cuban women. In the tourist industry women were drawn into service in two ways—as domestics at the many hotels that dotted the Havana skyline, and as cocktail hostesses, performers, and prostitutes in the many gambling casinos and nightclubs that served the tourist trade. The image of the Cuban woman that was portrayed by the tourist industry was not that of the "good" Cuban woman who stayed at home, nor was it that of the poorly paid, uneducated domestic servant. As Geoffrey Fox has so aptly put it, the women of the *calle* formed the tourist picture of Cuban women: "The tourist dollar made prostitution and live sex shows possible," and the "less inhibited guide books" advertised the sensuality of Cuban women as one of Cuba's most attractive tourist features.[15]

By 1959, the predominant social attitude in Cuba was dominated by a variety of male and female stereotypes that acted to limit women's social status. It was a man's role to rule inside the home and out—economically, politically, and sexually. In general, the "good" woman prepared herself for marriage and motherhood. In the Cuban upper class, a woman who worked outside the home fell under moral suspicion and brought shame to the family. In the small middle class, a certain number of professions, such as teaching or pharmacy, were considered possible stopgap jobs, but only until marriage. Before marriage, a woman was to stay under the protection of the men of her family for fear that her honor and the honor of her family would come into question. Following marriage, the role of protector would be transferred to her husband and his family.

For women who had no option but to work outside the home, there was little hope of maintaining their dignity. In general, they could accept poorly paid positions in domestic service or in a limited number of factory jobs, or they could become women of the *calle,* making more money, perhaps, but losing all social respect.

Since the Cuban Revolution, the entire social order of Cuba has been challenged, and in the process of the social transformation that has occurred, the traditional social roles of male and female have, of necessity, come under attack. This process of social transformation and the effect it has had on Cuban women's political power, economic position, and social status has been dramatic. Although all vestiges of the old order have yet to be removed, and Cuban women do not equally participate in or benefit from the new social order, much progress has been made, and many important lessons can be learned from what has transpired.

• **WOMEN'S POLITICAL POWER IN REVOLUTIONARY CUBA** •

With the overthrow of the Batista government and the victory of the July 26th guerrilla forces on January 1, 1959, a new social order began in Cuba. Although the new government did not proclaim itself socialist until 1961, and a new Cuban Communist party, combining elements of most groups that actively participated in the revolution, was not organized until 1965, the patterns of political power for the new Cuba began early on. Individuals who were engaged in the guerrilla struggle as well as their urban supporters assumed positions of direct political authority. For the first fifteen years, revolutionary mobilization, as opposed to the previous pattern of corporatist competition and electoral politics, characterized the political process. Although there were no direct elections, the new Cuban political ideology looked on political participation as the civic responsibility as well as the right of all citizens. However, because active political participation was not a tradition for the majority of Cubans, numerous mass organizations reflective of various interest groups were created by the revolutionary government to bring most Cubans into the political process. These organizations, in turn, became the major political organizations that, apart from the party, had major influence on Cuban policy. The organizations that developed and that have had continuity are the Committees for the Defense of the Revolution (CDR), the Federation of Cuban Women (FMC), the Confederation of Cuban Workers (CTC), and the National Association of Small Peasants (ANAP).

In the early years, most organization heads and government officials were drawn from the ranks of those who actively participated in the struggle against the former regime. Women as well as men had participated in the struggle, although not in as large numbers, and as a result, women came to hold positions of political authority in the new Cuban government, although in lesser numbers than men.[16] Over time, however, as more women participated in the mass organizations they gained greater influence and authority in these organizations and, as will be seen, greater influence on Cuban policy.

In 1975, a new Cuban constitution was inaugurated after lengthy discussion and debate throughout the country. Beginning in 1976, nationwide elections were held for the first time to elect delegates to municipal, provincial, and national Assemblies of People's Power. All these changes in the political life of the nation have affected Cuban women.

Women's Political Rights

Immediately after taking over the reigns of political power, the revolutionary government attempted to alter the material and cultural conditions in Cuba. Its principal expressed goal was to enforce the provisions of the 1940 constitution concerning equal economic, political, and social rights for all Cuban citizens. With regard to women's political rights, the equal rights provisions of the constitution continued to be the framework within which many revolutionary decrees proceeded. Although elections were not held initially, women had equal rights to participate in the revolutionary government and the mass organizations. In the 1975 constitution, women's political equality was again proclaimed, and in the 1976 nationwide elections women had the same rights as men to be nominated for and elected to political office. From the outset, however, Fidel Castro stated that equal rights, by themselves, would be insufficient to allow women equal participation in and benefit from the new society. Women, he declared, were doubly exploited: Women were exploited as workers in an underdeveloped, capitalist society, as were other groups, but they were simultaneously exploited and discriminated against as women.[17] As such, if women were to become fully integrated into the new society and were to equally benefit from the new social order, special efforts to integrate women's issues in the process of socialist transformation would have to be initiated.

Since 1959, economic and social legislation has been enacted that specifically addresses women's rights. Additionally, institutional arrangements have begun to develop that mitigate women's dual responsibilities in the public and private spheres. Further, an attempt at resocialization of male and female roles has begun. As a result of these combined efforts, although the number of women in positions of political authority is not equal to the number of men, women have had a growing influence on Cuban policy and have benefited from such influence.

Women's Political Authority

Prior to 1976, political authority was vested solely in the revolutionary government, which drew its membership, initially, from those who participated in the struggle against the Batista government, and later, both from this group and the newly formed Cuban Communist party. By the 1980s, women were still a small portion of party members, although the percentage of women had increased from 15 percent in 1975 to 19 percent by the end of the decade.[18] In the Central Committee of the party, a similar pattern of women's participation was in evidence: Female membership in the Central Committee rose from 5.4 percent in 1975 to 11 percent by 1983.[19] Women were, however, represented in other politically authoritative capacities. By the early 1970s, women already headed two ministries in the executive branch—Nina Fromenta was minister of Light Industry and Raquel Parez was minister of Social Welfare. Women also held the posts of vice-minister of Production and vice-minister of Education. Of the four mass organizations, women headed two: Vilma Espin was the head of the FMC, and Teresa Sanchez headed the CDR.[20] In the mass organizations, women were being elected to a variety of authoritative positions as well. By the early 1970s, women headed 15 percent of the provincial, 21 percent of the regional, and 24 percent of the municipal boards of government.[21] By the end of the decade, women had also begun to make their presence felt in the judicial arm of government, accounting for 20 percent of the Supreme Court judges and 24 percent of all judges nationwide.[22]

The nationwide elections held in 1976 for delegates to Assemblies of People's Power were preceded in 1974 by "experimental" elections conducted in Matanzas province.[23] Women fared poorly in these early elections; few women were nominated at the local level, and women were elected to only 3 percent of the seats in the municipal councils.[24] Castro, the party, and the FMC were dismayed at the number of women nominated and elected. On radio, television, and through the mass organizations, people were urged to elect more women. When elections to regional and provincial levels were held a week later, the percentage of women elected to office had risen, although not by much—to 6.9 percent and 16 percent respectively.[25]

During the 1976 and 1981 elections, the nationwide pattern was similar, and the government again intervened, calling upon the population to elect greater numbers of women. The results of these elections are displayed in Table 5.1.

Although even some critical commentaries on Cuba agree that there is "evidence of a government commitment to expanding the role of women in politics," twenty-odd years after the revolution women have yet to gain equal representation in positions of political authority.[26] Women have, however, made considerable gains when their position is viewed against the number of authoritative positions they held prior to the revolution, and as the level of elected office moves from the local to the national level, the proportion of women increases.

But the question remains: Why are so few women recruited at the local level? Interviews conducted by both the Cuban government and independent analysts suggest that quite often women decline nomination to run for office,

TABLE 5.1

Percentage of Women Elected to Positions
of Political Authority in Cuba

Office	1976	1981
Municipal Assemblies	6.6	8.0
National Assembly	22.0	22.7
Council of State	12.9	9.0

Sources: Jorge Dominque, Cuba: Order and Revolution (Cambridge: Harvard University Press, 1978), pp. 501-503; Alfred Padula and Lois Smith, Sex and Revolution: Women in Cuba, 1959-1985, forthcoming, p. 3.

citing that the combination of employment and household duties already leaves them with little free time.[27] This dual responsibility also explains, at least in part, the low percentage of women in the Communist party, where nomination comes from other party members, usually at the workplace or in mass organizations, and is offered to those individuals who have proven themselves exemplary by participation in such endeavors as voluntary labor. However, this explanation cannot be used as an excuse for the low percentage of women presenting themselves for election to office. Indeed, in recent years, both the government and the party have taken action to address what they consider an inequitable situation for women. New and better institutional arrangements that would help to mitigate women's double burden have been developed, and guidelines for party membership have altered to take responsibilities for home duties into consideration for both male and female candidates.

Women's Political Influence

Four mass organizations developed during the early years of the Cuban revolution. Beginning in 1959, the CTC, which existed prior to the revolution but represented only a small percentage of the labor force at the time, reorganized and expanded its jurisdiction to cover all employed persons in every occupational category. By 1979, between 96 and 98 percent of all Cuban workers were represented in the eighteen national trade unions.[28] In August of 1960, the FMC was organized with a nucleus of seventy-five women. Within months, its membership had grown to 17,000. By 1979, 80 percent of all Cuban women over the age of fourteen were dues-paying members of the FMC.[29] In September 1960, the CDR was formed to act as a local militia. During the years, the CDR has retained its militia function—CDR members, for example are the local police—while expanding both membership and functions. Organized at the block level and incorporating approximately 80 percent of the population by 1979, the CDR has become the largest mass organization in the nation with a variety of community development, health, and educational responsibilities.[30] The last of the mass organizations to be developed was the ANAP, which was designed in 1960 to provide organizational affiliation for individuals receiving or retaining private landholdings under the 1959 agrarian reform law.

Each of these organizations was conceived to have dual functions as a mobilization agent. On the one hand, they were created as instruments to mobilize support for the new revolutionary government and its plans for Cuban development. But on the other hand, and just as importantly, they offered the Cuban people vehicles through which they could have an influence on government policy. Speaking of the dual function of the FMC, its director, Vilma Espin, has been quoted as saying: "By mobilizing and incorporating women into the tasks of modernizing the country, the Federation sought to satisfy the specific goals of women and the common goals of the nation."[31] The FMC was to "provide a place where women could discuss the problems they faced as women and press for changes to alleviate these problems."[32]

Women's concerns are not viewed as solely the province of the FMC, however. Women are encouraged to participate in all of the mass organizations and to use these organizations to develop programs and policies that meet their needs. Approximately one-half of all CDR members are women, and in the CDR women participate in all activities, including police and guard duty. The smallest of the mass organizations, ANAP, did not originally mobilize women because it was constituted to represent the owners of small parcels of agricultural land who, for the most part, were men. By 1966, however, special ANAP women's brigades were organized to allow women, mostly the wives of ANAP members, full and equal representation in the organization. It was even mandated that women be represented on the ANAP's elected boards.[33]

Although women made up only 31 percent of the Cuban labor force by the end of the 1970s, their representation in the CTC had grown dramatically. Prior to 1959, the overwhelming majority of women workers were not represented by organized labor, but by 1979, 96 percent of employed women were members of the CTC. Although the role of the CTC will be analyzed more directly in the section on women's economic position, the degree to which women hold positions of authority in the organization is an important aspect of women's political influence in the new Cuba. At the local level, more than 40 percent of all CTC officials were women in 1976. At the national level, however, their numbers dropped; only 18 percent of national CTC officials were female.[34]

All of the mass organizations have political influence in the Cuban system of government. Elected representatives of these organizations at local, municipal, provincial, and national levels confer with the ministries of the government on policy formation and implementation, representing the interests of their particular organization. Proposed national legislation, such as the 1975 constitution and the family codes, is discussed in the organizations, and comment, criticism, and proposed changes are sent back to the government.[35] This consultative status of the mass organizations is recognized and outlined in Article 7 of the constitution.

Even though all the mass organizations deal with women's concerns, the FMC has been most active in mobilizing women and incorporating them into the new Cuba. Women have been incorporated in growing numbers into other mass organizations, but the FMC took responsibility for organizing the first women's militia that operated at the Bay of Pigs. The FMC also organized women to participate in the literacy campaign of 1961, developed special schools to educate and reeducate women to participate in productive and remunerated labor, and worked with the government and the other mass organizations to develop institutional supports for and change social attitudes toward women as they entered the labor force.

Women's Economic Position

Except for a small proportion of the agricultural sector that has remained privately owned, by 1961 Cuba's economy was transformed from a free enterprise to a socialist system, an economy essentially owned, operated, and planned by the Cuban state. Although the economy continues to be based primarily on agriculture, agricultural production has been diversified, increased, and to a large extent, mechanized. Cuban-controlled industrial production has increased as well.[36] Cuba remains, however, far from industrially developed, and the U.S.-initiated trade embargo begun against Cuba in the early 1960s has restricted the nation's trade possibilities and adversely affected its growth potential.[37] For the most part, the development and extension of social services, housing construction, and overall infrastructure development have come about within the confines of a limited economic base. It is within the context of such an economy that women's economic position in Cuba must be examined and assessed.

Women's Economic Rights

In revolutionary Cuba, women's economic rights are predicated on an ideology that views women's incorporation into remunerated economic production as beneficial both to women and to the nation. Women's overall social equality is considered a positive function of their participation in the labor force. Fidel Castro has maintained that "the whole question of women's liberation, of full equality of rights for women and the integration of women into society is to a great extent determined by their incorporation into production."[38]

However, the nation also needs women's labor if it is to increase its production and generate sufficient goods and services to better the national standard of living. Legislation, as such, must focus not only on drawing women into productive labor, but also on maintaining women's economic participation.

Women were encouraged to enter the labor force immediately after the revolution, and institutional arrangements were developed to assist them. Former domestic servants and prostitutes were retrained by the FMC to enter other occupations, and the economic provisions of the 1940 constitution regarding equal pay and maternity benefits were not only continued, but finally enforced. In addition, what was to become an extensive network of child-care centers began. It was not until 1968, however, that a campaign was initiated to draw greater numbers of women into the labor force and resulted in more specific legislation and government initiatives.

In order to draw more women into the labor force, and at the same time diffuse traditional objections to women's activities outside the home, a variety of actions were simultaneously undertaken. The Ministry of Labor, in consultation with the CTC, instituted Resolutions 47 and 48 of the labor code that reserved 400 jobs for women and prohibited women from working in 400 others that were "considered harmful to their health."[39] The FMC initiated a campaign to bring 100,000 women into full-time employment. Members of the FMC "went door-to-door and talked with over 600,000 women and their families, urging the women either to go to work or to enroll in educational classes." This individual message was reinforced by a media campaign linking women's entry into the labor force with national development and the process of socialist transformation.[40]

The 1969 sugar harvest and the national call for voluntary labor were also used to accustom the general population to having women in the work force. Although the goal of harvesting 10 million tons of sugar was not achieved, women did begin to be accepted as workers. For some women, it was the first time they had ever worked outside the home; others worked side by side with men for the first time. Not only did such activity give women confidence in their abilities, it also demonstrated to the male population the importance of women's labor in achieving national development goals. The mass organizations, especially the FMC, worked hard to translate this specific experience into a more general one wherein the need for women to be active in the public sphere of life would be viewed as a necessary precondition for the new social order. This more long-term goal would take time to incubate in the consciousness of the population, but the more specific goal of bringing more women into the work force was achieved. By the end of 1969, the FMC had helped to recruit 140,000 women into paid, full-time employment.[41]

During the same year, the Feminine Front was organized as a permanent secretariat of the CTC to "focus upon the problems of women in work centers."[42] In every work center employing ten or more women, Feminine Front delegates were elected to sit on the CTC executive boards at each level of union organization. In addition to enforcing women's economic rights and monitoring the number of female employees and the positions they hold in each work center, Feminine Front delegates are responsible for working with the CTC to develop and coordinate services that make women's participation in the labor force easier. For instance, the Feminine Front delegates in the executive committees of each union, "coordinate access to facilities provided through work centers, facilities such as laundry service, day care, places in boarding and semi-boarding schools." Further, Feminine Front delegates coordinate with the Ministry of Production in long-range planning and with work centers on a day-to-day basis to predict job openings so that once openings are determined, the Feminine Front can work closely with the FMC in the geographic area where the jobs are to become available. The FMC also makes women aware of employment opportunities and of the training necessary for such positions.[43]

Although legislation in 1971 required all able-bodied males to work or be enrolled in school, women were not required by law to be employed or studying.[44] Although women were perceived to have the same social duty to work as men, general consensus held that the material conditions of Cuba were still insufficient to afford all women equal treatment if they entered the labor force. Not wanting to cause unequal hardships for women through equal application of the requirement to work, the government exempted women from this law. Since that time, attempts have been made to generate additional support services for women and to promote social attitudes that would deem such services national priorities. Legislatively, for instance, maternity leaves have been extended and additional material allocations made for child-care and home services.

In discussing the maternity law of 1974, Benglesdorf and Hageman relate that it requires women to

> take an eighteen week paid leave of absence—six weeks prior to the birth and three months after. Pregnant women are granted six full days, or 12 half-days, off for pre-natal care. Mothers are entitled to one day per month during the first year after birth for the child's medical care; in practice, the father can also take responsibility for this assignment. At the end of the paid maternity leave, if the mother feels she needs or wants to continue to care for her child full-time she can take up to one year's leave without pay; at the end of the year she can return to her former position.[45]

Recognizing, however, that the majority of women continue to shoulder a double burden upon entering the labor force, in 1974 the 13th Workers Congress of the CTC adopted a proposal put forth by the 2nd Congress of Cuban

Women, which stated that "working mothers should automatically be granted labor merit." Labor merit is usually necessary for promotion, nomination to the category of exemplary worker, and nomination to the Communist party.[46] Both the Workers' and Womens' congresses called for a reexamination of Resolutions 47 and 48. As a result, the number of positions reserved for women and from which women are excluded has declined. However, certain jobs are still classified as harmful or potentially harmful to women, and women are not hired in those occupations or, when they are, they are restricted in their duties.[47] Although this policy affects women's occupational distribution, it does not necessarily have an adverse impact on women's wages.

The efforts of the Cuban government and the various mass organizations have had an impact on the number of women employed and, when combined with the greater employment and educational opportunities developed since 1959, have acted to alter women's occupational distribution as well.

Women's Economic Participation

Estimates suggest that 194,000 women were employed in 1959.[48] Although no definite figures exist for women's percentage of the labor force at that time, according to the last prerevolutionary census taken in 1953, women were estimated to make up between 10 and 11 percent of the work force, and the literature on the period 1953-1959 does not suggest that women were employed in any greater numbers during that six-year period.[49] By the end of 1969, and the first coordinated effort to incorporate women into the labor force, women's participation had grown to 22.9 percent.[50] In 1974, three and one-half times as many women were employed as in 1953, and women comprised one-quarter of the labor force.[51] By the end of the decade, 31 percent of the labor force was female, with 800,000 women gainfully employed.[52] Padula and Smith's recent study suggests the "nearly 40 percent of the workforce is female."[53]

Although women are still not employed in equal proportion with men, both male and female employment rates have increased since the revolution, the economy has grown and diversified, and the number of women employed has grown dramatically. Where women work has changed as well.

Women's Occupational Distribution

Before the revolution, the small number of employed women clustered in the lowest paying jobs of the service sector, with only a small proportion employed in industry or the professions. By 1974, the occupational distribution of women had changed dramatically, with women well represented in all areas of the economy except agriculture. In occupational sectors, the nature of women's work changed. Although women remained a majority of those employed in the service sector, by the late 1970s the majority of women in the service sector were working in public health (64 percent of all public health employees were women) and education (54 percent of all teachers and educational administrators were women). In the field of public health, 40 percent of all physicians were female. In all employment areas, women had moved into administrative positions in greater, although not equal, numbers. In education, for example, 40 percent of the school administrators were female by the mid-1970s. The same pattern was true in industry. Not only had women greatly diversified their areas of industrial employment, but they had become managers and administrators as well. For instance, in light industry, where women average 45 percent of the work force, women make up 22 percent of the administrators and managers.[54]

Women did not participate equally with men in all occupational categories by the end of the 1970s, nor did women hold the same jobs as men, but the remuneration women received for their labors had improved substantially.

Women's Remuneration

Although figures on male/female wage ratios are not available, certain aspects of Cuban wage policies, when combined with pertinent examples of women's wages, do give a clue as to this facet of women's economic position. In socialist Cuba, national wage rates are set jointly by the Ministry of Labor and the CTC, according to the "complexity of work, necessary educational qualifications and skill level." In 1979, a minimum wage of 85 pesos per month was guaranteed to individuals whose education was not above a sixth-grade level and whose jobs required either a limited level of skill or limited physical exertion. The average wage was 150 pesos per month. Individuals employed at a minimum wage were, however, granted free rent and free lunches at their work centers; others paid between 6 and 10 percent of the average salary of all employed family members for rent and a modest fee for lunches.[55]

As individuals increase their educational level and acquire additional skills, their salaries rise. Each workplace offers requalification courses, both during work hours and in the evening. But because women often retain primary responsibility for home and child care after working hours, women are less able than men to participate in evening classes. In order to mitigate this problem, the Feminine Front at each work center was given responsibility for seeing that women receive priority for daytime training.[56] Women actively, although not equally, take advantage of such opportunities. In 1977, for instance, 37.2 percent of all those enrolled in adult education and requalification classes were women.[57] Participation is encouraged through various incentives: For example, workers are given paid time off from work to increase their level of formal education—up to two hours per week or fifteen days per semester.

Because of this wage policy, even if women begin working with a low skill qualification or in an industry with a lower than average starting pay, they are encouraged to increase their wage rate through education and training. For example, in 1973, the lowest starting salary was found at the day-care assistant level. Many of the women employed as assistants had been domestics prior to the revolution and had begun their employment with little or no formal education. Although they were given basic literacy courses and some training prior to employment in the day-care centers, their own advancement and the welfare of the children placed in their charge necessitated that they continue their education and training.[58] As an incentive to do so, they were promised that with greater education and training, their salaries would increase. In 1974, assistant wages were 77 percent of the Cuban average wage.[59] In 1979 terms, although the assistant training is improved and wages are higher, the 1974 wage would be comparable to approximately 116 pesos, as opposed to a minimum wage of 85 pesos a month and an average wage of 150 pesos a month.

Although women are not permitted to engage in certain tasks, interviews conducted in 1980 with Digna Cires, head of the CTC Department of Women's Affairs, suggest that protective legislation does not adversely affect a woman's salary. As an example, following International Labor Organization guidelines, women are not allowed to work on outdoor scaffolding above five meters. Thus, when a work crew is assigned to paint a building, women work indoors or at ground level. However, the wages men and women receive for painting are not determined by who works on scaffolding and who does not. They are determined by the individual's level of education and training.[60]

An examination of the occupations in which women are employed by various labor ministries shows that women are fairly evenly spread out among various sectors, and in areas where women predominate, they are moving into administrative positions as well. In 1984, for example, in the occupations responsible to the Ministry of Public Health, 68.9 percent of those employed were female, as were 39 percent of the mid-level administrators. In the Ministry of Science and Technology, where nearly 48 percent of the employees were female, women were one-quarter of the mid-level administrators.[61]

The advances Cuban women have made in the field of public production are the direct result of various but interconnected factors. In order for the nation to modernize and industrialize, and in order for the nation to increase production to provide for the needs of its population, a larger and better educated work force is needed. In order to supply that work force, women must be brought into the realm of public production. The state has combined this social need for women's labor with social policies affording women equal opportunities to participate in and benefit from expanding employment possibilities. One such aspect of social policy is education, where women's participation has expanded dramatically since 1959.

Women's Education and Training

With the advent of the revolution, primary education was made compulsory, and schools were constructed throughout Cuba. As early as 1967, females represented 49 percent of those attending elementary schools, 55 percent of those at the junior high and secondary level, and 40 percent of the university students.[62] At school, female and male students took the same courses and did the same things "including productive work and combat preparation for the militia."[63] Women also became students at the Military Technical Institute, which trained officers for the revolutionary armed forces. At the university level, women were well represented in most fields by 1972 (see Table 5.2), and by 1975 women had greatly expanded their participation in key areas such as engineering and agricultural science, where they were 30 and 35 percent of all students respectively.[64] By the end of the 1970s, all Cubans had the equivalent of a sixth-grade education, and a movement had developed to increase overall educational levels to the ninth grade by the mid-1980s.[65]

Although women remain overrepresented in some areas, such as education, and underrepresented in others, the educational system is training more women and training them in a greater number of fields. Further, schools and other social institutions have been reeducating the population to develop new social attitudes so that once trained, women are expected and encouraged to use their skills.

TABLE 5.2

Percentage of Female College Students Enrolled by Field of Study (1972) in Cuba

Field of Study	Percentate
Humanities	63.0
Education	63.0
Fine Arts	44.4
Law	45.2
Social Sciences	44.7
Engineering	19.1
Medicine	48.3
Agricultural Science	26.7

SOURCE: Report of the Economic Commission for Latin America, Participation of Women in Development in Latin America, E/CONF. 66/BP/8 Add. 1 (may 13, 1975), p. 11.

• WOMEN'S SOCIAL STATUS: 1959-1979 •

Women's Social Rights

Cuban women have, perhaps, greater social rights than women in any other nation examined in this study. Developments in social legislation, especially the 1975 constitution and the family code, have given women even greater public rights than those outlined in the 1940 constitution and have expanded social rights and duties in the private spheres to apply equally to men and women. Not only are women and men afforded equal rights in marriage and divorce, but both sexes are given equal responsibilities as well. Under the provisions of Article 26 of the family code, for example, both parties in a marriage or consensual union "must participate to the extent of their capacity or possibilities in the running of the home."[66] Even if only one partner works outside the home, these provisions remain in effect. By law, then, both men and women must share in the housework that serves the family.

That legislation is passed does not, however, assure that the spirit of the law is obeyed. There seems to be general consensus that women in Cuba still continue to do the majority of household tasks, and that no one is thrown in jail for not sharing in home responsibilities. However, the family code has acted as a resocializing agent since it was proposed. According to Margaret Randall, although men were not always in favor of this new role, when the code was discussed in the mass organizations, "men seemed to understand the essential justice involved and, at least in this collective context, didn't contest their new role." Women felt that the code had importance over and above its legal suasion. Men, they felt, would more readily help at home "now that everyone's in the same boat."[67] Previously, even though Communist party regulations had stressed that men should help at home, the following story recounted by author Heidi Steffens was not uncommon prior to 1975: "A well known member of the Central Committee of the Communist Party of Cuba took over the job of doing the family laundry. However, he insisted that his wife hang it out and bring it in from the line—he didn't want his neighbors to see."[68]

In Cuba, if a marriage fails, and many do, each partner has the same rights to file for divorce, and the community property of the family is evenly divided.[69] If there are children, each parent has responsibility for their welfare. Even though each partner has the possibility of custody, it is usually the mother who gets custody of the children. Child support is the duty of the parent without custody. In 1979, payment of child support averaged about 40 pesos a month—the average salary being about 150 pesos a month—and was automatically deducted from the paycheck of the responsible party and sent directly to the parent with whom the child resided.[70]

Women, by law, have an absolute right to control their maternity; in practice, contraceptive devices are available at low cost, and abortions are free.[71] Responsible sexuality is emphasized throughout the media, and lately it has been the responsibility of the newly established Institute of Human Sexual Relations to make sure that the public is educated in general and in the schools about sexual matters and family planning.[72] Although the institute and other institutions emphasize that both men and women have responsibility for family planning, interviews conducted by this author suggest it is primarily women, not men, who accept this responsibility.[73]

In the realm of social legislation, statutes afford women and men equal rights and responsibilities. However, recognizing that resocialization takes a long time, legislation has also evolved that specifically recognizes women's dual responsibilities for production and reproduction and attempts to mitigate what, under the existing social order, is a double burden for women.

Recognition of Women's Dual Social Role

Perhaps the most comprehensive program recognizing women's dual social role is that of the *círculos,* or child-care centers. Begun in 1961 on a limited budget, and using converted mansions for facilities, the child-care system has grown tremendously, although the number of facilities is still not adequate to meet demand.[74] The majority of child-care facilities are *externados,* or day facilities, that operate from 6 A.M. to 7 P.M., six days a week. *Internados,* which provide twenty-four-hour care Monday through Saturday, are more limited, as are *mixtos,* or mixed facilities, which provide both types of services. By the early 1970s, only 600 facilities serving 50,000 children were available.[75] By the end of the decade, however, the capacity had almost doubled with 782 centers serving 96,000 children.[76]

Child care was initially free, but during the 1970s a sliding scale of fees was instituted, with parents paying from three to forty pesos a month depending on the average per capita family income. Parents who bring their children to the centers are, by law, allowed to remain at the center without loss of pay until their children have adjusted to the routine of the center and are actively participating in its activities.[77] In an attempt to limit the time parents would have to spend on cooking and washing at home, each center provides three hot meals a day as well as clothing for the children to wear while at the center.[78]

In addition to publicly sponsored child care, other programs have developed in Cuba to mitigate the double burden women traditionally acquire when they enter public production. In all places of employment, worker's dining rooms provide low-cost meals; all have lunch programs, and many provide three meals a day.[79] In the 1970s, two experimental programs were initiated. In 1974, the *Jaba,* or Shopping Bag, Plan began. Under this plan a working woman could either drop off a shopping list at the neighborhood store and pick up the items ordered at a prearranged time, or she could shop herself, but to eliminate waiting, had first priority in line. Special days and certain hours were set aside in all stores just for working women, and hard-to-obtain items were often marked "these articles only for sale to working women."[80] Although these particular programs ended, others have emerged. In addition to laundry services that are run through work centers and pick up and deliver washing, a growing number of neighborhood laundromats have opened with special hours set aside in the evenings and on weekends for working women or the husbands of working women.[81]

Although women still bear the brunt of home responsibilities, the services described above attempt to mitigate the problems that women encounter when undertaking employment. That such services are geared, at present, solely toward women may have an adverse effect, however. Given the economic constraints placed on the Cuban economy, choices must be made about allocation of scarce resources. To the degree that such services are not viewed as a national priority or are considered almost exclusively in the context of women's issues, there could be a tendency to keep such projects low on the allocative agenda. To the extent that women are not in positions of political authority, such a possibility increases. Indeed, economic constraints have been cited as the reason for limited funding for increased services in these areas.[82] Further, the tendency to view such services as aiding women might well act to reinforce existing female/male social roles. In recent years, however, the government has shown an increasing commitment to these areas of social services as well as a commitment to resocialize male and female roles.

Women's Social Identity

Billboards and posters abound in Cuba. Rather than promoting products, they are primarily used to educate and resocialize the population. Two examples of the way women are portrayed in such billboards suggest how the government perceives women's social role. Throughout the 1970s, printed on large billboards along with brightly colored graphics showing women working, were two slogans: "Women—the Revolution Within the Revolution," and "The Revolution of Women is Greater than the Revolution Itself." Geoffrey Fox suggests that "the revolutionary leadership identifies itself with the changes in women's roles; sex, like race, has become a political issue in Cuba."[83] Displays of sexism, like racism, are not socially acceptable in Cuba.

From their earliest experience in day care, citizens of Cuba are bombarded with a new conceptualization of male and female social roles. Men and women are acknowledged to be physically different, but their physical differences are not seen as indicative of different and unequal social roles. In day care, for example, children play an imitative game called "family" in which they learn that in a family, men and women have the same duties to both provide for the family through employment and to maintain the family and home through cooking, cleaning, and washing.[84] Films, television programs, and magazines all attempt to redefine "family relations—and thus the meaning of womanhood and manhood."[85]

From its inception, the revolutionary government of Cuba has utilized its control of the media to focus on the specific problems women confront and to promote discussion of these problems, especially with regard to private or familial relations. In the 1960s, for example, the movie *Lucia* focused on the conflict that arose between a woman and her husband as she attempted to attend literacy classes. Lucia's struggle against the tradition of patriarchy, and her desire to educate herself to actively participate in the new society being created, was one focus of the film. On another level, the personal relationships between women and men were also explored, and the necessity for change in this most private realm was developed. A similar theme was explored in *Retrata de Teresa* (Portrait of Theresa), produced in the late 1970s. This later film was produced specifically as a vehicle for nationwide discussion of the need to develop a new consciousness concerning male and female social roles. Together with government pronouncements, television and radio programs, and newspaper articles, *Portrait of Theresa* was part of a massive effort to have the nation reexamine familial, sexual, and social roles in the context of the new Cuba.

In the mass organizations as well, a new image of female and male social roles is fostered. Although attempts at resocialization have not always been successful, and at best take time to develop, in reporting attitudinal surveys conducted in the 1960s concerned with female and male roles, Jorge Dominguez concludes that the independent variable of organizational affiliation was "significantly and strongly" related to acceptance of the new social roles the government sought to inculcate.[86] Specifically, "those who belonged to mass organizations were much more likely to approve of women's working outside the home, to mention the need for supporting services to permit it, and, if the respondents were housewives, to want to work themselves."[87]

Not all Cubans have found such resocialization to their liking, however. In interviews conducted with Cuban exiles, Geoffrey Fox found that "the alleged destruction of the family—that is, of the patriarchy—is a favored theme." The exiled males complained of women's position in revolutionary Cuba, commenting that "neither the father, nor the husband rules her anymore."[88]

Perhaps Margaret Randall, a U.S.-born author who has lived many years in Cuba, most vividly summarized the emerging social identity of the new Cuban woman when in the early 1970s she wrote:

> The Cuban woman today drives a tractor, hoes a field, and carries an AK-47 as part of her militia duty. She is very likely to do any or all of these with her hair up in curlers, so she will look attractive and feminine to her man at night. The militia and the Army give her a choice between wearing pants or a skirt. And she sees no contradiction between her new emancipation on the work and fighting fronts, and her desire to look, appear and feel feminine.[89]

Not all Cubans have accepted the new social roles for men and women advanced by the government. However, the attempt at resocialization seems to have had a positive effect on the position of Cuban women. Although women are not yet equal to men in political power, economic position, or social status, movement toward greater equality in each of these spheres of life has been considerable.

• SUMMARY •

The Cuban attempt to equally incorporate women into the process of national development has been predicated on a Marxist strategy that envisions a threefold process of social transformation. Within this strategy, changes in the material conditions of social relations are viewed as preconditions for positive alterations in women's economic position, political power, and social status. The first step in this process is the development of a socialist political economy. However, socialism itself is not viewed as sufficient to allow women greater equality. In addition, the society must recognize women's dual roles in production and reproduction and, as a result, direct its surplus toward provision of material services and systems of support for women that would afford them equal opportunity. Specifically, the society must assume responsibility for those material burdens associated with maternity, childrearing, and the auxiliary functions traditionally associated with female family responsibilities; burdens that are viewed as having hampered women's chances for equal opportunity in the past.

Change in the social attitudes toward male and female social roles is the third facet of social transformation in the Cuban interpretation of this Marxist strategy. Here, in order to positively affect women's equality in the transformation to socialism, the state must actively promote new social roles for both men and women that will act to foster the development of the socialist society. In sum, material changes conditioning all three aspects of social transformation must occur in order for women to achieve the equal opportunity necessary for them to participate in and benefit from all forms of social relations.

Although Cuban women have not achieved equal economic position, political power, or social status in the years since the start of the revolution, they have made significant gains toward equality in all aspects of social relations, public as well as private. Especially since 1969, women have increasingly joined men in the arena of public production. Women in Cuba do not yet participate equally in production, nor are they equally represented in all occupational categories, but the training women receive prepares them for most occupations, and the new social norms stress that such training be put to use. Despite the fact that Cuban women do not always hold the same jobs as Cuban men, women have increased their share of high-status and administrative positions, and although data on remuneration is scarce, patterns of remuneration that are available suggest that there is no *de jure* discrimination against women. When *de facto* discrimination is uncovered, interviews undertaken in 1980 suggest that corrective measures are readily available.[90]

Women have also gained a greater degree of political power. Women in Cuba are not equally represented in positions of political authority, but they have effectively organized as a group and developed a significant degree of influence on public policy through participation in mass organizations. This is conveyed most dramatically in the role played by the Federation of Cuban Women. However, even though women's issues are the primary concern of the FMC, neither women nor women's issues are confined to this organization. Indeed, even cursory studies of other mass organizations illuminate a substantial degree of female participation and organizational activity of specific consequence for women. The development of a politically influential women's organization and the incorporation of women's concerns in other influential organizations have combined to dramatically alter the political power position of Cuban women.

It is in the area of women's social status, however, that Cuban women may have made the most striking progress. Although no observer of Cuba would claim that traditional attitudes toward female and male social roles have been completely transformed, none can fail to be impressed with the degree of transformation that has occurred. Moreover, resocialization attempts have focused on expanding the perception of male as well as female roles; both men and women are portrayed as having equal rights, responsibilities, and roles in the public as well as private spheres.

An examination of the transformation of Cuban society since 1959 suggests that patterns of female equality and inequality have been conditioned by two factors: (1) the level of Cuban economic development and (2) the particular policies Cuba has employed to implement women's equality in the context of overall development processes. Specifically, although Cuba has expanded its production base tremendously since 1959, Cuba is still far from industrialized and must promote economic growth at the same time as it attempts a more equitable redistribution of the benefits of that growth. Such material constraints, it may be argued, have adversely affected Cuba's ability to provide women with the support services necessary to assure them equal opportunity to participate in public affairs.

Recognition of women's dual responsibilities in production and reproduction has found concrete form in legislation and in institutional and material support systems for women, but the present level of support services is insufficient to allow all women to assume public responsibilities without also assuming a double burden. Within the parameters of this limited economic base and limited support system, however, Cuban women have made some tremendous strides toward equality that must be explained. At least partial explanation may be found in a particularly Cuban interpretation of the dynamics in which the threefold process of Marxist social transformation unfolds.

A comparison of Cuban and Soviet societies suggests that a Marxist logic concerned with women's equality and social transformation may be variously interpreted. Rather than the Soviet strategy, which might be characterized as a mechanistic view of social transformation in which alterations in male and female roles come about as the direct and *automatic* result of transformations in the material condition of life, Cuban policy seems to reflect a belief that direct government intervention and positive policy in support of women's equality are necessary both to *condition* perceptual changes and to *reinforce* progress in the transformation of material conditions.

In the Cuban context, for example, it becomes obvious that public employment for women is viewed as only one precondition for progress toward women's equality. Although government policy has increasingly stressed the need to develop material support systems for women so that they might more easily enter public employment, it has endeavored at the same time to intervene in the society in order to enhance the chances of such systems developing. Specifically, it has intervened to mobilize women politically and to alter social attitudes so as to support and reinforce the changing social roles of men and women. Direct intervention in support of positive public policy concerned with women's equality may help explain why Cuban women have made such remarkable progress in a limited network of support systems, and why positive projections for the future of women in Cuba are common.

The creation of the FMC and other politically influential mass organizations was a conscious decision on the part of the Cuban government. The creation of these organizations and the mandates given to them have afforded women specific opportunities that may help explain the positive changes that have occurred since 1959. First, within the FMC, women were officially recognized not only as a distinct social group having specific needs, but also as an integral part of the new society that was to emerge. Women were mobilized to give support to the emergent socialist society and to develop programs that would allow them to equally participate in and benefit from this new society. The dual functions of the organization merged women's needs with the national goal of socialist transformation. Each became officially identified with the other, and, thus, policies in support of women's equality were not as likely to be perceived as solely women's issues, nor as concerns that could wait until the development of an expanded socialist economy. Second, once mobilized, Cuban women became conditioned to view their needs as legitimate social concerns and to accept struggle on behalf of those needs as their right. Third, as support for the FMC developed and membership grew to encompass the vast majority of Cuban women, women acquired the political and organizational training that would allow them to actively participate in public endeavors. They also received the social sanction and support that reinforced such actions.

Similar arguments could be made with regard to government policies concerning women and their role in other mass organizations. The specific inclusion of the Feminine Fronts in the CTC in the late 1960s, for example, may also have helped women to merge the goals of equality with a specific goal of the new socialist society—increased production—and in this manner have helped to ensure that movement toward one goal was considered a function of progress toward the other.

The identification of the Cuban government with programs and policies stressing women's equality pervades Cuban life. This identification may help to explain why, even with a limited economic base, the development of support systems for women finds general approval, and it also may explain why attitudes toward male and female social roles have begun to alter. Not only are such attitudes stressed in schools and in the media, but new patterns of male and female behavior are publicly recognized, reinforced, and rewarded in important areas of social life, such as qualification procedures for exemplary worker and Communist party membership. Positive reinforcement is offered to those who modify their beliefs and actions, and negative social sanctions condemn those who do not. With such material incentives, it becomes easier to alter behavior patterns.

A Marxist logic would agree that the Cuban policy of linking women's equality with socialist transformation is a major factor conditioning attitudinal change and reinforcing progress in the transformation of other material conditions that afford women greater opportunities. Further, this logic foresees even greater opportunities for women's equality emerging as the economic base of the nation expands.

Although a Marxist logic contends that greater social direction by governing institutions has conditioned positive movement toward women's equality in Cuba, it is precisely this governmental control and direction of policy that a liberal logic sees as a potential problem for Cuban women. Greater movement toward equality, this logic argues, is predicated on government whim. While the economy is industrializing and needs greater inputs of female labor, concessions may well be made to the particular needs of women and women's equality equated with national needs. However, what happens if the economy stagnates? Will women's equality and societal needs be separated, with women's needs sacrificed to a new perception of a more general social need? Who will make such determinations? The Cuban government. Because women in Cuba do not hold a significant number of politically authoritative positions, they would have little political clout to influence such choices were they to become necessary. This logic argues, further, that Cuban women's political influence is not secure; the FMC and other politically influential organizations were created by the government and might just as easily be dismissed by it. When combined with the capitalist logic that foresees limited potential for economic growth in a socialist system, such choices become almost inevitable, and a liberal/capitalist logic suggests that Cuban women's progress toward equality will be the victim of such choices.

That Cuban women have made a substantial degree of progress toward economic, political, and social equality since 1959 cannot be disputed. However, in

Cuba, as in the other cases examined, there is considerable disagreement as to the reasons for this progress, the factors that have impeded progress, and the future for women's equality. The degree to which either the Marxist or the liberal/capitalist logic offers a compelling strategy for women's equality, or offers sufficient explanation for the lack of it still demonstrated in each of these cases, is a major focus of analysis in the next chapter.

• CHAPTER SIX •
What Have We Learned and Where Do We Go?

Women's political power, economic position, and social status differ in each of the nations previously examined, but in none do women equally participate in or benefit from the full range of economic, political, or social relations that characterize the society. However, although the condition and status of women fall short of equality in all cases, a comparative analysis provides insights into those factors that may be key in conditioning greater equality for women and into the capacity of either the liberal/capitalist or Marxist strategy to move a society in this direction.

A comparison among the four nations studied suggests that a positive thrust toward greater equality for women is conditioned by the following: (1) the degree to which a nation has a growing industrial base; (2) the degree to which reproductive and auxiliary home responsibilities are lifted off the shoulders of women; and (3) the degree to which both male and female social roles are redefined. Additionally, the degree to which a separate, nationwide women's organization emerges and is recognized as a legitimate political force with institutionalized access to policymaking conditions the manner in which women are affected by industrialization. It also determines the propensity of the state to adopt policies that facilitate women's entrance into the public realm and promote a redefinition of social roles. Further, although none of the nations examined has successfully integrated all factors of importance to women's equality into its development strategy, a comparison of national efforts, and the various emphases that characterize them, gives insight as to how these factors are key in conditioning equality for women and whether the logic of either strategy shows promise for engendering women's equality in the future.

• A COMPARISON OF WOMEN'S EQUALITY AND STATUS •

The Liberal/Capitalist Strategy

An examination of women's condition in the United States and Mexico brings into question the liberal assumption that industrial growth and suffrage will facilitate movement toward greater political power for women. In each of these cases, the combination of equal political rights and industrialization has not been sufficient to afford women the degree of social mobility necessary to alter their economic position or social status, and as a result, women have not had the opportunity to equally and effectively compete with men for political influence and authority.

In both nations, women do not generally participate in those socioeconomic sectors that either have political influence or act as recruiting agents for positions of political authority. In Mexico, no national women's organization has emerged to successfully include women's issues on the national development agenda. Although the government has variously proclaimed women's equality as part of its development scheme and an increased number of women has been elected to the national legislature, women's issues have never placed high on the national policy agenda. One explanation for this is the fact that in those organizations that do have legitimate political influence, prerequisites for membership act to effectively exclude most women. Prevailing social attitudes tend to further inhibit women's active political participation.

Recently, a greater number of women began to be elected to the national legislature; the long-term effect of this trend on government policy is unclear, however. Historically, the president and the PRI, not the legislature, have set the public policy agenda in Mexico. To the extent that the increase in the number of women legislators represents a recognition on the part of the PRI of the importance of women's issues, legislative initiatives benefiting women may result. On the other hand, the PRI's support of women for legislative office may have the effect of coopting any emergence of women as an independent political force, thereby muting the pressure for legislative change.

In the United States, on the other hand, despite the fact that single, nationwide women's organization has emerged with legitimate, institutionalized access to policymaking, various organizations whose concerns are specific to women have developed. Because these organizations have attempted to influence policy on a variety of issues, and at many levels of government, evaluation of their effectiveness is difficult. However, most have pressured government to pass the Equal Rights Amendment (ERA), and on this issue, the effectiveness of women's organized political influence can be evaluated. In particular states such groups have been effective in getting the ERA passed. At the national level, however, effectiveness varies. Women's organizations were effective in pressuring the U.S. Congress to extend the deadline for ratification of the ERA, but they were not effective in generating additional votes for ratification in the various states. Neither were they particularly effective in generating support for the ERA from more politically influential groups.

Female membership has increased in organizations that traditionally have wielded political influence in the United States, but women are not yet numerically equal with men in these groups. Additionally, female members have not been demonstrably successful in organizing such groups to actively support issues of concern to women that would normally fall under the competence of these organizations. Although each of the major political parties gives lip service to issues of concern to women, and women have increased their numbers in both Republican and Democratic circles, women have not successfully generated party backing for concrete and comprehensive legislation in support of women's equality.

One explanation for women's failure to achieve political influence in the United States is that women have not tended to enter occupations that act as springboards to positions of political influence and authority. Additionally, social attitudes defining sex roles continue to weigh heavily against women who seek a public career. Women may now be accepted in the workplace, but the pressure at home often precludes their committing the time necessary to compete for and hold public office. As a result, political parties and politicians have demonstrated only a limited commitment to legislation that would provide women with the support services necessary to compete equally with men.

In both the United States and Mexico, women have not achieved either the occupational or social mobility that the liberal/capitalist strategy posits. The only measurable differences that can be attributed to a greater rate of industrialization and suffrage are an increase in the number of women that join the labor force and an increase in the proportion of the female labor force that is married or has children. Little change is seen in women's occupational distribution or status, and the remuneration ratio between men and women continues to be disturbingly large and, at times, even increasing.

Although the United States is educating women in greater numbers, that education is not necessarily preparatory to lifelong careers. In general, the view that a job is something to be undertaken before marriage and family continues as a battered, but still strong, element of the social ethos. Women who do otherwise tend to have done so out of necessity, or out of conscious decisions to go their own way and break with tradition. As a result, women are not skilled in the same areas as men, whose primary function is placed in the public arena. Today, as has been true historically, married women tend to enter public production only when the male labor force is insufficient to meet production demands or when family circumstances require two incomes. The tendency to view women's employment as a temporary phenomenon usually means that women are employed in occupations with low social status that command lower wages than men.

Mexican society has not incorporated women into the paid labor force in as large numbers as their northern neighbor. This factor lends support to the idea that industrialization has had a positive impact on women. Although a similar pattern of low-status, low-paying employment for women in Mexico has the same rationale as in the United States, the difference in women's labor force participation rates needs further explanation. Mexico industrialized later than and under circumstances different from the United States. Both factors conditioned the impact of industrialization on Mexican women.

Because Mexico began to industrialize in a global economy that already contained advanced industrial states, it has had to compete with these states in attracting capital and promoting its products. In order to draw capital and industry into the country and to be competitive on the international market, Mexico has drawn on what are considered to be its comparative advantages—cheap labor and a relative wealth of raw materials. The results of this form of development have been a large unemployed and a large underemployed labor force that together act to keep wages low, as various groups within the society compete with each other for the available jobs. Under these circumstances, the economy creates little pressure to draw women into paid production. Rather, women tend to remain a labor reserve; a group drawn into employment in the modern sector only when the demands of male labor are too high to retain a competitive advantage. There is, then, little social and economic pressure on women to enter the cash economy and, conversely, few rewards that might generate pressure in the opposite direction—women making demands on society. Consequently, society neither prepares women, nor do women prepare themselves, to fulfill a public role. Rather, socialization cultivates aspirations toward a domestic role and education in the skills necessary to be a good wife and mother.

Because Mexican society does not view women as a necessary part of the modern labor force, and because it still perceives women's function in a domestic context, it demonstrates little commitment to legislation giving women greater economic opportunities and has generated few social services that would facilitate dual social roles for women. Except for the small proportion of the female population that is wealthy, or that is in a position to be protected by union and government regulations, women who work outside the home tend to do so by assuming jobs that do not preclude their primary task as wife or mother, and in doing so, assume a double burden. All these factors act to limit women's opportunities for greater social mobility.

The prevalent social attitudes toward male and female social roles is an important factor conditioning women's political power and economic position in the United States and Mexico. In each nation, the dominant perception of what women and men should do tends either to condition women away from participation in public activities, or to place a double burden on those women who attempt to combine public and domestic life.

The prevailing social attitude in the United States generally defines women as either employed persons, or wives and mothers. In states without an equal rights amendment, legislation concerned with family law often reflects this dichotomy. As a wife and mother, a woman has legal definition within a family context where she is assumed to be protected and provided for by a man. The man's responsibility to provide for his family and his rights to the property acquired through his labors are often considered dominant as long as the family unit remains.

When a marriage dissolves, the law usually views a woman as the nurturing specialist and awards her custody of any children. However although the courts usually view women as the primary parent and generally assume that women will continue to require financial assistance to fulfill this role, little legal provision is made to assure continued financial responsibility by the father. Further, a little legal provision is made to assure that women themselves will not require such support. Stated quite simply, the dichotomization of women's social roles does not tend to afford women the equal economic opportunities necessary to support themselves.

Although a large and growing number of employed women are married or are single parents, except for a brief period during World War II when women's labor was viewed as important for winning the war, there has not been a sustained effort to provide employed women with those services that would mitigate a double burden when they assume dual social roles. If women work outside the home, they are somehow assumed to forego their right to maternity or are forced to make personal and ad hoc arrangements for child care. Unless a woman makes a large salary, allowing her in turn to employ household help, she must assume a double burden with household responsibilities. Additionally, the dominant social attitude has conditioned males and females alike to assume that such duties are the primary responsibility of the female.

In the United States, legislation has altered to recognize women's individual rights to control their maternity. However, recognition of a woman's right in this regard is not constitutionally safeguarded, and legislation in this area is continually being rewritten and contested.

In Mexico, the traditional social roles for male and female have altered even less than in the United States. Women are still generally perceived and portrayed in the domestic sphere and men exclusively in the public arena. On paper, women have equal rights with men, but the accepted social roles for men and women as well as the economic options offered to women if they choose not to accept this role inhibit women's ability to use such rights. Because women are socialized to view themselves almost exclusively as wives and mothers, because attitudes still persist that regard males as the dominant authority in the family, and because women have limited access to educational and employment opportunities that would afford them status or financial security outside of a domestic context, women usually marry, stay married, and attempt to gain status and security through their husbands and children.

The Marxist Strategy

In the Soviet Union and Cuba, greater equality for women has emerged. However, this trend toward greater female equality is inhibited in the case of the Soviet Union by a limited change in male social roles and a lack of governmental commitment to developing surrogate domestic services for women. The trend is hindered in the Cuban case by a limited economic base.

In both nations, although women are still a small proportion of Communist party membership, in most other areas of political life women have gained a greater degree of political power and influence. Although no national women's organization currently acts as a separate voice for Soviet women, women tend to be well represented in those groups that advise the government and thus influence policy. In trade unions, for example, women are close to numerical parity with men, and special women's branches exist to assure that issues of concern to women are considered. Here, however, women's issues must compete with other concerns for attention, and issues of concern to women have not always fared well.

The low rate of female participation in the Communist party is often explained by women's lack of free time to participate in those activities leading to party membership. A similar explanation is given for the lesser numbers of women elected to public office. Because women in the Soviet Union are generally employed outside the home, the development of publicly sponsored childcare and surrogate domestic services is an important variable in determining the amount of free time women will have. Here, the Soviet strategy for women's equality breaks down. Although legislation has granted women equal rights, and support structures have emerged to promote equal opportunities on the job, once women leave work, the lack of commitment to a redefinition of male domestic roles and the lack of surrogate domestic services for home maintenance tend to place a double burden on Soviet women, thus limiting the amount of time they have to spend on political activities.

In Cuba, as in the Soviet Union, women have increased their political power and influence. The government has made an effort to mobilize women into organizations that wield political influence, even creating one organization especially for women—the Federation of Cuban Women. The pattern of women's participation in positions of political authority is not as definitive as in the Soviet Union, however. Few women are in positions of political authority at local levels of elective office; however, at the levels of government closer to the national level, a greater proportion of women is found.

The double burden women must undertake if they assume a public as well as a domestic role is, again, the most common explanation offered for the fact that women are a small minority of those elected at the local level and remain a small minority of Communist party members. Although there is an obvious governmental commitment to transforming the social definition of male and female roles, and institutional arrangements supporting these new roles are increasing, a low level of industrial development has limited such services. The lack of these services not only limits the number of women that can be absorbed into the labor force without assuming a tremendous double burden, but also lessens the amount of free time women have to participate in political activities.

Even with such constraints, however, in the area of public production women in the Soviet Union and Cuba have made tremendous strides toward a more equal economic position. In both nations, women have equal rights with men to employment and wages. In addition, women's productive as well as reproductive capacities are recognized, and comprehensive maternity benefits are guaranteed to all. In both of these nations, protective legislation has limited women's participation in certain occupations. However, in these cases, the wage disparity between male and female does not tend to be as great as it is in the United States and Mexico.

Level of industrialization makes a difference in women's labor force participation in nations attempting a Marxist development strategy, just as it does in nations attempting a liberal/capitalist one, and the Soviet Union has incorporated a greater proportion of women into the labor force than has Cuba. However, although level of industrialization makes a difference in this regard, it does not tend to make any great difference with regard to women's occupational distribution or training. In both the Soviet Union and Cuba, women tend to be fairly well dispersed throughout the various occupational categories examined.

Women do, however, tend to continue dominating those employment sectors that serve what are traditionally viewed as nurturing functions, such as child care. They have only recently made inroads into traditionally male fields, such as engineering. With these exceptions, however, there do not seem to be major categories of employment deemed women's work or men's work.

Trends toward increased female labor force participation in these societies may be traced to the fact that in both countries women's employment is encouraged; populations are socialized to view women as having public roles, and the educational systems train women to acquire the skills needed to participate in public production. However, the degree to which each government demonstrates a commitment to a complete resocialization of roles for men and women also differentially impacts on women's equality.

In the Soviet Union, although women are viewed as having dual social roles, traditional attitudes toward male social roles have not altered significantly, and the social role of Soviet men has not expanded to include a greater domestic function. This perception of separate social roles for men and women becomes harmful to women's equality when it is reflected in public policy concerned with the development of surrogate domestic services. Viewed solely as women's issues, such services have not always had a high place in the overall national development agenda. Women receive a greater proportion of those services that are seen to contribute to women's participation in economic production, but the government has not been as quick to provide services to lessen women's household work or to change attitudes that define such responsibilities as female.

In Cuba, on the other hand, although there is a greater demonstration of commitment to altering both male and female social roles, economic constraints have limited the development of many services that would lessen the domestic burden for men or women. Such material considerations have not, however, hindered the development of what is possibly the most comprehensive and most equitable social legislation to emerge in the four nations of this study.

In Cuba, women not only have equal rights with men in marriage and divorce, and the right to exercise control over their maternity, they have also succeeded in securing legislation that makes household duties the responsibility of both men and women. Although all portions of the adult population have not been resocialized to accept such equal rights and responsibilities, younger generations are being socialized to view men and women as having equal social roles, both domestically and in the public arena.

• WHAT HAVE WE LEARNED? •

As the preceding discussions suggest, although women do not enjoy equality in any of the societies examined, a comparison of women's status reveals certain factors as key in generating movement toward greater equality. The degree to which a nation has a growing industrial base will condition the social demand for women to develop a public role through paid employment. It will further condition the economic product available to provide support services that allow women participation free of a double burden. The degree to which a society views provision of such services as a national priority, and the degree to which males and females are socialized to have both domestic and public roles, will further condition the availability of such services and, thus, the degree of social mobility allowed to women.

Earlier discussions also suggest that progress in both instances will be a function of the willingness of the society to trade some measure of its economic efficiency for greater social equality, and that this, in turn, will be conditioned by the degree to which the governing bodies and institutions of the society stress that such trade-offs are important for, and compatible with, overall national development policy. Further, the degree to which governments intervene in society to positively alter the material and ideological structures in support of women's equality is positively associated with the degree to which women are successfully organized into legitimate, political influence groups.

Although none of the nations studied has placed issues of women's equality at the top of its development agenda, those nations that have pursued a strategy for women's equality reflective of a Marxist logic have tended to do so to a greater extent than those that have followed a liberal/capitalist logic. In many ways, the present formulations of capitalism and liberal democracy act to constrain progress toward women's equality. Although a socialist political economy does not automatically engender equality for women, elements of the Marxist logic suggest why movement in the direction of equality tends to be greater in the socialist states examined here.

Both Marxist and liberal logics have built on the political tradition of the Enlightenment, but each has evolved in different directions with regard to the role of the state. Specifically, the liberal logic assumes that a democratic and pluralist system of government should, at any given time, reflect the existing will of the electorate when defining citizen rights and responsibilities. Although social relations will change over time, a further assumption holds that such changes will be incremental and can occur within the broad framework of existing political and economic relations. From this perspective, the role of government is limited to that of arbiter among various interest groups contending for benefit within the existing set of socioeconomic relations. As such, government need not have a vision of the future; its role is not to create a new social order but simply to mediate between contending groups within the parameters that define the existing one. Marxist theory, on the other hand, does not view the state as neutral; this logic has infused into its theory of the state and general social relations elements of dialectical materialism and the theme of social engineering.

A Marxist logic views all social relations as historically conditioned and manipulable. Social relations are the creations of humankind; they come into being because of particular sets of material conditions, are perpetuated because they serve the existing socioeconomic order, and are reinforced by attitudes and institutions that emerge to reflect these material conditions. Because social relations are historically and materially conditioned, they can be changed.

In a capitalist political economy, the state acts as the organ for maintaining and adjusting the sets of relations that will perpetuate capitalist control and benefit. When a socialist government assumes state power, it has a different function. Here, the state must act to transform the material conditions of life that affect social relations. Specifically, the state must (1) have a vision of the society it wishes to create; (2) generate the material conditions that make this vision possible; and (3) mould new social attitudes that will bolster the new set of social relations it wishes to engender.

These perspectives on the nature of social relations and the role of the state help to explain why, at least theoretically, there may be a greater tendency for states acting within a Marxist logic to intervene in society in support of women's equality. But it is within the particular ideologies derived from such logics, especially as they condition policy formation and implementation, that the importance of this tendency becomes clear.

In a system of competitive capitalism, such as that employed in both Mexico and the United States, economic efficiency guides business decisions. Although greater social equality may be a desired goal for some, the promotion of such a social goal is not presumed to be the function of the business community, especially if policies promoting equality would adversely effect production efficiency and profit. With regard to policies facilitating women's equality, this functional priority has important consequences. Were an individual firm to assume the costs of providing surrogate support services, such as paid maternity leave or subsidized child care, such policies might well have a positive impact on women's economic and social mobility but an adverse impact on the firm's rate of profit. Such provisions might well increase the firm's production costs relative to other firms that did not offer such services, thereby limiting its ability to compete profitably in the market. Under such circumstances, policies promoting greater services for women would only come about if the costs of providing such services were not viewed as adversely effecting efficiency and profit, or, as in the case of the United States during World War II, when such services were necessary to attract and maintain necessary female labor.

In the context of a capitalist ideology, however, the state could intervene in the market and require all firms to provide such services, if such services were viewed as necessary for maintenance of the socioeconomic order, or were considered collective goods that were achievable only at the state level. Such actions are rare, however, and tend to run counter to the prevailing political ideology in both the United States and Mexico.

Hence, within the liberal, pluralist tradition of both nations, the role of government tends to be more circumscribed, especially as regards women. The governments of these nations have functioned, at best, to assure that women, as all other groups, have equal civil rights, that women do not forego the same rights as men simply because they are women. In both nations, governing structures have been created for the purpose of assuring that such conditions obtain. The political institutions of these nations do not have the constitutional mandate to go beyond the provision of equal rights by developing legislation that would give women special or unequal rights or benefits.

Although the original theories of Marx and his contemporaries assumed that a socialist society would be created out of an advanced capitalist economy, thereby allowing sufficient surplus to be more equitably divided through policies of the new socialist state, attempts at socialist transformation have not occurred in this way. As the studies of the Soviet Union and Cuba illustrate, policies designed to promote greater social equity have had to occur alongside policies designed to further industrialization and economic growth. This fact has had a major impact on the manner in which these two governments have attempted policies in support of women's equality and has variously conditioned the degree to which each has intervened.

An analysis of the Soviet attempt at socialist transformation suggests that the need for economic efficiency in the pursuit of industrialization and economic growth has often overshadowed concern for women's equality. By limiting support services to those necessary to ensure female entry into economic production, the state forced women to assume a disproportionate share of the social costs of development. Additionally, such policies have acted to reinforce traditional male and female domestic roles because women were resocialized to have a public as well as domestic persona, but men were not resocialized in the same manner or to the same degree.

However, in those areas of social life where the government has intervened in order to assure women equal opportunities, evidence suggests that movement toward women's equality has been facilitated. The Soviet case also suggests that state control of allocative and reallocative decisions is not, by itself, sufficient to provide greater equality for women. Rather, evidence suggests that without the presence of a separate women's organization capable of articulating women's needs within policymaking bodies, women's issues can easily become part of a secondary social agenda, something to strive for after other national priorities have been attained, but not needed in conjunction with such a process. The importance of these factors is demonstrated even more clearly in the Cuban case.

In comparison with the other nations in this study, Cuba has done quite well in promoting women's equality. At least partial explanation for this may be found in the Cuban policy of linking progress toward women's equality with progress toward national development. By equating women's equality with development, the government has been able to generate support for allocating scarce resources to services that allow women more equal opportunities. This linkage is also shown to have a positive effect on the resocialization of attitudes toward male and female social roles.

The degree to which the existence of the Federation of Cuban Women has been an important instrument conditioning government policies in this regard is not clear, but this study and others suggest that the FMC has played an important role in influencing public policy decisions. As such, the importance of women's organized political influence is once again highlighted.

The need to alter social consciousness emerges as a crucial factor conditioning women's equality in each case. Because "social engineering" allows for greater manipulation in this regard, governments following a Marxist logic have had greater comparative success. The present lack of full female equality in these states is, thus, particularly damning, as it suggests that governments have been either unwilling or unable to develop conditions that fully alter consciousness. The liberal/capitalist model, on the other hand, posits that "social engineering" is inefficient and therefore to be avoided. Consequently, or perhaps conveniently, an ideological barrier exists inhibiting conscious attempts to change the social ethos.

• WHERE DO WE GO FROM HERE? •

The preceding comparative examination of women's status suggests that certain conditions must obtain in order for women to move toward greater equality with men: industrialization and economic growth, the public provision of support services for women, the redefinition of male and female social roles, and the emergence of a politically influential women's organization. However, because the findings presented here emerge from the study of a limited number of cases, a much larger number of comparative studies needs to be undertaken to assess their reliability. I hope that such studies proliferate and that the results of this work contribute to a more comprehensive understanding of what is necessary to facilitate equality for women.

This study also suggests that in future studies, and with regard to policy formulation, new definitions and categories for analysis must be used. There is a need not only to redefine what has come to be called women's equality issues and development issues, but also the relationship that exists between women's equality and national development. Women's equality must be defined as an integral part of development because, if isolated and separated from overall national development, policies that act to promote women's equality can easily be postponed until more overarching, national needs are fulfilled. Similarly, the traditional separation between the public and private domains of social relations must dissolve and the areas of social life deemed appropriate for policy manipulation in support of women's equality expanded to include the personal realm of familial relations.

Certain general conclusions derived from this study also suggest what must be done on a more practical level. Although they must remain on a more general level here, I would hope that others attempt to use them to develop strategies for women's equality appropriate to various national conditions.

Industrialization and economic growth must be bolstered if women in the majority of nations are to be drawn into public production in a manner that allows them to attain equality with men. At the international level, efforts to restructure the international system of trade and exchange must be intensified, or the condition of debt and underdevelopment prevalent in so many nations will limit domestic efforts to foster equality for women. On the national level, change must occur as well.

In order to promote women's equality and development, governments must begin to revamp their public policies and resocialize their populations so that women's dual functions in production and reproduction are both recognized and supported. In order to facilitate movement in this direction, women's groups must develop that can effectively pressure governments for appropriate legislation.

Changes at either the international or domestic level will not be easy. Such changes necessitate a major restructuring of how most peoples and governments have been conditioned to view the world. Further, the present sets of global and domestic relations that act to limit women's equality are beneficial to others who may well act to maintain their position. As such, change may not be without conflict. Unfortunately, the changes necessary to facilitate women's equality will take time. However, if we don't begin today to bring about change, those born tomorrow will have an even harder road ahead.

Notes

• **CHAPTER ONE: WOMEN AND DEVELOPMENT** •

1. For an excellent review of the literature of this time, the reader should consult the annotated bibliography in Irene Tinker, Michele Bo Bramsen, and Mayra Buvinic, eds., *Women and World Development* (New York: Praeger, 1976), pp. 244–375.

2. For the reader who wishes to consult the key works on modernization theory that were used in this study, the following would be helpful: Gabriel Almond and G. Bingham Powell, *Comparative Politics: A Developmental Approach* (Boston: Little, Brown, 1966); David E. Apter, *The Politics of Modernization* (Chicago: University of Chicago Press, 1965); Karl Deutsch, "Social Mobilization and Political Development," *American Political Science Review* (September 1961):493–514; Bert F. Hoselitz, *Sociological Factors in Economic Development* (New York: Free Press, 1960); Samuel P. Huntington, *Political Order in Changing Societies* (New Haven; Conn.: Yale University Press, 1968); Walt W. Rostow, *The States of Economic Growth* (Cambridge; England: Cambridge University Press, 1960).

3. Margaret Mead, "A Comment on the Role of Women in Agriculture," in Tinker, *Women and World Development*, p. 10.

4. Joel Aronoff and William D. Crano, "A Re-Examination of the Cross-Cultural Principles of Task Segregation and Sex-Role Differentiation in the Family," *American Sociological Review*, 40 (1975).

5. United Nations General Assembly, *Report of the World Conference of the United Nations Decade for Women*, Doc.A/Conf.94/35:13.

6. This conclusion and the examples that follow are drawn from Blumberg, "Fairy Tales and Facts," in Tinker, *Women and World Development*, pp. 18–19.

7. Numerous challenges to modernization theory emerged during the 1960s and 1970s. These challenges ranged from mild critiques that sought to modify elements of the theory all the way to rejection of modernization and the subsequent formulation of new development theories. For two excellent works that review this literature, see Ronald H. Chilcote, *Theories of Development and Underdevelopment* (Boulder, Colo.: Westview, 1984) and Ronald H. Chilcote, ed. *Dependency and Marxism* (Boulder, Colo.: Westview, 1982).

8. The increase in information since 1975 is extremely important. However, a review of the data compiled for the 1985 Nairobi Conference that reviewed the UN Decade for Women suggests that a great deal more is needed to ensure comparable, time-series data both within and between nations.

9. UN, Doc.A/Conf.94/35:8.

10. Elaine Sciolino, "U.N. Finds Widespread Inequality for Women," *The New York Times,* June 23, 1985, p. 10.

11. See, for example, Ruth Leger Sivard, *Women . . . a world survey* (Washington, D.C.: World Priorities, 1985).

12. UN, Doc.A/Conf.94/35:11.

13. Throughout this study the term liberal/capitalist is used to refer to the theories of political rights derived from the liberal Enlightenment conceptualizations of democracy and the modern interpretations of capitalist economic relations. Taken together, these ideas set the parameters for government actions in the United States and Western Europe and are the cornerstones of modernization theory. The reader should refer to note 2, above, for authors relevant to this tradition.

14. These assumptions are addressed in the following works: Mary Wollstonecraft, *A Vindication of the Rights of Women* (New York: Penguin, 1978) and John Stuart Mill and Harriet Mill, *Essays on Sexual Equality,* ed. Alice Rossi (Chicago: University of Chicago Press, 1970).

15. The reader who is unfamiliar with general Marxist theories of the state and revolution may wish to consult the following: Lewis S. Feuer, ed., *Marx and Engels: Basic Writings* (Garden City, N.J.: Anchor, 1959); V. I. Lenin, *The State* (Peking: Foreign Language Press, 1965); David Gold, Clarence Lo, and Erik Olin Wright, "Recent Development in Marxist Theories of the Capitalist State," *Monthly Review* (November 1975): 36–51.

16. For a more detailed discussion, see Fredrick Engels, *The Origin of the Family, Private Property and the State,* ed. Eleanor Leacock (New York: International Publishers, 1975); and V. I. Lenin, *Women and Society* (New York: International Publishers, 1938).

17. Disagreement continues among Marxists as well as non-Marxists concerning the character of the Soviet state and its relationship with the proletariat. Although this debate is recognized, it is not the focus of this study.

18. Michael Harrington, *The Twilight of Capitalism* (New York: Touchstone, 1975), pp. 174–175.

19. The only other nations that might fit into this category are those of Eastern Europe. However, although the industrial capacity of these nations is sometimes even greater than that of the USSR and a strategy for women's equality similar to that of the USSR exists, their condition of coming into being—their "revolutions"—is even more questionable.

20. This perspective is usually articulated by such nations as Cuba and China. It is also woven throughout the literature on dependency and neo-Marxism (see Chilcote, 1982 and 1984 in note 7 above).

21. Although some might argue that Nicaragua is also a Marxist state because some of the members of the government are Marxist, I reject this contention.

22. For a representative sample of such national reports, see: United States National Commission for UNESCO, *Report on Women in America* (Washington, D.C.: Government Printing Office, 1977); Instituto Cubano del Libro, *Memories: Second Congress of the Cuban Women's Federation* (Havana: Editorial Obre, 1975); Centro de Estudios Historicos del Movimiento Obrero Mexicano, *La Mujer y el Movimiento Obrero Mexicano en el Siglo XIX* (Mexico, D.F.: Centro de Estudios Historicos del Movimiento Obrero Mexicano, 1975); and N. A. Kovalsky and Y. P. Blinova, eds. *Women Today* (Moscow: Progress Publishers, 1975).

23. Such international reports include the following: United Nations Fund for Population Activities, *Women, Population and Development* (New York: United Nations

Fund for Population Activities, 1976); United Nations General Assembly, *Report of the Secretary General*, E/CN.6/598 (New York: United Nations, July 21, 1976).

24. Evelyn Sullerot, *Women, Society and Change* (New York: McGraw-Hill, 1971), p. 15.

• **CHAPTER TWO: THE LIMITS OF SUFFRAGE** •

1. The United States National Commission for UNESCO, *Report on Women in America* (Washington, D.C.: Government Printing Office, 1977), p. 2 (hereafter referred to as UNESCO, *Report).*

2. By 1900, for example, women were more likely than men to have completed high school, and although many of the nation's colleges continued to refuse female students, women earned 20 percent of all bachelor's degrees. Marjorie Lansing, "Political Changes for the American Woman," Lynn B. Iglitzin and Ruth Ross, eds., *Women in the World: A Comparative Study* (Santa Barbara, Calif.: Clio Press, 1976), p. 178.

3. For specifics see Eleanor Flexner, *Century of Struggle,* (New York: Atheneum, 1974), pp. 193 and 230; and Rosalyn Baxnell, Linda George, and Susan Reverby, eds., *America's Working Women* (New York: Random House, 1976), pp. 232-235, 405.

4. William Chafe, *The American Woman: Her Changing Social, Economic and Political Roles, 1920-1970* (New York: Oxford University Press, 1972), p. 55.

5. Baxnell, *America's Working Women,* p. 232.

6. All information from Flexner, *Century of Struggle,* pp. 193-202.

7. Ibid., p 148.

8. Ibid.

9. The quote is from Blackstone's *Commentaries,* as cited in the United States Department of Labor, *1975 Handbook on Women Workers* (Washington, D.C.: Government Printing Office, 1975), p. 370 (hereafter referred to as U.S. Department of Labor, *1975 Handbook).*

10. National Commission on the Observance of International Women's Year, . . . *To Form A More Perfect Union* (Washington, D.C.: Government Printing Office, 1976), p. 41 (hereafter referred to as IWY, *Union).*

11. Chafe, *The American Woman,* p. 27.

12. Ibid., p. 23.

13. UNESCO, *Report,* p. 7; and Chafe, *The American Woman,* p. 36.

14. Chafe, *The American Woman,* p. 45.

15. The variety of women's groups active at this time are discussed in UNESCO, *Report,* p. 7.

16. As quoted in Ellen Goodman, "Battle of the Sexes Moves into Payroll Departments," *Los Angeles Times,* October 22, 1978, part 4, p. 5.

17. The specific conference recommendations as well as the later legislative record are discussed in A. Gillian, "How Feminists' Resolutions in Houston Fared in Washington," *Los Angeles Times,* November 21, 1978, part 1, pp. 6-7; and Bella Abzug and Mimi Kelber, *Gender Gap* (Boston: Houghton Mifflin, 1984), pp. 53-75.

18. As quoted in Abzug, *Gender Gap,* p. 77.

19. Ruth Leger Sivard, *Women . . . a world survey* (Washington D.C.: World Priorities, 1985), p. 35.

20. As quoted in Chafe, *The American Woman,* p. 38.

21. George Anderson, "Women in Congress," *Commonweal* 4 (March 13, 1929): 532–534.
22. IWY, *Union*, p. 41.
23. Abzug, *Gender Gap*, p. 25.
24. Ibid., p. 54.
25. Sivard, *Women . . . a world survey*, p. 35.
26. IWY, *Union*, pp. 34, 144.
27. Abzug, *Gender Gap*, p. 55.
28. For statistics from the 1970s, see IWY, *Union*, pp. 44–45.
29. A summary of this report can be found in IWY, *Union*, p. 344.
30. As quoted in Abzug, *Gender Gap*, p. 168.
31. For an excellent discussion of Democratic and Republican party attitudes toward female candidates, see ibid., pp. 175–180.
32. Chafe, *The American Woman*, p. 135.
33. U.S. Department of Labor, *1975 Handbook*, p. 11.
34. Chafe, *The American Woman*, pp. 180–181.
35. Ibid., p. 162.
36. Figures for 1974 from U.S. Department of Labor, *1975 Handbook*, p. 11; figures for 1980 from Howard Haygbe, "Marital and Family Patterns of Workers: An Update," *Monthly Labor Review* 105, no. 2 (Washington, D.C.: U.S. Department of Labor, 1982), p. 54.
37. According to Janet M. Hooks, *Women's Occupations Through Seven Decades*, (Washington, D.C.: U.S. Department of Labor, 1975), bulletin no. 218, the following occupations predominated: domestic servant, teacher, farm laborer, typist or stenographer, clerk, laundress, saleswoman, bookkeeper or cashier, cook, waitress, apparel and accessories operative, and nurse.
38. All statistics are from Chafe, *The American Woman*, pp. 60, 89, 93.
39. Ibid., p. 141.
40. Ibid., pp. 142–143.
41. Abbott L. Ferris, *Indicators and Trends in the Status of American Women* (New York: Russell Sage Foundation, 1971), p. 369.
42. Ibid., p. 179.
43. The percentage of women employed in various blue-collar occupations can be found in U.S. Department of Labor, *1975 Handbook*, p. 93.
44. Ibid., pp. 91, 92, 96.
45. Ellen Goodman, "Another Equal Pay Insult," *The Boston Globe*, January 31, 1984, p. 19.
46. U.S. Department of Labor, *1975 Handbook*, pp. 89, 95.
47. 1973 figures from ibid., pp. 89, 95, 151; 1980 figures from Sivard, *Women . . . a world survey*, p. 20.
48. "Women's Work is Never Done," editorial, *The Boston Globe*, April 18, 1984.
49. U.S. Department of Labor, *1975 Handbook*, p. 93; UNESCO, *Report*, p. 6.
50. Spencer Rich, "More Women Join Managerial Ranks," *The Boston Globe*, April 11, 1984, p. 1.
51. As cited in Ferris, *Indicators and Trends*, p. 117.
52. U.S. Department of Labor, *The Earnings Gap Between Women and Men* (Washington, D.C.: Government Printing Office, 1976), p. 6.

53. Robert Pearl, "Earnings Gap is Narrowing Slightly," *The New York Times*, October 3, 1983.
54. Abzug, *Gender Gap*, p. 112.
55. Ferris, *Indicators and Trends*, p. 397.
56. Abzug, *Gender Gap*, p. 112; and Pearl, "Earnings Gap."
57. Chafe, *The American Woman*, p. 85.
58. Ibid., p. 86.
59. Ibid., pp. 155-156.
60. Ibid., p. 157.
61. Ibid., p. 158.
62. For a discussion of the various protective laws and their effect on women, see Chafe, *The American Woman*, pp. 79-83, 85-87, 127-28.
63. For a colorful description of some of these changes, see LaVerne Bradley, "Women at Work," *The National Geographic Magazine*, (August 1944): 196-197.
64. U.S. Department of Labor, *1975 Handbook*, p. 289.
65. For an examination of the specific categories of employment exempted at this time and the effects such exemptions had on women's employment, see IWY, *Union*, p. 289.
66. Ibid., p. 350.
67. Ibid., p. 281.
68. As this book is being written, the U.S. Department of Justice is challenging the whole concept of affirmative action.
69. IWY, *Union*, pp. 281-282.
70. Ibid., p. 310.
71. Ibid., pp. 303-305.
72. Sivard, *Women . . . a world survey*, p. 15.
73. IWY, *Union*, p. 351.
74. Survey cited in ibid, p. 354.
75. William Meyers, "Child Care Finds A Champion in The Corporation," *The New York Times*, August 4, 1985, p. F6.
76. Figures for 1975 from U.S. Department of Labor, *1975 Handbook*, p. 76; figures for 1984 from U.S. Department of Labor, *Employment and Earnings* (Washington, D.C.: Government Printing Office, 1985).
77. Chafe, *The American Woman*, p. 89.
78. Ibid., p. 137.
79. Bradley, "Women at Work," pp. 211-212.
80. U.S. Department of Labor, *1975 Handbook*, p. 214.
81. U.S. Department of Education, *Digest of Educational Statistics, 1982* (Washington, D.C.: Government Printing Office, 1982), pp. 113, 117, 119-120, 124, 127 (hereafter referred to as U.S. Department of Education, *Digest*).
82. U.S. Department of Labor, *1975 Handbook*, p. 208.
83. U.S. Department of Education, *Digest*, p. 126.
84. As quoted in Chafe, *The American Woman*, p. 104.
85. For an interesting discussion of nontraditional education during this period, see Chafe, *The American Woman*, p. 138.
86. This study is cited in UNESCO, *Report*, p. 28.
87. Ibid., pp. 28-29.

88. Ibid., p. 29.
89. U.S. Department of Education, *Digest*, pp. 70-71.
90. Chafe, *The American Woman*, p. 99.
91. Ibid., pp. 99-100.
92. Baxnell, *America's Working Women*, pp. 245-246.
93. As quoted in Chafe, *The American Woman*, p. 176.
94. For a discussion of this phenomenon, see ibid., p. 147.
95. Baxnell, *America's Working Women*, p. 246.
96. As cited in Chafe, *The American Woman*, p. 148.
97. Ibid., p. 177.
98. Both surveys are quoted in ibid., p. 178.
99. Baxnell, *America's Working Women*, p. 383.
100. Various analyses of periodicals and magazines of this period can be found in Chafe, *The American Woman*, pp. 199-207.
101. Both quotes from ibid., pp. 207-208.
102. An analysis of female roles in U.S. film and television can be found in Steven Zuckerman, "T.V. Programming: Sexist and Ageist," *The Guardian*, December 12, 1979. p. 5.
103. Kathleen Newland, "Media Maketh (Wo)man!" *Development Forum*, (April 1979): 10.
104. Quote and information taken from Chafe, *The American Woman*, pp. 159-162.
105. For a discussion of the types of services instituted by war industries, see Baxnell, *America's Working Women*, p. 291.
106. Quote and statistics drawn from ibid., pp. 291, 193-194.
107. Ibid., p. 295.
108. Chafe, *The American Woman*, p. 187.
109. Studies reported in U.S. Department of Labor, *1975 Handbook*, p. 35.
110. Chafe, *The American Woman*, p. 241.
111. Abzug, *Gender Gap*, p. 113.
112. U.S. Department of Labor, *1975 Handbook*, p. 39.
113. Ibid., p. 133.
114. Meyers, "Child Care," p. F6.
115. As reported in Steven Zuckerman, "Survey Finds Many Men Agree They Should Help on Housework," *Los Angeles Times*, July 18, 1979, part 1-A, p. 4.
116. U.S. Department of Labor, *1975 Handbook*, p. 121.
117. Ibid., p. 368.
118. Both quotations from ibid., pp. 368-370.
119. In February 1984, the Oklahoma House rejected legislation that would have repealed a statute making the husband automatic head of household.
120. Abzug, *Gender Gap*, p. 140.
121. As reported in IWY, *Union*, p. 79.
122. For a list of these states and their relevant laws, see ibid., p. 82.

• **CHAPTER 3: THE *CASA* PREVAILS** •

1. Under both Spanish law and the Napoleonic codes the concept of community

property in marriage prevailed. Under both legal systems marriage was a religious as well as civil matter, and Catholic canon law forbidding divorce was reflected in civil law. Certain other laws, such as the Napoleonic code forbidding a wife's employment without the express consent of her husband, were also in effect. Child custody was considered to be a male prerogative, although divorce was not allowed.

2. Ward M. Morton, *Woman Suffrage in Mexico* (Gainesville, Fla.: University of Florida Press, 1962), p. 1.

3. Roderic A. Camp, "Women and Political Leadership in Mexico: A Comparative Study of Female and Male Political Elites," *The Journal of Politics* 41, no. 2 (May 1979):418.

4. Morton, *Woman Suffrage in Mexico*, p. 3.

5. For a discussion of the variety of local and national women's organizations of this time, see ibid., p. 9; and Camp, "Women and Political Leadership," p. 418.

6. Camp, "Women and Political Leadership," p. 419.

7. William Blough, "Political Attitudes of Mexican Women: Support for the Political System Among a Newly Enfranchised Group," *Journal of Inter-American Studies and World Affairs* 14, no. 2 (1972):202.

8. Camp, "Women and Political Leadership," p. 418.

9. For a discussion of the changes that occurred with women's suffrage and the role of women's organizations, see ibid., p. 418; and Morton, *Woman Suffrage in Mexico*, pp. 9, 11–12.

10. Camp, "Women and Political Leadership," pp. 418-419.

11. Ibid., p. 421. This position is similar to a judgeship on the U.S. Court of Appeals.

12. Blough, "Political Attitudes," p. 203.

13. Ibid.

14. Thomas G. Sanders, "Mexican Women," *American Universities Field Staff Reports* 3, no. 6 (1975):6.

15. Morton, *Woman Suffrage in Mexico*, p. 5.

16. Ester Boserup, *Women's Role in Economic Development* (New York: St. Martin's, 1970), p. 60.

17. Ibid., p. 187.

18. In addition, it must be understood that in the cities, the population was a racial mix of Indian, Spanish, and *mestizo* (mixed blood). In the countryside, the overwhelming majority of persons were of Indian descent, though as time went by a large number was *mestizo*. Almost without exception, socioeconomic class and race had a high correlation: the wealthiest and most prestigious groups reflected a pure Spanish or French persona; the poorest were Indians. Although in present-day Mexico the proportion of *mestizos* is by far the most overwhelming, the Indians tend to remain at the bottom of the socioeconomic pyramid.

19. Morton, *Woman Suffrage in Mexico*, p. 2.

20. Ibid., p. 1.

21. For a discussion of Mexico's economic growth and the effects of industrialization, see Merilee Serrill Grindle, *Bureaucrats, Politicians, and Peasants in Mexico* (Berkeley: University of California Press, 1977), introduction, pp. 80–81.

22. Lourdes Arizpe, "Women in the Informal Labor Sector: The Case of Mexico City, Wellesley Editorial Committee, ed., *Women and National Development: The*

Complexities of Change (Chicago: University of Chicago Press, 1977), p. 31.

23. Cornelia Butler Flora, "The Passive Female and Social Change: A Cross-Cultural Comparison of Women's Magazine Fiction," Ann Pescatello, ed., *Female and Male in Latin America* (Pittsburgh, Pa.: University of Pittsburgh Press, 1973), p. 65.

24. Elizabeth Jelin, "Migration and Labor Force Participation of Latin American Women: The Domestic Servants in the Cities," Wellesley Editorial Committee, ed., *Women and National Development;* p. 131.

25. The legal protection of workers under the constitution was restricted to those who either had a specific labor contract, those in large industrial enterprises and those who were part of a labor union, or those who worked for the government. Domestic service and street peddling rarely qualified for such protection.

26. Statistics from Sanders, "Mexican Women," p. 7.

27. Morton, *Woman Suffrage in Mexico,* p. 1.

28. Evelyn P. Stevens, *"Marianismo:* The Other Face of *Machismo* in Latin America," Pescatello, *Female and Male in Latin America,* p. 90.

29. For a discussion of the psychological aspects of *machismo* and its origins, see ibid., especially pp. 90–92.

30. Ibid., p. 91.

31. Sanders, "Mexican Women," pp. 1–2.

32. For descriptions of the accepted mores of Mexican women during the colonial period, see June E. Hahner, *Women in Latin America History* (Los Angeles: University of California at Los Angeles Press, 1976), various excerpts, pp. 113–163.

33. For a discussion of preconquest sex role patterns, see Sanders, "Mexican Women," p. 6; and Morton, *Woman Suffrage in Mexico,* p. 9.

34. Sanders, "Mexican Women," p. 2.

35. Ibid.

36. Reported by Rogelio Diaz Guerrero, *Psychology of the Mexican* (Austin: University of Texas Press, 1975), p. 67, as quoted in Camp, "Women and Political Leadership," p. 419.

37. As quoted in Blough, "Political Attitudes," p. 203.

38. Sanders, "Mexican Women," p. 1.

39. The official parties of Mexico during this period were the People's Party (PP), the National Action Party (PAN), the Party of the Mexican Revolution (PNM), and the Authentic Party of the Mexican Revolution (PARM).

40. For a discussion of the lack of research on women's influence in the authoritarian and corporatist governments of Latin America, see Jane S. Jaquette, "Female Political Participation in Latin America," Lynne B. Iglitzin and Ruth Ross, eds., *Women in the World: A Comparative Study* (Santa Barbara, Calif.: Clio Books, 1976), p. 66.

41. For a discussion of corporatism in general as well as an excellent description of the Mexican case, see James D. Cockcroft, "Mexico," Ronald H. Chilcote and Joel C. Edelstein, eds., *Latin America: The Struggle with Dependence and Beyond* (New York: Wiley, 1974), pp. 286–294.

42. For a discussion of the PRI and women's groups, see Morton, *Woman Suffrage in Mexico,* pp. 30–49.

43. Ibid., p. 90.

44. Sanders, "Mexican Women," p. 4.

45. Blough, "Political Attitudes," p. 206.
46. As reported in ibid.
47. 1976 figures from Camp, "Women and Political Leadership," p. 425; 1980 figures from Ruth Leger Sivard, *Women . . . a world survey* (Washington, D.C.: World Priorities, 1985), p. 35.
48. Camp, "Women and Political Leadership," pp. 421-422.
49. Ibid., p. 425.
50. Ibid., p. 432.
51. Sanders, "Mexican Women," p. 3.
52. Camp, "Women and Political Leadership," pp. 434-436.
53. Sanders, "Mexican Women," p. 6.
54. Inter-American Commission of Women, *News Bulletin* 31 (September 1974): p. 20.
55. Economic Commission for Latin America (ECLA), *Participation of Women in Development in Latin America*, E/Conf.66/BP/8/Add.1 (May 13, 1975):11.
56. Camp, "Women and Political Leadership," pp. 437, 440.
57. Interviews conducted by Margaret Leahy with women in Mexico City, January and February 1980.
58. Sanders, "Mexican Women," p. 7 for 1950 figures; Sivard, *Women . . . a world survey*, p. 35 for 1980 figures.
59. Figures 1960 and 1970 from ECLA, *Participation of Women*, annex, p. 3; figures for 1980 from Sivard, *Women . . . a world survey*, p. 35.
60. Arizpe, "Women in the Informal Labor Sector," p. 29.
61. ECLA, *Participation of Women*, annex, p. 3.
62. Sanders, "Mexican Women," p. 7.
63. Arizpe, "Women in the Informal Labor Sector," p. 30.
64. Sanders, "Mexican Women," p. 7.
65. ECLA, *Participation of Women*, annex, p. 19.
66. Sanders, "Mexican Women," p. 7.
67. Ma. Elena Muñoz and Guadelupe Murayama, "Las obreras y la industria maquiladora," *fem* 1, no. 3 (Mexico, D.F.: April-June 1977).
68. For a description of the labor conditions of women working in U.S. border factories, see Robert Montemayor and Ed Sylvestor, "Mixed Blessings: Dollars Flow to Mexico's Border Land," *Los Angeles Times*, part I, pp. 1, 14, 15.
69. ECLA, *Participation of Women*, p. 19; and Sanders, "Mexican Women," p. 7.
70. According to Olivia Benavente, "¿Sobrevives como mujer profesionista?" *fem* 1, no. 3 (Mexico, D.F.: April-July 1977), p. 21, the percentage of women in various professions was as follows:

architect and engineers	3.4%
lawyers, economists, social scientists	11.1%
medicine, dentists and veterinarians	12.7%
chemists and biologists	31.7%
mathematicians, accountants, and astronomers	12.0%

71. A. McGrath, *The Unfinished Assignment: Equal Education for Women*, Worldwatch Monograph #7 (Washington, D.C.: Worldwatch Institute, 1976), p. 34.
72. Secretaría de programación y presupuesto, *La población de México, su ocupación y sus rivelos de bienestar*, serie manuales de información básica de nación 2 (Mexico, D.F.: 1979), pp. 82-83.

73. Sanders, "Mexican Women," p. 7.
74. Arizpe, "Women in the Informal Labor Sector," p. 32.
75. Sivard, *Women . . . a world survey,* p. 35.
76. Secretaría de programación y presupuesto, *La población de México,* p. 238.
77. Anilu Elias, "El complot de la natalidad," *fem* 2, no. 8 (Mexico, D.F.: July-September 1978), pp. 31–34.
78. For a discussion of women's educational goals, see Sanders, "Mexican Women," p. 52. For a breakdown of women's fields of study, see ECLA, *Participation of Women,* p. 1; and Elena Urrutia, "Que escribe la mujer en México," *fem* 3, no. 10 (Mexico, D.F.: July-October 1979), p. 9; UNESCO *Statistical Yearbook, 1981,* p. 338, Table 3.12.
79. For a description of rural women's lives, especially their attitudes toward marriage, see Perdita Huston, *Message from the Villages* (New York: Epoch B. Foundation, 1978), pp. 109–32; and Sanders, "Mexican Women," p. 1.
80. This discussion of the civil code is drawn from Carmen Lugo, "La legislación familiar," *fem* 2, no. 7 (México, D.F.: April-June 1978), pp. 28–31.
81. Thomas G. Sanders, "Population Factors and Ideology in Mexico's Elementary Textbooks," *American University Field Staff Reports* 3, no. 2 (1975):3.
82. For a discussion of such material constraints, see Huston, *Message from the Villages,* pp. 109–110.
83. Pat Morrison, "The Church Today: A Rich Ritual, a Women's Faith," Special Supplement, "Mexico: Crisis of Poverty," *Los Angeles Times,* July 15, 1979, pp. 22–27.
84. Lucia Miery Teran de Munoz, as quoted in Huston, *Message from the Village,* p. 109.
85. Sanders, "Mexican Women, p. 1.
86. Information on the forms of child care that are available, who uses what types, and the availability of facilities was developed through interviews conducted by the author in Mexico City during January and February 1980.
87. Robert Montemayor and Ed Sylvestor, "Mexican Family Dilemma: Working Women Find Tension at Home," *Los Angeles Times,* September 19, 1979, part 1, pp. 15–16.
88. Sanders, "Mexican Women," p. 2.
89. Flora, "The Passive Female," p. 60.
90. Ibid, pp. 69, 71–74.
91. Kathleen Newland, *The Sisterhood of Man* (New York: Norton, 1979), p. 88.
92. In the 1970s for example, one of the top TV programs in Mexico was a U.S. import, "Charlie's Angels." This program has often been cited as an example of the tendency of the U.S. media to stress women's bodies over their brains. See the section on women's social identity in the chapter on the United States presented earlier in this volume for a more thorough discussion of women in the U.S. media.

• **CHAPTER 4: EQUALITY CREATES A DOUBLE BURDEN** •

1. Dorothy Atkinson, "Society and the Sexes in the Russian Past," Dorothy Atkins, Alexander Dallin, and Gail Warshofsky Lapidus, eds., *Women in Russia* (Stanford, Calif.: Stanford University Press, 1977), p. 33.
2. Ibid., p. 29.

3. William M. Mandel, *Soviet Women* (Garden City, N.Y.: Anchor, 1975), p. 12.
4. Atkinson, "Society and the Sexes," pp. 31-32.
5. Ibid., p. 32.
6. Gail Warshofsky Lapidus, *Women in Soviet Society* (Berkeley: University of California Press, 1978), pp. 32-33; and Rose L. Glickman, "The Russian Factory Woman, 1880-1914," Atkins, *Women in Russia*, p. 77.
7. Lapidus, *Women in Soviet Society*, pp. 45-50; Glickman, "The Russian Factory Woman," p. 78; and Clara Zetkin, *Reminiscences of Lenin* (New York: International Publishers, 1934), pp. 110-111.
8. Mandel, *Soviet Women*, p. 38.
9. Glickman, "The Russian Factory Woman," pp. 64-67.
10. Lapidus, *Women in Soviet Society*, p. 164.
11. Ibid., pp. 49, 164.
12. Ibid., p. 49.
13. Statistics and quotation from Glickman, "The Russian Factory Woman," pp. 69-70.
14. George St. George, *Our Soviet Sisters* (New York: Robert B. Luce, 1973), pp. 20-21.
15. United Nations Educational, Scientific and Cultural Organization, *National Inventory on the Status of Women in the USSR* (Paris: UNESCO, February 18, 1977), ED-77/WS/11, annex 1.
16. Glickman, "The Russian Factory Woman," p. 73.
17. St. George, *Our Soviet Sisters*, p. 25.
18. Lapidus, *Women in Soviet Society*, pp. 28, 30, 31.
19. Norton T. Dodge, *Women in the Soviet Economy* (Baltimore, Md.: John Hopkins, 1966), p. 103.
20. Glickman, "The Russian Factory Woman," p. 63.
21. Jessica Smith, *Women in Soviet Russia* (New York: Vanguard, 1928), p. 4.
22. Ibid.
23. St. George, *Our Soviet Sisters*, p. 24.
24. Ibid.
25. Atkinson, "Society and the Sexes," p. 33.
26. Lapidus, *Women in Soviet Society*, p. 59.
27. Vladimir Barnashov, trans., *Soviet Legislation on Women's Rights* (Moscow: Progress Publishers, 1978), p. 28.
28. N. A. Kovalsky and Y. P. Blinova, eds., *Women Today* (Moscow: Progress Publishers, 1975), p. 31.
29. Lapidus, *Women in Soviet Society*, p. 63.
30. Gail Warshofsky Lapidus, "Sexual Equality in Soviet Policy: A Development Perspective," Atkins, *Women in Russia*, pp. 121, 123.
31. Lapidus, *Women in Soviet Society*, p. 65.
32. Ibid., p. 121.
33. Lapidus, "Sexual Equality," p. 123.
34. Jerry F. Hough, "Women and Women's Issues in Soviet Policy Debates," Atkins, *Women in Russia*, p. 361.
35. Lapidus, *Women in Soviet Society*, p. 39.
36. As quoted in St. George, *Our Soviet Sisters*, p. 33.
37. Y. D. Yemelyanova, "The Social and Political Activity of Soviet Women,"

N. A. Kovalsky and Y. P. Blinova, eds., *Women Today* (Moscow: Progress Publishers, 1975), p. 60.

38. Lapidus, *Women in Soviet Society*, pp. 204, 219.
39. Ibid., p. 215.
40. Ruth Leger Sivard, *Women . . . a world survey* (Washington, D.C.: World Priorities, 1985), p. 36.
41. Lapidus, *Women in Soviet Society*, pp. 205, 206.
42. Kovalsky, *Women Today*, p. 48.
43. UNESCO, *Report*, p. 5.
44. Both Hough, "Women and Women's Issues," p. 356, and Lapidus, "Sexual Equality," p. 216 give figures of women's participation rates in the Communist party and the Central Committee of the Communist party between 1920 and 1975.
45. Sivard, *Women . . . a world survey*, p. 36.
46. Yemelyanova, "Social and Political Activity," p. 66.
47. St. George, *Our Soviet Sisters*, p. 64.
48. For a more detailed discussion of these and other decrees that had impact on women's economic rights, see Kovalsky, *Women Today*, pp. 28–29.
49. As quoted in Smith, *Women in Soviet Russia*, p. 16.
50. Lapidus, *Women in Soviet Society*, pp. 98–99.
51. Mandel, *Soviet Women*, p. 112.
52. UNESCO, *Report*, p. 7.
53. For a description of the rationales as well as particulars on some of the International Labor Organization conventions, see Vladimir Barnashov, trans., *Soviet Legislation on Women's Rights* (Moscow: Progress Publishers, 1978), p. 205; and Mandel, *Soviet Women*, p. 112.
54. UNESCO, *Report*, p. 8.
55. Dodge, *Women in the Soviet Economy*, p. 70.
56. Lapidus, *Women in Soviet Society*, p. 126.
57. Data for 1922 from Yemelyanova, "Social and Political Activity," p. 60; for 1975, UNESCO, *Report*, p. 5.
58. Kovalsky, *Women Today*, p. 49.
59. A discussion of the studies mentioned here is contained in Lapidus, *Women in Soviet Society*, p. 125.
60. Ibid., p. 99.
61. Sivard, *Women . . . a world survey*, p. 36. Since World War II, the female proportion of the labor force has tended to reflect almost exactly the female proportion of the working age population.
62. Michael Paul Sacks, "Women in the Industrial Labor Force," Atkins, *Women in Russia*, p. 199, uses data on 1926 that suggest that more than one-half, and in certain age cohorts near 80 percent, of the women were economically active and receiving wages for their work. Given the overwhelming number of studies that discuss the impediments rural women had to overcome before their incorporation into the paid labor force, and the many discussions of the impact of collectivization of the 1930s as well as the resistance to the *zhenotdyel* during this time in Central Asia, I cannot give too much credence to Sacks' conclusions.
63. Statistics and explanation taken from Lapidus, *Women in Soviet Society*, p. 169.
64. Sivard, *Women . . . a world survey*, p. 36.
65. Statistics for the 1930s from Dodge, *Women in the Soviet Economy*, p. 46; 1940

information from Lapidus, *Women in Soviet Society*, p. 172.
66. Mandel, *Soviet Women*, pp. 130–131.
67. UNESCO, *Report*, p. 9; Lapidus, *Women in Soviet Society*, pp. 173, 189.
68. Lapidus, *Women in Soviet Society*, p. 183.
69. Norton T. Dodge, "Women in the Professions," Atkins, *Women in Russia*, pp. 215–216, 222.
70. Smith, *Women in Soviet Russia*, p. 26.
71. Lapidus, *Women in Soviet Society*, p. 193.
72. Janet G. Chapman, "Equal Pay for Equal Work," Atkins, *Women in Russia*, pp. 225–242.
73. Mandel, *Soviet Women*, p. 107.
74. The study described here as well as others conducted during the past two decades is reported in Lapidus, *Women in Soviet Society*, p. 193.
75. Chapman, "Equal Pay for Equal Work," p. 233.
76. UNESCO, *Report*, p. 9.
77. Chapman, "Equal Pay for Equal Work," p. 239. This conclusion is reinforced by observations made in United Nations General Assembly, *Report of the World Conference of the United Nations Decade for Women*, Doc. A/Conf.94/35:11 (New York: April 1980).
78. Lapidus, *Women in Soviet Society*, p. 137.
79. The particular quotas at various levels of education and training as well as in particular areas of specialization as enumerated in Lapidus, *Women in Soviet Society*, p. 148.
80. Richard B. Dobson, "Educational Policies and Attainment," Atkins, *Women in Russia*, pp. 267–268.
81. G. P. Sergeyeva, "Women's Education and Scientific and Technological Progress," T. N. Sidorova, ed., *Soviet Women* (Moscow: Progress Publishers, 1975), p. 86.
82. Dobson, "Education Policies and Attainment," pp. 268, 287.
83. Classifications and statistics from Lapidus, *Women in Soviet Society*, p. 149.
84. Ibid., p. 143.
85. Dobson, "Education Policies and Attainment," p. 288.
86. The particular educational and admissions policies discussed here are found in greater detail in Lapidus, *Women in Soviet Society*, p. 148; and Dobson, "Education Policies and Attainment," p. 272.
87. Lapidus, *Women in Soviet Society*, pp. 60, 61, 83.
88. Beatrice Brodsky Farnsworth, "Bolshevik Alternatives and the Soviet Family: The 1926 Marriage Law Debate," Atkins, *Women in Russia*, p. 146.
89. Lapidus, *Women in Soviet Society*, pp. 116, 142.
90. Both Peter H. Juviler, "Women and Sex in Soviet Law," Atkins, *Women in Russia*, p. 254, and St. George, *Our Soviet Sisters*, p. 85, discuss the problems of children born in the occupied regions of German fathers, and the ways in which the government attempted to modify the resentment much of the population had both for the women who bore such children and the children themselves.
91. Juviler, "Women and Sex in Soviet Law," p. 255.
92. Bernice Madison, "Social Services for Women: Problems and Priorities," Atkins, *Women in Russia*, p. 314.
93. Farnsworth, "Bolshevik Alternatives," p. 160.
94. Smith, *Women in Soviet Russia*, p. 187.

95. Mandel, *Soviet Women*, p. 71.
96. Juviler, "Women and Sex in Soviet Law," p. 255.
97. St. George, *Our Soviet Sisters*, p. 186.
98. Lapidus, *Women in Soviet Society*, p. 129.
99. In 1914, the number of children's playgrounds and kindergartens has been placed at around 275. These facilities were either charitable institutions or reserved for the children of wealthy parents. For a more complete account of child care prior to the revolution, see A. M. Fonarev, "Preschool Education in the USSR," *Soviet Women* (Moscow: Progress Publishers, 1975), p. 149.
100. V. S. Yazykova, "The Socialist Mode of Life and Women's Free Time," T. N. Sidorova, ed., *Soviet Women*, p. 120.
101. Madison, "Social Services for Women," p. 322.
102. UNESCO, *Report*, annex 4.
103. Ibid.
104. Dodge, *Women in the Soviet Economy*, p. 98.
105. Kovalsky, *Women Today*, p. 59.
106. Z. A. Yankova, "The Woman and the Family," T. N. Sidorova, ed., *Soviet Women*, p. 145.
107. Lapidus, *Women in Soviet Society*, p. 106.
108. Ibid., p. 122.
109. For a description of Soviet media portraits of women in the 1920s, see Kovalsky, *Women Today*, pp. 32-33.
110. St. George, *Our Soviet Sisters*, p. 52.
111. Mollie Schwartz Rosenhan, "Images of Male and Female in Children's Readers," Atkins, *Women in Russia*, p. 302.
112. St. George, *Our Soviet Sisters*, p. 81. In the Soviet Union, the commercial distribution of pornography is a crime.
113. Rosenhan, "Images of Male and Female," p. 302.
114. Y. Z. Danilova, "Forming a New Attitude to Women," T. N. Sidorova, ed., *Soviet Women*, p. 80, reports on these and other studies.
115. Yankova, "The Woman and the Family," p. 139, discusses this report.
116. Mandel, *Soviet Women*, pp. 231-232, 235-236.

• **CHAPTER FIVE: THE REVOLUTION IN THE REVOLUTION** •

1. For excellent descriptions of this period, see Donald W. Bray and Timothy F. Harding, "Cuba," Ronald H. Chilcote and Joel C. Edelstein, eds., *Latin America: The Struggle with Dependency and Beyond*, (New York: Wiley, 1974), pp. 590-600; and Jorge I. Dominguez, *Cuba: Order and Revolution* (Cambridge, Mass.: Harvard University Press, 1978), pp. 11-53.
2. For a good discussion of women's status under the Spanish civil codes, see Lowry Nelson, *Rural Cuba* (Minneapolis: University of Minnesota Press, 1951), pp. 76-77.
3. Susan Kaufman Purcell, "Modernizing Women for a Modern Society: The Cuban Case," Ann Pescatello, ed., *Female and Male in Latin America* (Pittsburgh, Pa.: University of Pittsburgh Press, 1973), p. 260.
4. The figures as well as the conclusion are drawn from Nelson, *Rural Cuba*, pp. 144-145.

5. Dominguez, *Cuba*, pp. 56, 95.

6. These figures come from Margaret Randall, *Cuban Women Now* (Toronto: Woman's Press, 1974), p. 9; also, Max Azicri, "Women's Development through Revolutionary Mobilization: A Study of the Federation of Cuban Women," *International Journal of Women's Studies* 2, no. 1 (January-February 1977), p. 40, gives similar evidence.

7. For an excellent discussion of this topic, see Edward Boorstein, *The Economic Transformation of Cuba* (New York: Monthly Review, 1968), which discusses in pp. 1-16 the economic base of Cuba and the employment situation prior to 1959.

8. Vilma Espin, "The Early Years," Elizabeth Stone, ed., *Women and the Cuban Revolution* (New York: Pathfinder, 1981), p. 38.

9. According to Azicri, "Women's Development," p. 41, in 1953 women made up the following percentage of these occupations: domestics, 89%; clerk typists, 53%; administrators and managers, 5%; agricultural and fishing employees, 1%; miners, 2%; artisans and factory workers, 15%; lawyers, 7%; doctors, 13%; engineers, 5%.

10. Ibid., p. 37.

11. Carollee Benglesdorf and Alice Hageman, "Emerging from Underdevelopment: Women and Work," *Cuba Review* (September 1974):4.

12. The studies of Cuban university women prior to the revolution are discussed in Randall, *Cuban Women Now*, p. 12. Most women at the university were found to study in three fields—philosophy and letters, education, and pharmacy. According to Randall, "In medicine, there were almost none. In law, just a few."

13. Randall, *Cuban Women Now*, p. 12, discusses this society. Interestingly enough, it grew in importance as slavery ended. By the 1950s, it acted as a protective association, and its members, by this time white and mulatto as well as black, controlled most of the port jobs in Havana and other cities.

14. Specific legislation from the Spanish civil codes, the 1901 constitution, and the 1940 constitution can be found in Nelson, *Rural Cuba*, pp. 176-179.

15. These quotations as well as a description of the ways in which many of the tourist attractions of Cuba sexually exploited Cuban women can be found in Geoffrey E. Fox, "Honor, Shame and Women's Liberation in Cuba: Views of Working-Class Emigre Men," Pescatello, *Female and Male in Latin America*, pp. 277-278.

16. Many women were involved in the revolution. In the mountains, there was a special brigade of women who fought side by side with men. Women were present at the storming of the Moncada Barracks in 1953 and afterward were jailed along with men. Almost all accounts of the revolutionary struggle give mention to the role played by women.

17. Purcell, "Modernizing Women for a Modern Society," pp. 261-262.

18. Figures for 1975 from Dominguez, *Cuba*, p. 503; figures for 1980 from Espin, "The Early Years," p. 20.

19. 1975 figure from Dominguez, *Cuba*, p. 503; 1983 figure from Alfred L. Padula and Lois M. Smith, *Sex and Revolution: Women in Cuba, 1959-1985*, forthcoming, p. 3.

20. Purcell, "Modernizing Women for Modern Society," p. 268; Heidi Steffens, "FMC: Feminine, Not Feminists," *Cuba Review* (September 1974):23; Randall, *Cuban Women Now*, p. 18.

21. Azicri, "Women's Development," p. 45.

22. From Margaret Leahy, interviews with officers of the FMC, Havana, Cuba, January-February 1980.

23. Here the term experimental is used with regard to procedure, not with respect to whether or not elections would become national.
24. Dominguez, *Cuba,* p. 287.
25. Figures drawn from ibid, p. 282.
26. Ibid, p. 503.
27. Particulars are drawn from ibid., the above-cited Leahy interviews, and Communist party of Cuba, "Thesis: On the Full Exercise of Women's Equality," Stone, *Women and the Cuban Revolution,* pp. 90–91.
28. Leahy, interview with Digna Cires, head of the Department of Women's Affairs of the CTC, Havana, Cuba, January 31, 1980.
29. Azicri, "Women's Development," p. 29.
30. Leahy, interviews with FMC. With regard to judicial functions, in each CDR local residents are elected to serve as people's judges and are empowered to try minor offenses that occur in the neighborhood.
31. Azicri, "Women's Development," p. 31.
32. Espin, "The Early Years," p. 9.
33. Both the transcript of the 2nd Congress of the Cuban Women's Federation, Instituto Cubano del Libro, *Memories: Second Congress of the Cuban Women's Federation* (Havana: Editorial Obre, 1979), p. 43; and Dominguez, *Cuba,* pp. 296–297, discuss the Women's Brigades of the ANAP.
34. Leahy, interview with Cires cited in note 28.
35. For a discussion of this process, especially with regard to the family code, see Margaret Randall, "Introducing the Family Code," *Cuba Review* (September 1974): 31.
36. For a specific discussion of the agrarian sector, see J. R. Morton, "Agriculture and Rural Development," John Griffiths and Peter Griffiths, eds., *Cuba: The Second Decade* (London: Writers and Readers Publishing Cooperative, 1979), pp. 84–100; and for an overview of the economy with emphasis on industry, see Chris Logan, "Economy in the 1970s," ibid., pp. 53–69.
37. The trade embargo initiated against Cuba by the United States was later adopted by most nations in the Organization of American States; Mexico was the exception. With this one exception, the embargo effectively cut off all Cuban trade with Latin America. Although Mexico has continued to trade with Cuba, and some Latin American governments have begun trade relations, U.S. legislative and executive actions stipulate that no U.S. company or subsidiary can buy a product that in any part of its production process uses materials bought from Cuba, nor can such companies or their subsidiaries sell products to Cuba.
38. Azicri, "Women's Development," p. 38.
39. Ibid., p. 42. For a discussion of the rationale here, see Randall, *Cuban Women Now,* p. 20.
40. Espin, "The Early Years," p. 13.
41. The figures cited are from Benglesdorf and Hageman, "Emerging from Underdevelopment," p. 6.
42. Carollee Benglesdorf, "The Frente Feminino," *Cuba Review,* (September 1974): 27.
43. Ibid., pp. 27–28.
44. For a discussion of the 1971 vagrancy law, see Benglesdorf and Hageman, "Emerging from Underdevelopment," p. 6.
45. Ibid., p. 11.

46. Ibid.
47. From Leahy, interview with Cires; see note 28.
48. Instituto Cubano del Libro, *Memories*, p. 19.
49. Figures from Azicri, "Women's Development," p. 40; and Randall, *Cuban Women Now*, p. 9.
50. Dominguez, *Cuba*, p. 499.
51. Azicri, "Women's Development," p. 41.
52. From Leahy interview with Cires. Also see, Fidel Castro, "Into the Third Decade," Stone, *Women and the Cuban Revolution*, p. 114.
53. Padulla, *Sex and Revolution*, p. 19.
54. Preceding figures all from Instituto Cubano del Libro, *Memories*, p. 19; and Leahy, interview with Cires.
55. Leahy, interview with Cires.
56. Ibid. However, Cires complained that often the Feminine Front and the National Office of the CTC have to work hard to see that such assurances become reality.
57. Commission on the Status of Women of the United Nations Economic and Social Council, *Report of the Secretary General*, E/CN.6/611 (February 17, 1978):25.
58. Leahy, interviews with officers of the Institute for Early Childhood Education, Havana, January 1980. At present, all new assistants must have an eighth-grade education and, in addition, must complete a special four-year course in early childhood education.
59. Dominguez, *Cuba*, p. 501.
60. Leahy, interview with Cires.
61. Padula, *Sex and Revolution*, p. 9. In their work, Padula and Smith translate the Cuban term *mujeres dirigentes* as second-tier female administrators. I have used the term mid-level administrators.
62. Azicri, "Women's Development," p. 37.
63. Randall, *Cuban Women Now*, p. 22.
64. Azicri, "Women's Development," p. 37.
65. Leahy, interviews at the Institute for Human Sexuality and the FMC, Havana, January 1980.
66. "The Cuban Family Code," *Center for Cuban Studies Newsletter* 2, no. 4 (1975):6.
67. Quotations from Randall, "Introducing the Family Code," p. 31.
68. Heidi Steffens, "A Woman's Place" p. 29.
69. Chapter 2, sections 2–5 of the family code concern property rights. Chapter 3, sections 1–4 discuss divorce.
70. Leahy, interviews with FMC.
71. Purcell, "Modernizing Women for a Modern Society," p. 265.
72. With regard to policies, see Instituto Cubano del Libro, *Memories*, p. 66.
73. Leahy, interviews with staff from the Institute for Human Sexuality.
74. Marvin Leiner, *Children are the Revolution: Day Care in Cuba* (Middlesex: Penguin, 1978), gives an excellent account of Cuban child care in the 1960s and early 1970s.
75. Dee Hopkins, "Ya brotan las semillas," *Cuba Review* (September 1974):32–33.
76. Benglesdorf and Hageman, "Emerging from Underdevelopment," p. 8; and Espin, "The Early Years," p. 18.
77. Leahy, interview with directors of the Institute for Early Childhood Education.

78. For a discussion of the services of the centers, see Leiner, *Children are the Revolution*, pp. 119–154.

79. Purcell, "Modernizing Women for a Modern Society," p. 265; and Azicri, "Women's Development," p. 47.

80. As reported in Benglesdorf and Hageman, "Emerging from Underdevelopment," p. 9; and confirmed by Leahy in interviews conducted in Havana, January 1980.

81. Instituto Cubano del Libro, *Memories*, p. 39.

82. For a discussion of these services as well as the ways in which the economic constraints of underdevelopment and the embargo condition them, see Benglesdorf and Hageman, "Emerging from Underdevelopment," p. 8.

83. Fox, "Honor, Shame and Women's Liberation in Cuba," p. 275.

84. The use of imitative games is described in Hopkins, "Ya brotan las semillas," p. 31.

85. This comes from Steffens, "A Woman's Place," p. 30. Diana Mansfield, "Television and Radio," Griffiths, *Cuba: The Second Decade*, pp. 239–240, also argues in the same vein when she discusses a television series popular in Cuba during the 1960s— *Detrás de la Fachada* (Behind the Facade)—in which young persons in the family ridiculed traditional sex roles. *Mujeres* (Women), the magazine of the FMC, women are portrayed in a variety of roles.

86. Dominguez, *Cuba*, p. 495.

87. Ibid., pp. 495–496.

88. Quotations from Fox, "Honor, Shame and Women's Liberation in Cuba," pp. 279, 287.

89. Randall, *Cuban Women Now*, p. 23.

90. Enforcement is carried out directly at the workplace, or immediately after a phone call to the CTC officer in charge. When the author was interviewing Digna Cires, Cires received a call from a woman who charged that her manager was not following the law. After citing the example of infringement, she asked Cires to look into the matter. With codebook in hand, Cires assured the woman that she would make a call to the manager as soon as I had left. In explaining the process of investigation, Cires said she would first call the manager and listen to his side of the story. Because she was sure that the code was quite specific in this case, he could have no alibi if the allegations were true. The following day she would go to the work center to determine that the situation had been rectified. If the manager did not comply immediately, she would go to the ministry responsible for that particular workplace and ask to have the manager removed.

Bibliography

Abzug, Bella with Kelber, Mimi. *Gender Gap*. Boston: Houghton Mifflin Company, 1984.
Allendorf, Marlis. *Women in Socialist Society*. New York: International Publishers, 1975.
Almond, Gabriel, and Powell, G. Bingham. *Comparative Politics: A Developmental Approach*. Boston: Little, Brown, 1966.
Amundsen, Kirsten. *A New Look at the Silenced Majority*. Englewood Cliffs, N.J.: Prentice-Hall, 1977.
Anderson, George. "Women in Congress." *Commonweal* 4 (March 13, 1929): 532–534.
Anthony, Susan B. "Voices of Revolution." *The Guardian* (March 4, 1980), p. 22.
Apter, David E. *The Politics of Modernization*. Chicago: University of Chicago Press, 1965.
Arizpe, Lourdes. "Women in the Informal Labor Sector: The Case of Mexico City." In *Women and National Development: The Complexities of Change,* edited by the Wellesley Editorial Committee. Chicago: University of Chicago Press, 1977.
Aron, Raymond. "Social Structure and the Ruling Class." *The British Journal of Sociology,* 1 (March–June 1950).
Aronoff, Joel and Crano, William D. "A Re-Examination of the Cross-Cultural Principles of Task Segregation and Sex-Role Differentiation in the Family." *American Sociological Review* 40 (1975).
de Arturo, Hector. "Something to Think About." *Cuba Review* (September 1974).
Atkinson, Dorothy. "Society and the Sexes in the Russian Past." In *Women in Russia,* edited by Dorothy Atkins, Alexander Dallin, and Gail Warshofsky Lapidus. Stanford, Calif.: Stanford University Press, 1977.
Avrnturin, Elzea. "The Division of Labor and Sexual Inequality: The Role of Education." In *Women Workers and Society*. Geneva: International Labor Organization, 1976.
Azicri, Max. "Women's Development through Revolutionary Mobilization: A Study of the Federation of Cuban Women." *International Journal of Women's Studies* 2, no. 1 (January-February 1977): pp. 27–50.
Baer, Werner. "The Brazilian Growth and Development Experience: 1964–1974." In *Brazil in the Seventies,* edited by Riordan Roett. Washington, D.C.: American Enterprise Institute, 1976.
Barber, Mary. "Riveting In On Rosie the Riveter." *Los Angeles Times,* October 18, 1979, part 4, p. 23.
Barnashov, Vladimir, trans. *Soviet Legislation on Women's Rights*. Moscow: Progress Publishers, 1978.

Baskina, Ada. *About Women Like Me.* Moscow: Novosti Press, 1979.
Baxnell, Rosalyn, George, Linda, and Reverby, Susan, eds. *America's Working Women.* New York: Random House, 1976.
Becklund, Laurie, and Montemayor, Robert. "Land Reform: The Revolution That Failed." Special Supplement, "Mexico: The Crisis of Poverty." *Los Angeles Times,* July 15, 1979, pp. 21-24.
Benavente, Olivia. "¿Sobrevives como mujer profesionista?" *fem* 1, no. 3 (Mexico, D.F.: April-July 1977), pp. 18-23.
Bendell, Ben. "1980: The Year of Unemployment." *The Guardian* (January 5, 1980), p. 5.
Bendix, William, and Lipset, Seymour Martin, eds. *Class, Status and Power.* Garden City, N.Y.: Doubleday, 1962.
Benglesdorf, Carollee. "The Frente Feminino." *Cuba Review* (September 1974): 3-12.
Benglesdorf, Carollee, and Hageman, Alice. "Emerging from Underdevelopment: Women and Work." *Cuba Review* (September 1974): 3-12.
Benitez, Jose A. "Celia Sanchez Manduley." *Granma* (January 20, 1980): 1-16.
Berman, Joan. "Women in Cuba." *Women: A Journal of Liberation* 1. no. 4 (Summer 1970): 10-14.
Blair, Emily Newell. "Are Women a Failure in Politics?" *Harpers* (October 1925): 513-522.
Blough, William. "Political Attitudes of Mexican Women: Support for the Political System Among a Newly Enfranchised Group." *Journal of Inter-American Studies and World Affairs* 14, no. 2 (1972): 201-224.
Blumberg, Rae Lesser. "Fairy Tales and Facts: Economy, Family, Fertility and the Female." In *Women and World Development,* edited by Irene Tinker, Michele Bo Bramsen, and Mayra Buvinic. New York: Praeger, 1976.
Blumenthal, Irene, and Benson, Charles. *Educational Reform in the Soviet Union: Implications for Developing Countries.* Washington D.C.: World Bank, 1978.
Boles, Janet K. *The Politics of the Equal Rights Amendment.* New York: Longman, 1979.
Boorstein, Edward. *The Economic Transformation of Cuba.* New York: Monthly Review Press, 1968.
Boserup, Ester. "Preface." In *Women and National Development: The Complexities of Change,* edited by the Wellesley Editorial Group. Chicago: University of Chicago Press, 1977.
_____. *Woman's Role in Economic Development.* New York: St. Martin's Press, 1970.
Boulding, Elise. *The Underside of History: A View of Women Through Time.* Boulder, Colo.: Westview, 1976.
Bradley, LaVerne. "Women at Work." *The National Geographic Magazine* (August 1944):193-220.
Bray, Donald W., and Harding, Timothy F. "Cuba." In *Latin America: The Struggle with Dependency and Beyond,* edited by Ronald H. Chilcote and Joel C. Edelstein. New York: John Wiley and Sons, 1974.
Breslin, Jimmy. "A Wife Should Get Part of Her Husband's Paycheck—And in Her Own Name." *Los Angeles Times,* January 3, 1980, part 2, p. 7.
Brownlee, W. Elliot, and Brownlee, Mary M. *Women in the American Economy.* New Haven, Conn.: Yale University Press, 1976.

Buvinic, Mayra. "Woman and World Development: An Annotated Bibliography." In *Women and World Development,* edited by Irene Tinker, Michele Bo Bramsen, and Mayra Buvinic. New York: Praeger, 1976.

Camancho, Nicolasa, and Cruz, Delgadillo. "El majoramiento de la mujer y la sociedad, 'Las clases productas.' " In *La mujer y el movimiento obrero Mexicano en el siglo XIX.* Mexico, D.F.: Centro de Estudios Historicos del Movimiento Obrero Mexicano, 1975.

Camp, Roderic A. "Women and Political Leadership in Mexico: A Comparative Study of Female and Male Political Elites." *The Journal of Politics* 41, no. 2 (May 1979):417–441.

Carr, E. H. *Studies in Revolution.* New York: Grosset & Dunlap, 1976.

Castro, Fidel. Excerpts from July 26th Speech. *Cuba Review* (September 1974):35.

_____. "Into the Third Decade.: In *Women and the Cuban Revolution,* edited by Elizabeth Stone. New York: Pathfinder Press, 1981.

_____. Speech at Jose Martí Vocational School in Holguin, Cuba, September 1, 1977. As reprinted in *Bulletin of Information: Central Committee of the Communist Party of Cuba* 3 (1977):54–60.

_____. Speech at the second period of sessions of the National Assembly of Peoples' Power, December 12, 1977. As reprinted in *Bulletin of Information: Central Committee of the Communist Party of Cuba* 1 (1978):4–16.

Centro de Estudios Historicos del Movimiento Obrero Mexicano. *La mujer y el movimiento obrero Mexicano en el siglo XIX.* Mexico, D.F.: Centro de Estudios Historicos del Movimiento Obrero Mexicano, 1975.

Chafe, William. *The American Woman: Her Changing Social, Economic and Political Roles, 1920–1970.* New York: Oxford University Press, 1972.

Chapman, Janet G. "Equal Pay for Equal Work." In *Women in Russia,* edited by Dorothy Atkins, Alexander Dallin, and Gail Warshofsky Lapidus. Stanford, Calif.: Stanford University Press, 1977.

Chilcote, Ronald H., ed. *Dependency and Marxism.* Boulder, Colo.: Westview Press, 1982.

Chilcote, Ronald H. *Theories of Development and Underdevelopment.* Boulder, Colo.: Westview Press, 1984.

Chinchilla, Norma. "Industrialization, Monopoly Capitalism, and Women's Work in Guatemala." In *Women and National Development: The Complexities of Change,* edited by the Wellesley Editorial Group. Chicago: University of Chicago Press, 1977.

Cimon, Marlene. "Memories of a Pioneering Suffragette." *Los Angeles Times,* January 16, 1980, part 4, pp. 1, 6.

_____. "The War on Sexism in the Nation's Schools." *Los Angeles Times,* January 17, 1980, part 4, pp. 1, 13, 15.

Clements, Barbara Evans. *Bolshevik Feminist.* Bloomington: Indiana University Press, 1979.

Cockburn, Cynthia. "People's Power." In *Cuba: The Second Decade,* edited by John Griffiths and Peter Griffiths. London: Writers and Readers Publishing Cooperative, 1979.

_____. "Women and the Family in Cuba." In *Cuba: The Second Decade,* edited by John Griffiths and Peter Griffiths. London: Writers and Readers Publishing Cooperative, 1979.

Cockcroft, James D. "Mexico." In *Latin America: The Struggle with Dependence and Beyond*, edited by Ronald H. Chilcote and Joel C. Edelstein. New York: John Wiley and Sons, 1974.

Collier, Jane Fishburne. "Women in Politics." In *Women, Culture and Society*, edited by Michelle Zimbalist Rosaldo and Louise Lamphere. Stanford, Calif.: Stanford University Press, 1974.

Comisión de la Condición Jurídica y Social de la Mujer. *Informe del Secretario General.* E/CN.5/611. febrero, 17, 1978.

Commission on the Status of Women of the United Nations Economic and Social Council. *Report of the Secretary General.* E/CN.6/611. February 17, 1978.

"The Cuban Family Code." *Center for Cuban Studies Newsletter* 2, no. 4 (1975).

Dahl, Robert. *A Preface to Democratic Theory.* Chicago: University of Chicago Press, 1966.

―――――. *Who Governs? Democracy and Power in an American City.* New Haven, Conn.: Yale University Press, 1971.

Dallin, Alexander. "Conclusion." In *Women in Russia*, edited by Dorothy Atkins, Alexander Dallin, and Gail Warshofsky Lapidus. Stanford, Calif.: Stanford University Press, 1977.

Danilova, Y. Z. "Forming a New Attitude to Women." In *Soviet Women*, edited by T. N. Sidorova. Moscow: Progress Publishers, 1975.

Darling, Martha. *The Role of Women in the Economy.* Paris: Organization for Economic Cooperation and Development, 1975.

Deutsch, Karl. "Social Mobilization and Political Development." *American Political Science Review* (September 1961): 493–514.

Dobson, Richard B. "Educational Policies and Attainment." In *Women in Russia*, edited by Dorothy Atkins, Alexander Dallin, and Gail Warshofsky Lapidus. Stanford, Calif.: Stanford University Press, 1977.

Dodge, Norton T. "Women in the Profession." In *Women in Russia*, edited by Dorothy Atkins, Alexander Dallin, and Gail Warshofsky Lapidus. Stanford, Calif.: Stanford University Press, 1977.

―――――. *Women in the Soviet Economy.* Baltimore, Md.: Johns Hopkins Press, 1966.

Dominguez, Jorge I. *Cuba: Order and Revolution.* Cambridge, Mass.: Harvard University Press, 1978.

Dunn, Ethel. "Russian Rural Women." In *Women in Russia*, edited by Dorothy Atkins, Alexander Dallin, and Gail Warshofsky Lapidus. Stanford, Calif.: Stanford University Press, 1977.

Economic Commission for Latin America. *Participation of Women in Development in Latin America.* E/Conf.66/BP8/Add.1. May 13, 1975.

―――――. *Report of the Regional Conference on the Integration of Women in the Economic and Social Development of Latin America.* E/Cepal/1042/Rev.1. November 21, 1977.

Elias, Anilu. "El complot de la natalidad." *fem* 2, no. 8 (Mexico, D.F.: July-September 1978):31–34.

Elmendorf, Mary. "The Dilemma of Peasant Women: A View from a Village in Yucatan." In *Women and World Development*, edited by Irene Tinker, Michele Bo Bramsen, and Mayra Buvinic. New York: Praeger, 1976.

Engels, Fredrick. *The Origin of the Family, Private Property and the State.* Edited by

Eleanor Leacock. New York: International Publishers, 1975.

_____. "Socialism: Utopian or Scientific." In *Marx and Engels: Basic Writings in Politics and Philosophy.* Edited by Lewis S. Feuer. Garden City, N.Y.: Anchor, 1959.

Espin, Vilma. "The Early Years." In *Women and the Cuban Revolution,* edited by Elizabeth Stone. New York: Pathfinder Press, 1981.

Farnsworth, Beatrice Brodsky. "Bolshevik Alternatives and the Soviet Family: The 1926 Marriage Law Debate." In *Women in Russia,* edited by Dorothy Atkins, Alexander Dallin, and Gail Warshofsky Lapidus. Stanford, Calif.: Stanford University Press, 1977.

Feinsilber, Mike. "Caucus Fighting for More Women on Federal Bench." *Los Angeles Times,* May 24, 1979, part 1B, p. 4.

Ferris, Abbott L. *Indicators and Trends in the Status of American Women.* New York: Russell Sage Foundation, 1971.

de Figueroa, Teresa Orrego. "A Critical Analysis of Latin American Programs to Integrate Women in Development." In *Women and World Development,* pp. 35-44. Edited by Irene Tinker, Michele Bo Bramsen, and Mayra Buvinic. New York: Praeger, 1976.

de Flaquer, Concepción Gimeno. "La obrera Mexicana." In *La mujer y el movimiento obrero Mexicano en el siglo XIX.* Mexico, D.F.: Centro de Estudios Historicos del Movimiento Obrero Mexicano, 1975.

Flexner, Eleanor. *Century of Struggle.* New York: Antheneum, 1974.

Flora, Cornelia Butler. "The Passive Female and Social Change: A Cross-Cultural Comparison of Women's Magazine Fiction." In *Female and Male in Latin America: Essays,* edited by Ann Pescatello. Pittsburgh, Pa.: University of Pittsburgh Press, 1973.

Fonarev, A. M. "Preschool Education in the USSR." In *Soviet Women,* edited by T. N. Sidorova. Moscow: Progress Publishers, 1975.

Fox, Geoffrey E. "Honor, Shame and Women's Liberation in Cuba: Views of Working-Class Emigre Men." In *Female and Male in Latin America: Essays,* edited by Ann Pescatello. Pittsburgh, Pa.: University of Pittsburgh Press, 1973.

Frank, Andre Gunder. "Sociology of Development and the Underdevelopment of Sociology." In *Dependence and Underdevelopment: Latin America's Political Economy,* edited by James Cockcroft, Andre Gunder Frank, and Dale Johnson. New York: Anchor, 1972.

Gerassi, John, ed. *Venceremos: The Speeches and Writing of Ernesto Che Guevara.* New York: Simon and Schuster, 1968.

Germain, Adrienne. "The Status and Roles of Women as Factors in Fertility Behavior: A Policy Analysis." Unpublished paper prepared under the auspices of the Ford Foundation, New York, 1974.

Giddens, Anthony. *Capitalism and Modern Social Theory.* New York: Cambridge University Press, 1979.

Gillian, A. "How Feminists' Resolutions in Houston Fared in Washington." *Los Angeles Times,* November 21, 1978, part 1, p. 6.

Girson, Rochelle. "Women's Status Fifty Years After the Vote." In *Women and Society,* edited by Diana Reiche. New York: H. W. Wilson Co., 1972.

Glickman, Rose L. "The Russian Factory Woman, 1880-1914." In *Women in Russia,* edited by Dorothy Atkins, Alexander Dallin, and Gail Warshofsky Lapidus.

Stanford, Calif.: Stanford University Press, 1977.
Goodman, Ellen. "Another Equal Pay Insult." *The Boston Globe*, January 31, 1984.
_____. "Battle of the Sexes Moves into Payroll Departments." *Los Angeles Times*, October 22, 1978, part 4, p. 5.
Gough, Kathleen. "The Origin of the Family." In *Towards an Anthropology of Women*, edited by Rayna R. Reiter. New York: Monthly Review Press, 1975.
Grant, Linda. " 'Miracle' Boom: Millions Are Left Behind." Special Supplement, "Mexico: Crisis of Poverty." *Los Angeles Times*, July 15, 1979, pp. 11–12.
Grindle, Merilee Serrill. *Bureaucrats, Politicians, and Peasants in Mexico: A Case Study in Public Policy*. Berkeley: University of California Press, 1977.
Grossman, Allyson Sherman. "More than Half of All Children Have Working Mothers." *Monthly Labor Review* 105, no. 2. Washington, D.C.: U.S. Department of Labor, 1982.
Guardian Bureau. "Violence Against Women." *The Guardian* (January 16, 1980):7.
Guzman, Alba. "Cuando se hable de educación." *fem* 2, no. 8 (Mexico, D.F.: July-September 1978):6–9.
Hahner, June E. *Women in Latin American History*. Los Angeles: UCLA Latin American Center Publishing, 1976.
Hamsher, Caroline D. "Eleanor Roosevelt: A Study of Irony." In *Women in Politics: Studies in Role and Status*, edited by Marian R. McKeod. Sydney, Australia: Wentworth Press, 1974.
Hansen, Joseph. *Dynamics of the Cuban Revolution: The Trotskyist View*. New York: Pathfinder Press, 1978.
Harrington, Michael. *The Twilight of Capitalism*. New York: Touchstone, 1976.
Haygbe, Howard. "Marital and Family Patterns of Workers: An Update." *Monthly Labor Review* 105, no. 2, Washington, D.C.: U.S. Department of Labor, February 1982.
Herrera, Antonio Jose, and Rosenkranz, Hernan. "Political Consciousness in Cuba." In *Cuba: The Second Decade*, edited by John Griffiths and Peter Griffiths. London: Writers and Readers Publishing Cooperative, 1979.
Hoch, Nancy. "Porn Legitimizes Hatred of Women." *The Guardian* (December 26, 1979):8.
Hollist, W. Ladd. "Constancy and Change: The Perpetuation of Dependence Amidst Brazilian 'Development.' " Unpublished paper prepared for an NSF Conference on "Constancy and Change: The Political Economy of Global Differentiation," Ojai, California, November 14–17, 1979.
Holly, Douglas. "Education." In *Cuba: The Second Decade*, edited by John Griffiths and Peter Griffiths. London: Writers and Readers Publishing Cooperative, 1979.
Holt, Alix. *Selected Writings of Alexandra Kollantai*. Westport, Conn.: Lawrence Hill and Co., 1977.
Hooks, Janet M., *Women's Occupations Through Seven Decades*. Washington, D.C.: U.S. Department of Labor, 1975, bulletin no. 218.
Hopkins, Dee. "Ya brotan las semillas." *Cuba Review* (September 1974):32–34.
Hoselitz, Bert F. "Social Stratification and Economic Development." *International Social Science Journal* 16, no. 2 (1964).
_____. *Sociological Factors in Economic Development*. New York: Free Press, 1960.
Hough, Jerry F. "Women and Women's Issues in Soviet Policy Debates." In *Women in Russia*, edited by Dorothy Atkins, Alexander Dallin, and Gail Warshofsky Lapidus.

Stanford, Calif.: Stanford University Press, 1977.
Howland, Elizabeth. "Sexual Stereotyping Dies Hard." *Los Angeles Times,* September 28, 1979, part 2, p. 7.
Huntington, Samuel P. *Political Order in Changing Societies.* New Haven, Conn.: Yale University Press, 1968.
Huston, Perdita. *Message from the Villages.* New York: Epoch B. Foundation, 1978.
Instituto Cubano del Libro. *Memories: Second Congress of the Cuban Women's Federation.* Havana: Editorial Obre, 1975.
Inter-American Commission of Women. *News Bulletin* (September 1964).
_____. *News Bulletin* 31 (September 1974).
International Bank for Reconstruction and Development. *Report on Cuba.* Washington, D.C.: International Bank for Reconstruction and Development, 1951.
International Labor Organization. *Employment, Growth and Basic Needs: A One-World Problem.* New York: Praeger, 1977.
International Labour Office. *Women at Work.* Geneva: ILO, 1977.
Jain, Devaki. "Women Are Separate." *Development Forum* (August 1978).
Jancar, Barbara Wolfe. "Women in Cuba." In *Women Under Communism,* edited by Barbara Wolfe Jancar. Baltimore, Md.: Johns Hopkins University Press, 1978.
_____, ed. *Women Under Communism.* Baltimore: Johns Hopkins University Press, 1978.
Jaquette, Jane S. "Female Political Participation in Latin America." In *Women in the World: A Comparative Study,* edited by Lynne B. Iglitzin and Ruth Ross. Santa Barbara, Calif.: Clio Books, 1976.
_____. "Literary Archetypes and Female Role Alternatives: The Woman and the Novel in Latin America." In *Female and Male in Latin America; Essays,* edited by Ann Pescatello. Pittsburgh, Pa.: University of Pittsburgh, 1973.
_____. "Women and Development in Latin America: The Problem of Power." Unpublished paper prepared for delivery at the 1978 Annual Meeting of the American Political Science Association, New York, August 31–September 3, 1978.
Jelin, Elizabeth. "Migration and Labor Force Participation of Latin American Women: The Domestic Servants in the Cities." In *Women and National Development: The Complexities of Change,* edited by the Wellesley Editorial Committee. Chicago: University of Chicago Press, 1977.
Johnson, John J. *Political Change in Latin America: The Emergence of the Middle Sectors.* Stanford, Calif.: Stanford University Press, 1958.
Juviler, Peter H. "Women and Sex in Soviet Law." In *Women in Russia,* edited by Dorothy Atkins, Alexander Dallin, and Gail Warshofsky Lapidus. Stanford, Calif.: Stanford University Press, 1977.
Kantner, J. F., and Zelnik, M. "Contraception and Pregnancy: Experience of Young Unmarried Women in the United States." *Family Planning Perspective* (May 21, 1973):23, 24.
King, Marjorie. "Cuba's Attack on Women's Second Shift." *Latin American Perspectives* 4, nos. 1 and 2 (Winter and Spring 1977):106–119.
Korolyov, Yuri. *Soviet Family and the Law.* Moscow: Novosti Press, 1977.
Kovalsky, N. A., and Blinova, Y. P., eds. *Women Today.* Moscow: Progress Publishers, 1975.
Kuznetsova, Larissa. "That Eternal Women's Question." *Soviet Life* (March 1978):28–29.

———. "Women in Soviet Society." *Women in the Land of the Soviets.* Moscow: Novosti Press, 1978.
Lamos, Marta. "Madre Soltera." *fem* 3, no. 9 (October-December 1978):71–72.
Lansing, Marjorie. "Political Changes for the American Woman." In *Women in the World: A Comparative Study,* edited by Lynn B. Iglitzin and Ruth Ross. Santa Barbara, Calif.: Clio Press, 1976.
Lapidus, Gail Warshofsky. "Changing Women's Roles in the USSR." In *Women in the World: A Comparative Study,* edited by Lynne B. Iglitzin and Ruth Ross. Santa Barbara, Calif.: Clio Press, 1976.
———. "Sexual Equality in Soviet Policy: A Developmental Perspective." In *Women in Russia,* edited by Dorothy Atkins, Alexander Dallin, and Gail Warshofsky Lapidus. Stanford, Calif.: Stanford University Press, 1977.
———. *Women in Soviet Society.* Berkeley: University of California Press, 1978.
Leahy, Margaret. Interviews Conducted with Women in Mexico City. January and February 1980.
———. Interviews with Cuban Women. January and February 1980.
Leiner, Marvin. *Children Are the Revolution: Day Care in Cuba.* Middlesex: Penguin Books. Ltd., 1978.
Lenin, V. I. *Collected Works.* Vol. 3. New York: International Publishers, 1920.
———. "Soviet Power and the Status of Women." *Socialism: Theory and Practice* (March 1978):56–59.
———. *The State.* Peking: Foreign Language Press, 1965.
———. *Women and Society.* New York: International Publishers, 1938.
Lipset, Seymour M. *Political Man: The Social Basis of Politics.* Garden City, N.Y.: Anchor, 1963.
Lipset, Seymour M., and Solari, Aldo, eds. *Elites in Latin America.* New York: Oxford University Press, 1967.
Logan, Chris. "Economy in the 1970s." In *Cuba: The Second Decade,* edited by John Griffiths and Peter Griffiths. London: Writers and Readers Publishing Cooperative, 1979.
Loper, Mary Lou. "The Working Mother's Crisis." In *Women and Society,* edited by Diana Reiche. New York: H. W. Wilson Co., 1972.
Lozano, Itziar. "La presencia de las no invitadas." *fem* 2, no. 8 (Mexico, D.F.: July-September 1978):44–49.
Lugo, Carmen. "Derechos del niño?" *fem* 2, no. 8 (July-September 1978):66–71.
———. "Esmeralda Arboleda Cuevas: una feminista en la ONU." *fem* 3, no. 9 (Mexico, D.F.: October-December 1978):41–44.
———. "La legislación familiar." *fem* 2, no. 7 (Mexico, D.F.: April-June 1978):24–32.
Luna, K. H. "Letters to the Editor." *Los Angeles Times,* January 19, 1980, part 2.
Madison, Bernice. "Social Services for Women: Problems and Priorities." In *Women in Russia,* edited by Dorothy Atkins, Alexander Dallin, and Gail Warshofsky Lapidus. Stanford, Calif.: Stanford University Press, 1977.
———. *Soviet Women.* Garden City, N.Y.: Anchor, 1975.
Mandel, William M. *Soviet Women.* Garden City, N.Y.: Anchor Press, 1975.
Mansfield, Diana. "Television and Radio." In *Cuba: The Second Decade,* edited by John Griffiths and Peter Griffiths. London: Writers and Readers Publishing Cooperative, 1979.

Marx, Karl. *Capital.* Vol. 1. New York: International Publishers, 1947.
———. "Excerpts from a Contribution to the Critique of Political Economy." In *Marx and Engels: Basic Writings in Politics and Philosophy.* Edited by Lewis Feuer. Garden City, N.Y.: Anchor, 1959.
McGrath, A. *The Unfinished Assignment: Equal Education for Women.* Worldwatch Monograph #7. Washington, D.C.: Worldwatch Institute, 1976.
Mead, Margaret. "A Comment on the Role of Women in Agriculture." In *Women and World Development,* edited by Irene Tinker, Michele Bo Bramsen, and Mayra Buvinic. New York: Praeger, 1976.
Meyer, Alfred G. "Marxism and the Women's Movement." In *Women in Russia,* edited by Dorothy Atkins, Alexander Dallin, and Gail Warshofsky Lapidus. Stanford, Calif.: Stanford University Press, 1977.
Meyers, William. "Child-Care Finds a Champion in the Corporation," *The New York Times,* August 4, 1985.
Miguel, Guillermo Wasmer. *La mujer en Cuba socialista.* Havana: Empresa Editorial Orbe, 1977.
Mill, John Stuart. "On the Subjection of Women." In *Essays on Sexual Equality,* by John Stuart Mill and Harriet Mill. Edited by Alice Rossi. Chicago: University of Chicago Press, 1970.
Mills, C. Wright. *Listen Yankee: The Revolution in Cuba.* New York: Ballantine, 1960.
Mody, Bella, and Rodgers, Everett M. "Women's Networks and Development Planning." Unpublished paper presented at the International Studies Association Conference, Toronto, Canada, March 21–24, 1979.
Monsivais, Carlos. "Notas sobre cultura popular en México." *Latin American Perspectives,* 16, vol. 5, no. 1 (Winter 1978):98–118.
———. "Nueva situatión del optimista." *fem* 3, no. 9 (Mexico, D.F.: October-December 1978):17–19.
Montemayor, Robert, and Sylvestor, Ed. "Mexican Family Dilemma: Working Women Find Tension at Home." *Los Angeles Times,* September 19, 1979, part 1, pp. 15–16.
———. "Mixed Blessings: Dollars Flow to Mexico's Borderland." *Los Angeles Times,* 1979, part 1, pp. 1, 14, 15.
Morrison, Pat. "The Church Today: A Rich Ritual, a Women's Faith." Special Supplement, "Mexico: Crisis of Poverty," *Los Angeles Times,* July 15, 1979, pp. 27–29.
Morrison, Pat, and Grant, Linda. "Tycoons and Squatters Share Industrial City: A Standoff That Works." Special Supplement, "Mexico: Crisis of Poverty," *Los Angeles Times,* July 15, 1979, pp. 13–14.
Morton, J. R. "Agriculture and Rural Development." In *Cuba: The Second Decade,* edited by John Griffiths and Peter Griffiths. London: Writers and Readers Publishing Cooperative, 1979.
Morton, Ward M. *Woman Suffrage in Mexico.* Gainesville, Fla.: University of Florida Press, 1962.
Moses, Joel C. "Women in Political Roles." In *Women in Russia,* edited by Dorothy Atkins, Alexander Dallin, and Gail Warshofsky Lapidus. Stanford, Calif.: Stanford University Press, 1977.
Moune, William, and Feldman, David. *Labor Commitment and Social Change in Latin America.* New York: Social Science Research Council, 1960.

Muñoz, Ma. Elena, and Murayama, Guadelupe. "Las obreras y la industria maquiladora." *fem* 1, no. 3 (Mexico, D.F.: April-July 1977):40–46.

Myrdal, Gunnar. *Asian Drama: An Inquiry into the Poverty of Nations.* New York: Pantheon, 1968.

Nash, Manning. "Introduction: Approaches to the Study of Economic Growth." *Journal of Social Issues* 19, no. 1 (January 1963).

National Commission on the Observance of International Women's Year. . . . *To Form a More Perfect Union.* Washington, D.C.: Government Printing Office, 1976.

Nelson, Harry. "Chronic Malnutrition: 100,000 Children Die Yearly." Special Supplement, "Mexico: Crisis of Poverty," *Los Angeles Times,* July 15, 1979, pp. 17–18.

Nelson, Lowry. *Rural Cuba.* Minneapolis: University of Minnesota Press, 1951.

Newland, Kathleen. "Media Maketh (Wo)man!" *Development Forum* (April 1979)

_____, *The Sisterhood of Man.* New York: W. W. Norton, 1979.

_____. *Woman and Population Growth: Choice Beyond Childbearing.* Worldwatch Paper #16. Washington, D.C.: Worldwatch Institute, 1977.

_____. *Woman in Politics: A Global Review.* Worldwatch Paper #3. Washington, D.C.: Worldwatch Institute, 1975.

New York City Commission on Human Rights. *Women's Role in Contemporary Society.* New York: Avion, 1972.

Novikova, E. Y. "How Trade Unions Regulate the Working Conditions of Working Women and Help Organize Their Everyday Life and Leisure." In *Soviet Women,* edited by T. N. Sidorova. Moscow: Progress Publishers, 1975.

Novosti Press. "Facts and Figures." *Women in the Land of the Soviets.* Moscow: Novosti Press, 1978.

_____. *The Rights and Freedoms of Soviet Citizens.* Moscow: Novosti Press, 1977.

Novosti Press Agency. *Yearbook: USSR.* Moscow: Novosti Press, 1979.

Ocompo, Jose F., and Johnson, Dale L. "The Concept of Political Development." In *Dependence and Underdevelopment:* Latin America's Political Economy, edited by James Cockcroft, Andre Gunder Frank, and Dale Johnson. New York: Anchor, 1972.

O'Connor, James. *Origins of Socialism in Cuba.* Ithaca, N.Y.: Cornell University Press, 1970.

Organization for Economic Cooperation and Development. *Equal Opportunities for Women.* Paris: OECD, 1979.

Orlova, Dina, "Must a Woman's Day Never Be Done?" *Women in the Land of the Soviets.* Moscow: Novosti Press, 1978.

Osario, Lilia. "Ambito de Sueños." *fem* 2, no. 8 (Mexico, D.F.: July-September 1978):63–65.

Packenham, Robert. *Liberal America and the Third World.* Princeton, N.J.: Princeton University Press, 1973.

Padula, Alfred L. and Smith, Lois M. *Sex and Revolution: Women in Cuba, 1959–1985* (forthcoming).

Parsons, Talcott. *The Social System.* New York: Free Press, 1951.

_____. *Structure and Process in Modern Societies.* New York: Free Press, 1960.

Pearl, Robert. "Earnings Gap is Narrowing Slightly." *The New York Times,* October 3, 1983.

Penalosa, Fernando. "Mexican Family Roles." *Journal of Marriage and the Family* 30 (November 1968):680–688.
Phelps-Brown, E. "The Underdevelopment of Economics." *Economic Journal* 1972).
Pisarevski, Gennadi. *Manpower and Jobs: How the Problem Is Tackled in the Soviet Union.* Moscow: Novosti Press, 1979.
Purcell, Susan Kaufman. "Modernizing Women for a Modern Society: The Cuban Case." In *Female and Male in Latin America: Essays,* edited in Ann Pescatello. Pittsburgh, Pa.: University of Pittsburgh Press, 1973.
Pye, Lucien. *Aspects of Political Development.* Boston: Little, Brown, 1966.
Pye, Lucien, ed. *Political Culture and Political Development.* Princeton, N.J.: Princeton University Press, 1965.
Randall, Margaret. *Cuban Women Now.* Toronto: Woman's Press, 1974.
_____. "Introducing the Family Code." *Cuba Review* (September 1974):31.
_____. *Mujeres en la revolución.* Mexico, D.F.: Siglo Veintiuno Editores, S.A., 1978.
_____. "Venceremos: Women in the New Cuba." *Canadian Dimension* (June 1975):48–54.
Randall, Margaret, ed. *Las mujeres.* Mexico, D.F.: Siglo Veintiuno Editores, S.A., 1970.
Raspberry, William. "Equal Rights: Should States Have Equal Rights to Shift?" *Los Angeles Times,* January 7, 1980, part 2, p. 5.
_____. "Numbers Game: 'Math Anxiety' among Females." *Los Angeles Times,* January 8, 1978, part 2, p. 5.
Reid, Elizabeth A. "Draft Report: International Workshop on Feminist Ideology and Structure." APCWD 18. United Nations Internal Report. New York: July 20, 1979. Unpublished report.
Rich, Spencer. "More Women Join Managerial Ranks." *The Boston Globe,* April 11, 1984.
Riddell, Adaljiza Sosa. "Female Political Elites in Mexico: 1974." In *Women in the World: A Comparative Study,* edited by Lynne B. Iglitzin and Ruth Ross. Santa Barbara, Calif.: Clio Books, 1976.
Rivera, Ignacio Borges. "Fases de la mujer Mexicana y su education." In *La mujer y el movimiento obrero Mexicano en el siglo XIX,* pp. 115–16. Mexico, D.F.: Centro de Estudios Historicos del Movimiento Obero Mexicano, 1975.
Robb, Carol, and Hageman, Alice. "Let Them be Examples . . . " *Cuba Review* (September 1974):19–21.
Rosaldo, Michelle Zimbalist, and Lamphere, Louise. "Introduction." In *Women, Culture and Society,* edited by Michelle Zimbalist Rosaldo and Louise Lamphere. Stanford, Calif.: Stanford University Press, 1974.
Rosenhan, Mollie Schwartz. "Images of Male and Female in Children's Readers." In *Women in Russia,* edited by Dorothy Atkins, Alexander Dallin, and Gail Warshofsky Lapidus. Stanford, Calif.: Stanford University Press, 1977.
Rossi, A. "The Biosocial Side of Parenthood" *Human Nature* (June 1978).
Rostow, Walt W. *The Stages of Economic Growth.* Cambridge, England: Cambridge University Press, 1960.
Rousseau, Isel, ed. *Children in Cuba: Twenty Years of Revolution.* Havana: Social Sciences Publishing, 1979.
Rousseau, Jean Jacques. *The Social Contract and Discourse.* Trans. by G. D. H. Cole.

New York: Everyman's Library, 1954.
Rubin, Gayle. "The Traffic in Women: Notes on the 'Political Economy' of Sex." In *Towards an Anthropology of Women*, edited by Rayna R. Reiter. New York: Monthly Review Press, 1975.
Ruiz, Jesus Orta. "Three Women." *Granma* (March 2, 1980):3.
Russell, Diana E., and Van de Ven, Nicole, eds. *The Proceedings of the International Tribunal on Crimes Against Women*. Millbrae, Calif.: Les Femmes Press, 1976.
Rzhanitsyna, Ludmila. *Soviet Family Budgets*. Moscow: Progress Publishers, 1977.
Saasta, Timothy. "Foundations Ignore the Largest 'Minority.'" *Los Angeles Times*, November 14, 1979, part 2, p. 7.
Sacks, Michael Paul. "Women in the Industrial Labor Force." In *Women in Russia*, edited by Dorothy Atkins, Alexander Dallin, and Gail Warshofsky Lapidus. Stanford, Calif.: Stanford University Press, 1977.
Salishcheva, N. "The New Constitution and Women's Rights." *Reprints from the Soviet Press* 26, no. 7 (April 15, 1978):14–21.
Samuelson, Robert J. "An Abstract Thought—No Reading Has to be Dull." *Los Angeles Times* January 6, 1980, part 2, p. 7.
Sanchez, Megaly. "Rights and Duties Go Together." *Cuba Review* (September 1974):13–14.
Sanday, Peggy R. "Female Status in the Public Domain." In *Women, Culture and Society*, edited by Michelle Zimbalist Rosaldo and Louise Lamphere. Stanford, Calif.: Stanford University Press, 1974.
Sanders, Thomas G. "Mexican Women." *American Universities Field Staff Reports* 3, no. 6 (1975).
_____. "Mexico." *Common Ground* 2, no. 1 (January 1976):45–55.
_____. "Mexico, 1974: Demographic Patterns and Population Policy." *American Universities Field Staff Reports* 2, no. 1 (1974).
_____. "Mexico's Food Problem." *American Universities Field Staff Reports* 3, no. 1 (1975).
_____. "Population Factors and Ideology in Mexico's Elementary Textbooks." *American Universities Field Staff Reports* 3, no. 2 (1975).
Scheuver, Harry N., ed. *United States Economic History: Selected Readings*. New York: Alfred A. Knopf, 1964.
Schmidt, Steffen W. "Political Participation and Development: The Role of Women in Latin America." *Journal of International Affairs* 30, no. 2 (1976–1977):243–260.
Schumpeter, Joseph. *Capitalism, Socialism and Democracy*. New York: Harper and Row, 1962.
_____. *The Theory of Economic Development*. Cambridge, Mass.: Harvard University Press, 1934.
Scott, Hilda. *Does Socialism Liberate Women?* Boston: Beacon Press, 1974.
Secretaría de programación y presupuesto, *La probación de México, su ocupación y sus rivelos de bienestar*, serie manuales de información básica de nación 2 (Mexico, D.F.: 1979).
Seers, Dudley. "The Limitations of the Special Case." *Bulletin of the Oxford Institute of Economics and Statistics* (May 1975).
Sergeyeva, G. P. "Women's Education and Scientific and Technological Progress." In *Soviet Women*, edited by T. N. Sidorova. Moscow: Progress Publishers, 1975.
Shulman, Colette. "The Individual and the Collective." In *Women in Russia*, edited by

Dorothy Atkins, Alexander Dallin, and Gail Warshofsky Lapidus. Stanford, Calif.: Stanford University Press, 1977.
Sidorova, T. N. "Labour in Social Production and the Shaping of the Women's Personality." In *Soviet Women,* edited by T. N. Sidorova. Moscow: Progress Publishers, 1975.
Sivard, Ruth Leger. *Women . . . a world survey.* Washington, D.C.: World Priorities, 1985.
Smith, Jessica. *Women in Soviet Russia.* New York: Vanguard Press, 1928.
Steffens, Heidi. "FMC at the Grass-roots." *Cuba Review* (September 1974):25–26.
──────. "FMC: Feminine, Not Feminist." *Cuba Review* (September 1974):22–23.
──────. "A Woman's Place . . . " *Cuba Review* (September 1974):29–30.
Stevens, Evelyn P. "Marianismo: The Other Face of *Machismo* in Latin America." In *Female and Male in Latin America: Essays,* edited by Ann Pescatello. Pittsburgh, Pa.: University of Pittsburgh Press, 1973.
St. George, George. *Our Soviet Sister.* New York: Robert B. Luce, Inc., 1973.
Stites, Richard. "Women and the Russian Intelligentsia: Three Perspectives." In *Women in Russia,* edited by Dorothy Atkins, Alexander Dallin, and Gail Warshofsky Lapidus. Stanford, Calif.: Stanford University Press, 1977.
Stone, Elizabeth, ed. *Women and the Cuban Revolution.* New York: Pathfinder Press, 1981.
Sturgeon, Wina. "A Woman's Invisible Years Are Frightening to See." *Los Angeles Times,* January 7, 1980, part 2, p. 5.
Sullerot, Evelyn. *Women, Society and Change.* New York: McGraw-Hill, 1971.
Sutton, Larry, and Miller, Herman. "Income Differences Between Men and Career Women." *American Journal of Sociology* (January 1973):73–98.
Sylvestor, Ed and Montemayor, Robert. "Mixed Blessings: Dollars Flow to Mexico's Border Land." *Los Angeles Times,* September 19, 1979, part 1, pp. 1, 14, 15.
Tinker, Irene, Bo Bramesen, Michele, and Buvinic, Mayra, eds. *Women and World Development.* New York: Praeger, 1976.
Tsyganov, Igor. "Women Watchmakers." *Soviet Life* (March 1978):14–21.
United Nations Educational, Scientific and Cultural Organization. *National Inventory on the Status of Women in the USSR.* ED-77/WS/11. Paris: UNESCO, February 18, 1977.
──────. "Table 3.12." Statistical Yearbook, 1981. Paris: UNESCO, 1981.
United Nations Fund for Population Activities. *Women Population and Development.* New York: United Nations Fund for Population Activities, 1976.
United Nations General Assembly. *Report of the Secretary General.* E/CN.6/598. New York: United Nations, July 21, 1976.
──────. *Report of the Secretary General.* A/32/216. New York: United Nations, October 3, 1977.
──────. *Report of the Secretary General.* A/32/216/Add.1. New York: United Nations, November 21, 1977.
──────. *Report of the Secretary General.* E/CN.6/611. New York: United Nations, February 17, 1978.
──────. *Report of the World Conference of the United Nations Decade for Women.* A/Conf.94/35. New York: United Nations, April 1980.
United States Department of Education. *Digest of Educational Statistics, 1982. (Washington, D.C.: Government Printing Office, 1982.*

United States Department of Labor. *The Earnings Gap Between Women and Men.* Washington, D.C.: Government Printing Office, 1976.
_____. *Employment and Earnings.* Washington, D.C.: Government Printing Office, 1985.
_____. *Minority Women Workers: A Statistical Overview.* Washington, D.C.: Government Printing Office, 1977.
_____. *1975 Handbook on Women Workers.* Washington, D.C.: Government Printing Office, 1975.
_____. *State Labor Laws in Transition: From Protection to Equal Status for Women.* Washington, D.C.: Government Printing Office, 1976.
_____. *20 Facts on Women Workers.* Washington, D.C.: Government Printing Office, 1978.
_____. *Women Workers Today.* Washington, D.C.: Government Printing Office, 1976.
_____. *Working Mothers and Their Children.* Washington, D.C.: Government Printing Office, 1977.
United States National Commission for UNESCO. *Report on Women in America.* Washington, D.C.: Government Printing Office, 1977.
Urrutia, Elena. "Que escribe la mujer en México." *fem* 3, no. 10 (Mexico, D.F.: July-October 1979):9-12.
Vanek, Joann. "Time Spent in Housework." *Scientific American* (November 1974):118.
Vaughan, Mary K. "Feminismo en la casa del lago." *fem* 2, no. 8 (Mexico, D.F.: July-September 1978).
_____. "Iglesia y mujer." *fem* 2, no. 8 (Mexico, D.F.: July-September 1978):41-43.
_____. "Women, Class and Education in Mexico: 1880-1928." *Latin American Perspectives* 4, nos. 1 and 2 (Winter and Spring 1977):135-152.
Vitek, Jan. "Women: Back to the Kitchen." *The World of Labor and Development.* Geneva: International Labor Organization, 1976.
Wellesley Editorial Group, eds. *Women and National Development: The Complexities of Change.* Chicago: University of Chicago Press, 1977.
Whitney, Craig R. "Women in Soviet Face a Stark Choice: Career or Children." *The New York Times,* August 26, 1979, part 1, p. 9.
Wollstonecraft, Mary. *A Vindication of the Rights of Women.* New York: Penguin, 1978.
Worswick, G. D. N. "Is Progress in Economic Science Possible?" *Economic Journal* (1972).
_____. "Women and Class Struggle." *Latin American Perspectives,* Special Issue (Winter-Spring 1977).
_____. *Women Today.* Moscow: Progress Publishers, 1975.
Yankova, Z. A. "The Woman and the Family." In *Soviet Women,* edited by T. N. Sidorova. Moscow: Progress Publishers, 1975.
Yazykova, V. S. "The Socialist Mode of Life and Women's Free Time." In *Soviet Women,* edited by T. N. Sidorova. Moscow: Progress Publishers, 1976.
Yemelyanova, Y. D. "The Social and Political Activity of Soviet Women." In *Soviet Women,* edited by T. N. Sidorova. Moscow: Progress Publishers, 1975.
Zasursky, Yasen, ed. *Soviet Mass Media.* Moscow: Novosti Press, 1979.
Zeitlin, Maurice, and Scheir, Robert. "CTC Resolutions." *Cuba Review* (September 1974):17-18.

───────. *Cuba: Tragedy in Our Hemisphere.* New York: Grove Press, 1963.
───────. *Family Code.* Havana: Official Publication of the Ministry of Justice, 1975.
───────. *La educación en revolución.* Havana: Instituto Cubano del Libro, 1975.
───────. "Maternity Law." *Cuba Review* (September 1974):15.
───────. *Mujeres* 1 (1980).
───────. "Report on the Third Congress of Cuban Women." *Bohemia* (March 14, 1980):48–56.
Zetkin, Clara. *Constitution (Fundamental Law) of the Union of Soviet Socialist Republics.* Moscow: Novosti Press, 1977.
───────. *Reminiscences of Lenin.* New York: International Publishers, 1934.
Zuckerman, Steven. "50 Protest at LA Magazine over Ad They Say Encourages Violence to Women." *Los Angeles Times,* December 27, 1979, part 2, p. 6.
───────. "For the Era, a Brushoff on High." *Los Angeles Times,* February 25, 1980, editorial, p. 6.
───────. "Impact at Home When Mother Takes a Job." *U.S. News and World Report* (January 15, 1979):69–70.
───────. "Male Dropouts Found to Outlearn College Women." *Los Angeles Times,* November 20, 1978, part 1, p. 4.
───────. "Sexual Harassment: A Federal Case." *The Guardian* (December 2, 1979):2.
───────. "Survey Finds Many Men Agree They Should Help on Housework." *Los Angeles Times,* July 18, 1979, part 1A, p. 4.
───────. "TV Programming: Sexist and Ageist." *The Guardian* (December 12, 1979):10.
───────. "TV's Blurred Image." *Los Angeles Times,* November 19, 1979, editorial, p. 8.
───────. "Women at Work: Still Fighting 'Stereotyped Roles.' " *U.S. News and World Report* (January 15, 1979):73–74.
───────. "Women in Politics." *Los Angeles Times,* November 9, 1978, part 1, p. 10.
───────. "Working Women—Joys and Sorrows." *U.S. News and World Report* (January 15, 1979):64–68.

Index

Abortion
  Cuba, 108
  Soviet Union, 82-83
  United States, 43
Africa, 1
Alimony
  Mexico, 51
Allen, Florence, 20
All-Russian League for Women's Equality, 66
All-Union Central Council of Trade Unions (U.S.), 76
American Association of University Women, 18
Appointed positions of women, 11
  Cuba, 92, 98
  United States, 20-21
Arizpe, Lourdes, 56
Armed forces
  Cuban women in, 101, 107, 143(n16)

Bay of Pigs, 101
Benefits, 12, 29
Betancourt, Anna, 91
Bird, Rose, 20
Birth control, 2
  Cuba, 108, 109
  Mexico, 59-60
  Soviet Union, 83
  United States, 43
Black women in United States, 24
Bolshevik party, 66-67, 70-71, 72, 83
Bradley, La Verne, 31
Brazil, 9
Bugbee, Emma, 20

Capitalism, 45-46, 63, 70, 89, 124-126
  See also Liberal/capitalist logic
Carter administration, women in, 20
Castro, Fidel, 97, 98, 102
Chafe, William, 18, 23
Child care, 12
  Cuba, 102, 103
  Mexico, 60, 62
  Soviet Union, 76, 80, 82, 83, 84, 87-88
  subsidization, 39-40, 45, 88
  United States, 39-40
Child-care benefits
  Cuba, 109
  Mexico, 55-56, 60,62
  Soviet Union, 77, 82, 83-84, 88
  United States, 39-41
Child-care facilities, 6, 12, 55-56, 60, 62, 109
Child custody, 12, 42-43 134(n1)
Child support, 12
  Cuba, 108
  Mexico, 51
  Soviet Union, 82
  United States, 42-43
Cires, Digna, 106, 146(n90)
Civil marriage (Mexico), 51
Civil Rights Act (U.S.) (1964), 28
Civil rights for women (Cuba), 91, 95, 113
Collective bargaining (Mexico), 55
Collectivization (USSR), 75, 77, 78
Commissariat of Enlightenment (USSR), 83
Committees for the Defense of the Revolution (CDR) (Cuba), 96, 98, 100

Common law, 41-42
Communist party
    Cuba, 96, 98, 104, 115, 121-122
    Soviet Union, 73-75, 121-122
Community property, 41-42, 134(n1)
Confederation of Cuban Workers (CTC), 96, 99, 100, 102, 103, 105, 106, 114
Confederation of Mexican Workers (CTM), 53
Constitution of Mexico (1917), 48, 49, 51
Contraception, 2
    Cuba, 108
    Mexico, 59-60
    Soviet Union, 83
    United States, 43
Cortines, Adolfo Ruiz, 52
Cuba, 9, 13, 91-116, 121-124, 126-127
Cuban Communist party, 96, 98, 104, 115, 121-122
Cuban Revolution (1959), 91, 106
Cuban Women's Federation, 93

Decree on Land (USSR), 74
Democratic pluralism, 5, 124-125
Dewson, Mary, 18
Divorce, 12
    Cuba, 95, 108, 123
    Mexico, 51, 59
    Soviet Union, 82
    United States, 42-43, 120-121
Dominguez, Jorge, 111
Dual social roles of women
    Cuba, 97, 99, 109-110, 112, 113, 122
    Mexico, 60, 120
    Soviet Union, 83-85, 86-89, 122, 123
    United States, 38-41, 119, 121
Duma, 66

Economic equality, 11, 12
Economic participation of women, 12
    Cuba, 104
    Mexico, 56
    Soviet Union, 77
    United States, 21-23
Economic position of women
    Cuba, 92-94, 101-107, 122
    Mexico, 49-50, 55-58, 120
    Soviet Union, 67-68, 74-81, 122
    United States, 14-15, 21-34, 43-44, 120
Economic rights of women
    Cuba, 101-104
    Mexico, 55-56, 63
    Soviet Union, 74-76
    United States, 27-30, 63
Education, 12
    Cuba, 93-94, 101, 103, 105-107
    Mexico, 49, 50, 55, 58
    Soviet Union, 68, 71, 80-81, 87
    United States, 15, 23, 26-27, 30-33, 119, 131(n2)
Elected positions of women, 11
    Cuba, 92, 97, 98
    Mexico, 54-55
    Soviet Union, 73, 87, 122
    United States, 20
Employee Retirement Income Security Act (U.S.) (1974), 29
Engineering
    Cuban women in, 107
    Soviet women in, 78
Equal Pay Act (U.S.) (1963), 28
Equal Rights Amendment (U.S.), 42, 44, 118, 120
Espin, Vilma, 93, 98, 100

Fair Labor Standards Act (U.S.), 27, 28
Family code
    Cuba, 108
    Soviet Union, 82-83
Family planning
    Cuba, 109
    Mexico, 59-60
    Soviet Union, 83
    United States, 43
Federation of Cuban Women (FMC), 96, 98, 99-101, 102-103, 113, 114, 115, 122, 127
Feminine Front (Cuba), 103, 105, 114
Ferris, Abbott L., 25-26

Five Year Plan (USSR) (1975-1980), 83-84
Flora, Cornelia Butler, 61
Fox, Geoffrey, 95, 110-111
Fromenta, Nina, 98

Garment industry (U.S.), 23
General Federation of Women's Clubs (U.S.), 19
Goodman, Ellen, 24-25
Grasso, Ella T., 20

Hiestand, Dale L., 25
Household responsibilities, 6, 12, 85-86, 123-124

Income tax credits for child care (U.S.), 40
Index of the Status of Occupations (U.S.), 25
Inheritance laws (Russia), 82
Institute of Human Sexual Relations (Cuba), 109
Institutional Revolutionary Party (PRI) (Mexico), 52-54, 55, 63, 118
International Women's Year (1975), 3

Jaba (Shopping Bag) Plan (Cuba), 109
Judgeships held by women
  Cuba, 98
  Mexico, 48, 54
  Soviet Union, 73
  United States, 20

Komsomal (Young Communist League) (USSR), 73, 74

Labor force, women in, 12
  Cuba, 93, 100, 102, 104, 112, 123
  Mexico, 50, 56, 119
  Soviet Union, 123
  United States, 15, 21-23
Land ownership
  Mexico, 49
  Soviet Union, 66, 74, 82
  United States, 16, 41-42
Lapidus, Gail Warshofsky, 71, 81

League of Women Voters (U.S.), 19
Legal profession, women in (U.S.), 21, 25
Legal rights of women
  Cuba, 91-92
  Mexico, 59
  Soviet Union, 69-70
  United States, 17
Lenin, 71, 72, 74
Liberal/capitalist logic, 5, 7, 10-11, 45-46, 47, 62-64, 89, 90, 116, 117-121, 124, 129(n13)
Liberal/democratic logic, 89
Library of Women Workers and Peasants (USSR), 85
Literacy (Mexico), 50, 58

McNutt, Paul, 39
Mandel, William, 83
Mandel, Ruth, 21
Marxist strategy, 6-7, 8-11, 45, 62-65, 86, 88, 90, 112, 113-115, 116, 117, 121-124, 125, 126-127
Maternity benefits, 6, 12
  Cuba, 93, 102, 103, 122
  Mexico, 49, 55-56, 62
  Soviet Union, 67, 74, 75-76, 77, 88, 122
  United States, 29-30, 44, 45
Maternity law (1974) (Cuba), 103
Mead, Margaret, 34, 41
Media portrayal of women
  Cuba, 110
  Mexico, 61
  Soviet Union, 85
  United States, 38, 61
Mexico, 9, 11, 47-64, 117-121, 125-126
  migration to cities, 50
Minimum wage
  Cuba, 93, 105
  Mexico, 55

National American Women's Suffrage Association, 18
National Association of Small Peasants (ANAP) (Cuba), 96, 100
National Confederation of Popular

Organizations (CNOP) (Mexico), 53, 54
National Federation of Business and Professional Women (U.S.), 18-19
National Organization for Women (U.S.), 19
National Peasant Confederation (CNC) (Mexico), 53
National Recovery Act (NRA) (U.S.), 27
National War Labor Board (NWLB) (U.S.), 27
National Women's Conference (U.S.), 19
Newland, Kathleen, 37
Nursing, women in
  Mexico, 57
  United States, 27

Occupational distribution of women, 12
  Cuba, 102, 104-105, 106, 112
  Mexico, 57-58, 119
  Soviet Union, 75-76, 77-79
  United States, 15, 23-25, 119
O'Connor, Sandra Day, 20
Organized labor
  Cuba, 92, 99-100
  United States, 15, 27-28, 30

Parez, Raquel, 98
Party of the Mexican Revolution, 53
Perkins, Frances, 20, 35
Petrograd Council of Trade Unions (USSR), 74-75
Physicians, women
  Cuba, 105
  Soviet Union, 68, 78, 80
  United States, 25
Political authority of women, 118
  Cuba, 96, 97-99, 122
  Mexico, 54-55
  Soviet Union, 72-74, 87, 122
  United States, 19-21
Political influence of women, 118, 124
  Cuba, 99-101
  Mexico, 52-54

Soviet Union, 67, 70-72
United States, 17-19, 118-119
Political party endorsement of women, 21
Political power of women
  Cuba, 91-92, 96-101
  Mexico, 47-48, 52-55, 62, 120
  Soviet Union, 65-67, 69-74, 86, 87
  United States, 16-21, 44, 120
Political rights of women
  Cuba, 97
  Mexico, 52, 62
  Soviet Union, 65-67
  United States, 43, 44
Pregnancy Discrimination Act (1978) (U.S.), 29
PRI. *See* Institutional Revolutionary Party (Mexico)
Professional homemaker concept, 37
Professional women
  Cuba, 105
  Mexico, 57, 137(n70)
  Soviet Union, 68, 72, 78, 80
  United States, 21, 25
Project on Human Sexual Development (U.S.), 41
Property laws
  Mexico, 49
  Soviet Union, 66, 74, 82
  United States, 16, 41-42

Randall, Margaret, 108, 111
Reagan administration, women in, 20
Remuneration of women versus men, 12
  Cuba, 93, 102, 105-106, 123
  Mexico, 58, 119
  Soviet Union, 68, 74, 75, 79-80, 87, 123
  United States, 15, 16-17, 23, 25-27, 28, 29, 119
Report of the World Conference of the United Nations Decade for Women (1980), 4
Reproduction, 2, 6-7, 8
Revolution of 1910 (Mexico), 47, 51, 53

Roosevelt, Eleanor, 18
Roosevelt, Franklin D., 18, 20
Ruckelhouse, Jill, 19
Russian Revolution (1917), 65, 90

Sanchez, Teresa, 98
Sanders, Thomas G., 60-61
2nd Congress of Cuban Women, 103-104
Sex education
  Cuba, 108-109
  Mexico, 59
  Soviet Union, 83
  United States, 43
Slavery (Cuba), 94-95, 143(n13)
Smeal, Eleanor, 19
Social identity of women
  Cuba, 110-112
  Mexico, 60-61
  Soviet Union, 85-86
  United States, 34-38
Social mobility of women, 124
  Mexico, 119
  United States, 44, 119
Social rights of women, 11, 12
  Cuba, 108-109
  Mexico, 59-60
  Soviet Union, 81-83
  United States, 41-43
Social roles of women
  Cuba, 122
  Mexico, 62, 63-64, 120
  Soviet Union, 122
  United States, 44, 63-64, 120
  See also Dual social roles
Social status of women
  Cuba, 94, 108-112
  Mexico, 50-52, 59-61
  Soviet Union, 68-69, 81-86
  United States, 15-16, 34-44
Socialism, 7, 8, 70, 89, 91, 101, 112, 114-115, 124
Soviet Union, 7-8, 13, 65-90, 121-124, 126-127
Steffens, Heidi, 108
Stimson, Henry, 35
Supreme Court of Mexico, 54

Teachers, women as
  Cuba, 105, 145(n58)
  Mexico, 57
  Soviet Union, 78
  United States, 23-24, 25
Third World, 1, 2
Trade embargo against Cuba, 144(n37)
Trade unions
  Cuba, 99-100
  Soviet Union, 76, 122
  United States, 15, 27-28, 30, 136(n25)

Unemployment (Mexico), 57, 120
United Nations (UN), 1
UN Decade for Women, 3, 129(n8)
UN Economic Commission for Latin America (ECLA), 56
UN Food Conference, 1-2
UN Population Conference, 1, 2
United States, 11, 14-46, 117-121, 125-126
U.S. Constitution
  Fifteenth Amendment, 16
  Fourteenth Amendment, 16
  Nineteenth Amendment, 17
  See also Equal Rights Amendment
U.S. House of Representatives, women in, 20
U.S. Senate, women in, 20
U.S. Supreme Court, women appointed to, 20

Vocational training of women
  Cuba, 105-107
  Mexico, 58
  Soviet Union, 68, 80-81, 87
  United States, 30-33, 34

Wages. *See* Remuneration of women versus men
War Manpower Commission (U.S.), 36, 39
Wartime employment of women (U.S.), 22-23, 24, 30-31, 35-36, 38-39, 121
Women's Bureau (U.S. Democratic party), 18

Women's Bureau (U.S. Department of Labor), 15, 36
Women's organizations, 11
  Cuba, 22
  Mexico, 48, 53-54
  Soviet Union, 66, 71, 121-122
  United States, 17-19, 118-119
  See also specific organizations
Women's periodicals (USSR), 71, 85
Women's suffrage, 11
  Cuba, 91
  Mexico, 48, 52
  Soviet Union, 66
  United States, 17-18

Young Communist League (USSR), 73, 74

Zhenotdyel 67, 71-72, 73, 83, 85, 140(n62)